A MATTER OF LIFE AND DEATH

The Brain Revealed by the Mind of Michael Powell

DIANE BROADBENT FRIEDMAN

AuthorHouse™
1663 Liberty Drive, Suite 200
Bloomington, IN 47403
www.authorhouse.com
Phone: 1-800-839-8640

© 2008 Diane Broadbent Friedman. All rights reserved.

No part of this book may be reproduced, stored in a retrieval system, or transmitted by any means without the written permission of the author.

First published by AuthorHouse 9/8/2008

ISBN: 978-1-4389-0945-5 (sc)

Library of Congress Control Number: 2008907478

Printed in the United States of America
Bloomington, Indiana

This book is printed on acid-free paper.

Front cover: Roger Livesey and David Niven,
A Matter of Life and Death (1946). Photograph by kind permission of Granada International

Back cover: Neurons and blood vessel (1991). Photograph by kind permission of Ralph Lydic PhD.

Table of Contents

Preface		xi
Introduction:	The Unrecognized Medical Science within a Creative Work	xix
Chapter One:	A Map to Search for Understanding	1
Chapter Two:	Sudden Losses and Medical Hope: The Story of *A Matter of Life and Death* and a Reflection of the Era	17
Chapter Three:	"Dr. Cushing, Have You Ever Seen the Soul?" An Introduction to the Workings of the Brain	29
Mini-Tutorial: What Michael Powell Learned about How the Brain Works		31
Chapter Four:	"Do You Think I'm Cracked?" The Neurological Evaluation of Peter Carter	47
Chapter Five:	"I Discovered I Had an Eye." References to Normal and Abnormal Vision	69
Mini-Tutorial: What Michael Powell Learned about Vision		71

Chapter Six:	How Did Michael Powell Acquire this Medical Information?	83
Chapter Seven:	Neurologic Hints, Echoes, and Possibilities	117
Chapter Eight:	Cinematic Equations, Neurologic Maps	139
Conclusion:	"We'll Invent the Greatest Lie in Medical History, You and I!"	151

| Appendix I: | Elaboration of Neurological Connections from Chapter Seven | 157 |

A. " She cannot wake. We are talking in space, not in time." 159

B. Poets and Neurologists: "I haven't much modern stuff in my library, but you're there…I hope we shall have some talks together…" 167

C. Music in *A Matter of Life and Death*: A Musical Aura, a Precipitant of a Seizure, a Tribute to the First Brain Surgery, or All Three? 174

D. "But it wouldn't explain how I could jump without a parachute and still be alive." "No, it couldn't do that, but there might be a practical explanation, even of that." 183

E. "Do You Think I'm Cracked?" 186

F. The Intersection of Neurology and Literature 194

G. Dr. Reeves asked Peter: "Was it a pleasant smell? Can you place it?" "Why yes … fried onions" 202

H. The Staircase and the Statues 205

I. "Frank's had an accident."   211

J. The Camera Obscura   215

K. "The trial takes place tonight, and that's why we must operate tonight." Echoes of Dr. James Collier (1870–1935)   218

L. The Authors of Two Brain Atlases—William Macewen, John Lizars and Landon Rives and the Names of the Three *AMOLAD* Doctors—Dr. McEwen, Dr. Leiser and Dr. Reeves: 222

M. A Joke in the History of Neurology   226

N. Why Chess?   228

O. "Abraham Farlan! The American War of Independence! Killed by a British bullet!"   232

Appendix II:	Some Additional Neurologic Ideas	235
Appendix III:	For Further Reading	243
Appendix IV:	"Chiasmal Arachnoiditis" by A.J.B. Goldsmith	249
Appendix V:	Emeric Pressburger's application for the British Museum Reading Room	257
Index		261

Socrates: And I, Meno, like what I am saying. Some things I have said of which I am not altogether confident. But that *we shall be better and braver and less helpless if we think that we ought to enquire,* than we should have been if we indulged in the idle fancy that there was no knowing and no use in seeking to know what we do not know;--that is a theme upon which I am ready to fight, in word and deed, to the utmost of my power.

Plato *Meno*

(How Peter saves himself.)

Preface

When each of us saw our first film by Michael Powell and Emeric Pressburger, we said to ourselves, "What an unusual and extraordinary film!" For me, it was 1990, and I had just put our two-year-old son to bed for an afternoon nap. I turned on the TV and saw from the very beginning, although without the titles and credits, *A Matter of Life and Death* (*AMOLAD*). Since I have experience in caring for people with epilepsy, I was shocked because I thought I recognized extensive, detailed neurologic information within the film. From that Saturday afternoon onward, I have wanted to understand more about the film and its makers. My challenge began with determining the title of the film I had just seen! The questions developed from there. Above all, I wanted to talk to the person who made this film.

As fate would have it, the day after I obtained a copy of Michael Powell's autobiography, *A Life in Movies*, from the library, I heard on National Public Radio that Mr. Powell had died on February 19, 1990, at the age of 88. I would never have the chance to ask him directly about the creation of the film. I bought a video of the film, and after watching it several more times, I decided I could present the detailed information from the film as a complete neurologic case history at the Second International Conference of Epilepsy Surgery in Cleveland, Ohio, in the spring of 1990. Wanting to understand more, I then decided to contact other people associated with the film. I was able to correspond with Powell's brother-in-law, Dr. Joe Reidy, and with the actress Kim Hunter, but they could tell me only a little about how the medical information was pulled together for the film.

Because Michael Powell credited David Thompson for inviting him to Dartmouth as an artist in residence, I sent Mr. Thompson a copy of my paper. He encouraged me to send a copy to Mr. Powell's widow, Mrs. Thelma Schoonmaker Powell. I did, never imagining receiving a reply. How wrong I was! How wonderfully supportive, kind, and encouraging she has been! She took my interests seriously and sent a copy of my work on to Ian Christie at the British Film Institute, who also was encouraging. Sadly, she told me that Mr. Powell's medical notes and other notes concerning the film were lost. I would never be able to look at them directly.

I published a paper on the medical case of the hero of the film, RAF pilot Peter Carter, in an English epilepsy journal, hoping that the article might be like a message in a bottle thrown into the ocean, in that a British neurologist might find it and contact me with more insights about the film.[1] Alas, no comments reached me.

I cannot explain the reason for what happened next. In his autobiography, Michael Powell had said he read medical textbooks and papers in the development of the script for the film.. Simply, I came to believe that I could find the medical papers that Michael Powell must have read. After all, how many could there be? Ah, the misguided wisdom of the uninformed!

At that time, internet searches and e-mails were not widely available to the general public. I used the Pub Med search engine when

I visited the National Library of Medicine in Bethesda, Maryland, in 1991. It was not possible at that time, as it is today, to search from a distant location for fragments of text or names with internet searches. In the spring of 2008, internet text searches are still not available for some medical journals written before 1950, although many are starting to come online.

I found all of the articles discussed in this book by personally locating articles referring to seizures, especially uncinate seizures, from 1880 through 1955, beginning with *Brain,* the neurological journal founded by John Hughlings Jackson. (I started there because, in the film *AMOLAD,* June mentions to Dr. Reeves that he must be a prominent neurologist as evidenced by his having been published in *Brain.*) I would read an article and then all of the articles listed in the references to compile a collection of articles and scientific works that were available to Michael Powell in 1945. My work included all the volumes of *Brain* published from 1878 through 1946; the tables of contents and indices of most of the volumes of *The Lancet* and the *British Medical Journal* in this time range; as well as the *Journal of the American Medical Association, The British Journal of Surgery, Epilepsia,* and articles in the *British Journal of Ophthalmology.* I searched through many of the neurological text books available to British medical students in 1945 on the hunch that Michael Powell would consult those same texts for explanations of the mechanisms he sought to understand. With this approach, I hoped to come upon the texts that Michael Powell used for dialogue.

As a wise person might have already guessed, this turned out to be a larger task than I foresaw at the beginning! Why did I do this? Apart from my being a little single-minded, it has been very interesting. And so tantalizing! Ultimately I did find some information that I feel sure Powell read as well as other material that I think he probably read. This is the basis of this book.

I like the image offered by Kevin Macdonald in the biography of his grandfather, Emeric Pressburger: "Confronted with the Powell-Pressburger partnership, they [critics] have tried to prise it apart, like an oyster, to see which side contains the pearl."[2] Emeric Pressburger did not leave detailed notes, while Michael Powell recorded his version of the process of creating *AMOLAD* in his autobiography.[3,4] While I cannot say for sure which moments of the film are one partner's contributions or the other, I can say that the final work of art represents the combined agreement of both artists. Typically the story would begin with Mr. Pressburger. They shared the manuscript between them, back and forth, making changes until they both concurred. While Michael Powell was the director, Emeric Pressburger would be on the set and would quietly mention his insights and preferences to Michael Powell. My assumption for this book is that Michael Powell was responsible for the medical scholarship of *AMOLAD* because that is what he says in *A Life in Movies*. However, the ultimate creation of the pearl was the product of both men's efforts. Possibly another researcher will be able to shed more light on this question some day.

The deeper understanding of how Emeric Pressburger and Michael Powell combined forces to make unique and wonderful films is not our purpose here. The purpose of this book is to show you, the reader, a neurological interpretation of what I see within *AMOLAD*. If I am successful, I hope you will share my feeling that this film represents remarkable medical scholarship and warrants an even stronger appreciation of the creation of The Archers.

I could not have come to this point in my understanding of *AMOLAD* without the generous, patient, and very kind help of so many librarians who were willing to assist me in locating articles and sometimes listening to me exclaim over a finding as I checked out books at the end of a day in the library. The first person to help me was Ned Comstock, Archival Librarian at the Cinema/Television Library, University of Southern California. I called the library on a chance on a Saturday afternoon. He answered the phone and provided me with the first information to help me understand what lay behind the title "The Archers." Esther Dell, Medical Reference Librarian at the Pennsylvania State University, Milton S. Hershey School of Medicine, George T. Harrell Library, was the first one to help me obtain information about the film though the medical library. So many other librarians were so kind: Louise Sheppard at the Institute of Neurology, The National Hospital Queen Square, London; and the abundant help and patience of the librarians of the Ruth Lilly Medical Library, Indiana University School of Medicine—especially the Interlibrary Loan staff, the Front Desk staff, and Nancy Eckerman of the History of Medicine collection.

Other very kind people who responded to my questions include Mr. Joseph Reidy, plastic surgeon and Michael Powell's brother-in-law; Niall MacGinnis's daughter, Sandra Jorgenson; Shelia Clarke, author of *Ashford: A Journey Through Time*, and Dick Fitzpatrick, both of Ballycullen, Ireland; Ms. Ruth Buckingham, magazine editor of the League of Charing Cross Hospital Nurses; Ms. Irene Spruce, nurse at Ashridge in 1944; Dr. Vivian Edwards, surgeon at Charing Cross/Ashridge 1944-1945 and his wife, attending nurse at Charing Cross/Ashridge 1939-1946; Joanne Turner, Assistant Curator of Dumfries Museum and Camera Obscura;[5] Morag Williams of the Dumfriesshire & Galloway Natural History and Antiquarian Society; Toby Whitaker of the Cinema and Television Benevolent Fund of the UK; Robert Greenwood, Assistant Librarian, Rare Books, Royal

Society of Medicine, and Mick Thompson, Archivist, Ashridge Business School.[6]

I have grateful appreciation to friends who have helped me along the way. Mrs. Mary Lundeen is a good friend, always ready for an adventure, who first suggested that I should consider transforming this long story into a book, after she traveled with me to Bangor Wales for the Michael Powell Centenary Conference in August 2005.

Thelma Schoonmaker Powell has helped me in so many significant ways. She allowed me to have a copy of the script and a copy of Mr. Powell's date book from 1944 and 1945. She gave me access to still photos from the film. She also gave me the generous gift of her insights and kind encouragement. Steve Crook is the indefatigable and insightful webmaster of a remarkably detailed and complete web site devoted to the understanding of the work of Michael Powell and Emeric Pressburger, the Powell-Pressburger pages of the Powell and Pressburger Appreciation Society.[7] He put my paper on his web site and started me thinking that there were some like-minded people who might be interested in learning more. And finally, my loving husband Marty, endlessly supportive and encouraging, sharing every moment along the way, who never once asked me if it might be time to put down something I started thinking about a long time ago.

1. Friedman, Diane Broadbent, "A Matter of Fried Onions." *Seizure* 1(1992): 307–10.
2. Macdonald, Kevin, *Emeric Pressburger: The life and death of a screen writer,* (London: Faber and Faber, 1994), xvii.
3. Powell, Michael, *A Life in Movies* (New York: Alfred A. Knopf, 1987).

4. Powell, Michael, *Million-Dollar Movie* (London: Heinemann, 1992).
5. Dumfries Museum and Camera Obscura. Dumfries, Scotland http://www.dumgal.gov.uk/museums
6. Ashridge Business School, Berkhamsted, England.
7. The Powell and Pressburger Pages. http://www.powell-pressburger.org/

Introduction:

The Unrecognized Medical Science within a Creative Work

My husband is fond of observing that a genius makes his or her actions look so easy that we can imagine ourselves capable of doing just the same—like David Beckham or Kiri Te Kanawa. That is, until we try kicking a ball or singing in the shower, when we know down deep that it is not so easy at all. In our failure to execute that effortless graceful gesture, turn of phrase, or insightful thought, we can sense the presence of complexity just out of our reach.

That sense of elusive complexity was an important part of the power of a Michael Powell and Emeric Pressburger film. People were drawn to their films without being able to completely articulate why. Michael Powell knew this and worked to produce that result in his films.

You may have picked up this book because Powell and Pressburger's 1946 film *A Matter of Life and Death* (AMOLAD) is one of your all-time favorites. It is romantic and funny, thought-provoking, brave, and gripping. There is one more layer of appreciation that you may have sensed but did not completely understand: the film is a complex neurological story of a psychologically normal man who believes a heavenly court has sentenced him to death. I have written this book to show you the wonderful richness of Michael Powell's medical scholarship in *AMOLAD*. It is in the dialogue, the structure of the story, the set dressing, and even seen through the lens of the camera. My goal is that Michael Powell's medical scholarship should be recognized and appreciated. Let's look at *AMOLAD* in a new way. Even if you are not a physician, you can still understand the neurologic underpinnings just as Michael Powell mastered them.

Not only was the medical scholarship within *AMOLAD* remarkable, but in addition, the film was made during wartime. Michael Powell and Emeric Pressburger created ten films in London while bombs were falling and while there was a very real possibility of poison gas attacks and invasion. To have a sense of the danger of that time, the reader is referred to an account and photographs of the bombing of the Royal Society of Medicine in London in 1941[1]. Four years later, *AMOLAD* was rewritten at sea near the end of the war. Remarkably and wonderfully, the work in *AMOLAD* embodies the frontier of new knowledge of the human mind in 1946—neurosurgery, neurology, psychiatry, ophthalmology, art, literature, history, action, and passion.

This film embodies the power of scientific thought, vision, and observation within the focus of the love of two people from different countries. Interwoven is the filmmakers' abiding love for England through references to literature and poetry. It is also a celebration of the new power of medical science, a large portion of which had been developed in England, Scotland, and Ireland within the preceding

Bombing of the Library of the Royal College of Physicians London 1940; "The Royal College of Physicians on the Occasion of its Recent Bombing," Proceedings of the Royal Society of Medicine vol 34 1940-1941 part 2 May-October pg 811-814, reproduced with the permission of the Royal Society of Medicine Press, London.

one hundred years. From our vantage point in the twenty-first century, we know that the many of the tools available to a British surgeon in 1945 had been developed to a practical significance in just the preceding ten years. Dilantin, developed in 1938, was the only drug available for treatment of seizures other than Phenobarbital. A powerful technique, the electroencephalogram (EEG), developed in 1929, was producing new information about precisely where in the brain a seizure was arising, thanks in part to research done in Cambridge in 1937. Penicillin had only been developed in 1943 by British researchers, but it would revolutionize the treatment of surgical infection and the treatment of syphilis. Techniques of brain surgery for epilepsy, including using subdural EEG during surgery, were becoming more sophisticated and could save more people who had complex and severe problems.[2] From the man-on-the street's point of view of 1946, these techniques were revolutionary. These techniques and the surgeons who used them were saving lives that could not have been saved in World War I. Many in the 1946 audience knew that these techniques were significantly developed by British and American scientists. So to fully appreciate this film, we need to recall what both physicians and filmmakers had available to them in 1945. This feeling of power and accomplishment can be summed up in a phrase from a British physician at the beginning of the war—the cream of British medicine would come to the fight.

That the neurology is present in accurate abundance is very plain to me. Why did Michael Powell do this; how did he do this? I have only partial answers. Does every possible neurologic explanation imply it was a purposeful scientific and artistic decision? I cannot be sure. I will make my case and the reader will decide.

As you read this book, you will encounter the names of authors when we are talking about medicine, and the names of surgeons and physicians when we are talking about literature. This is because *AMOLAD* is also a story of the interplay and overlap of significant people in medicine and literature. This is surely the result of the dynamic intellectual and creative life within the United Kingdom and connections with Europe and America. In completing this book, I have a far deeper admiration for the pure human energy of scientific and artistic creativity despite war, death, and destruction. While I am not sure if this moment of creativity in England is a product of unique circumstances, I do know that as I worked on my inquiry, the people from one realm—whether literature or science—would emerge in the other. So don't be surprised if you find that a neurosurgeon or an author appears in an unexpected portion of the story that follows.

A Note on Neurology

An audience watching a movie is made up of people with diverse backgrounds. For example, both scientists and non-scientists are drawn to the films *Apollo 13*, *A Beautiful Mind*, and *Awakenings*. The book you are holding may also have a diverse audience—possibly, and hopefully, both film-lovers and science-lovers. Just as in *AMOLAD*, when Peter travels between worlds, I hope to do the same. I will be explaining neurological information to some readers who already understand this in far greater complexity, and I will be describing elements of film-making to some readers who engage in this every day. If I am successful, I will have shown to each a little of what the other knows so well. That is what Michael Powell did far more creatively and gracefully in *AMOLAD*: he introduced neurology in cinema and cinema in neurology. I hope the gentle reader, whether scholar of film or medicine, will be patient with my explanations so that all readers can follow my interpretation, and if I am lucky, Mr. Powell's synthesis.

Cinematic Equations

These medical details are not just flavorings. It is the way the entire film is constructed.

The first equation: The neurological status of Peter Carter

Consider these images from the film, in order:

- Peter in the cockpit speaking with June on the radio
- On the beach Peter looks at his shadow while standing on one foot
- Conductor 71 with his hook
- June lost from view in the garden
- The visual test in Lee Wood House
- The wind blows, each time a little harder, as the film progresses

You can look at these pictures as the figures of a cinematic equation which can be added together to determine Peter's diagnosis, the location of the brain lesion, and needed treatment.

The second equation: A way to look

Combine these images in order:

- Looking at the sky
- The camera obscura
- The ping-pong game
- The ride on the motorcycle in the rain
- The onset of anesthesia
- The heavenly courtroom

Michael Powell is showing you how he has an eye.

In the film, there is one incidental moment that sums up the entire neurological story of *AMOLAD*. To fully appreciate this, I will save the best for last. In this book, I'll teach you how to understand the equations that Michael Powell created and solved. I hope to show you more of the way Michael Powell could see.

Let's begin!

1. *Proceedings of the Royal Society of Medicine* 34, part 2 (1940–1941, May–October): 811–14.
2. Penfield, Wilder and Erickson, Theodore, *Epilepsy and Cerebral Localization: A Study of the mechanism, treatment, and prevention of epileptic seizures.* (Springfield: Charles C. Thomas, 1941), 460.

Chapter One:

A Map to Search for Understanding

The first reading of Michael Powell's *My Life in Movies* is an experience of the very full life of Michael Powell—the movies he made, the places he visited, and the people he knew. But there is more imbedded within those vivid experiences to be found. Occasionally he reveals more about the power and direction of his mind. Taken together, those brief vignettes spread throughout the book may explain why *AMOLAD* was Michael Powell's favorite movie. I think that he believed that his medical scholarship represented some of his finest intellectual and artistic work—although I also think he was careful to erase most of the traces of that scholarship and just leave the natural residue of accuracy in service of the story.

Diane Broadbent Friedman

A Life in England

"What a mother for a man!"
Michael Powell believed that his adult creative spirit was greatly influenced by the spirit of his family, particularly his mother; where he was raised; and his exposure to literature. Michael Powell was born in Canterbury, Kent, in September 1905. He was exposed to literature and history from his earliest years by his mother, Mabel Corbett Powell. He loved her deeply and felt great pride in her zest for life. A family friend described her riding the most challenging horses named "The Giantess" and "The Terror": "She'll ride anything and put that monster of a horse at it, and if it's too high for him he'll just smash his way though and your mother on him and me right behind them both."[1] She was beautiful and vigorous. She was also energetic, cheerful, and adventurous. She loved animals, flowers, birds[2] and the English countryside[3] with a free, wide embrace. He was proud of her and secure in her love "as she coped with the changes in life and home by making new friends, new things out of adversity"[4]

Powell described very happy times with his mother. As an adult, he looked back with tenderness and gratitude that she allowed him to explore and have real adventure. In 1915, a Calvary unit moved near their village and began training with their horses.[5] "[At age ten] I was soldier mad," he said. "There was no chance of keeping either of us [the boy or his horse] out of the Camp."[6] Michael Powell was allowed to take his little pony and practice with the soldiers—"this was after my mother had made me a uniform to which the Quartermaster added Sergeant's stripes"—and to hang about the edges watching practice and listening to the soldiers talk. [7]

He told a wonderful story about a group of horses which, after having trained together and been in war together, finally spent their post-war days grazing in a pasture. He described them during a booming thunderstorm, in response to the thunder and lightning:

> What did the old cavalry horses who had seen and survived Albuera, Torres, Vedras, and Waterloo do? They formed in a line, wheeling and tramping and taking up their positions as if ghostly riders had gauntleted hands on their reins, and there they stood, facing the enemy, until the storm was over and they could turn to grazing again.[8]

Powell had his share of childhood scrapes and accidents. Even after he fell from a horse and was dragged over the ground, one foot caught in the stirrup, his head bobbing on the ground, his mother comforted him but did not keep him from continuing to ride. He noted this as, "One of the narrow escapes that colors a lifetime."[9]

When Michael Powell was twelve, mother and son began a bike trip to Stonehenge, a place that had ignited her imagination. A fierce storm blew up. Pedaling grew more and more onerous as the cold rain fell while they struggled to ride in muddy lanes. Eventually she had to stop and comfort her son, who was mentally and physically exhausted. She gave up her goal of seeing Stonehenge that day but did return seven years later, to sleep there overnight in her sleeping bag.[10] For Powell, this story was emblematic of her core of strength, imagination, and passion, and suggested to him the source of his similar qualities. "One of her exploits when freed from me was a tour of southern England on her bicycle," he later said. "She carried a hammock and slung it between trees in the new forest and elsewhere with a Macintosh to pull over her when it rained. What a mother for a man!"[11]

As he grew, he loved the freedom to roam over the countryside. He also appreciated the literary figures who also were men of Kent. Here he described himself as a fifteen year old in 1920:

> I was already an avid second-hand book buyer and every penny went on little editions of G.K. Chesterton, Hilaire Belloc and H.G. Wells who, excitingly, was a fellow inhabitant of Hythe, and could be seen cycling through the lanes of Romney Marsh, perhaps to call on Henry James at Rye or on Joseph Conrad in his farmhouse.[12]

Mrs. Powell was a great reader, and Michael Powell held on to her books until the end of his days. In 1918, as the war continued and she feared she would lose her older son John, to the army, she decided to make a wonderful month-long bike trip with her two boys, riding from Kent to Dorset along the Pilgrim's Way. "Anyone who traveled with my mother," Powell wrote, "had to be prepared for numerous detours made for their literary or historic associations."[13] He recalled reciting Kipling, Chaucer, and other poets as the family biked their wonderful adventure:

> The sheer size of it all… the sensation of being in a part of old England that had not changed or felt the plough since *The Doomsday Book* was compiled, the Forrest where Red William had died of an arrow shot by an unknown hand, where outlaws could hide and be undetected, where children –*the children of the New Forest*—could have incredible adventures among Roundheads and Cavaliers. It was beyond our dreams…[14]

The real life of literature

"Thanks to my mother and her sisters I had read and had read to me, poetry and legend, biography and fiction," Powell said. "I read and I listened and I remembered what I read and heard. The experience of farm life, of books, and of the life of the camps and barracks combined to make me a disconcerting little boy in conversation."[15]

In 1916, at age eleven, he became a border student at the Junior King's School at Canterbury. By his own account, he would devour books:

> [The school was ideally located in the center of town,] not more than four hundred yards from the two libraries that I patronized—...a lending library of modern novels, where my mother had a ticket which allowed me to take out two books at a time. Frequently on half-holidays I would take out two novels, say by Edgar Jepson or E.F. Benson, devour them standing at the counter or walking about the town, return and change them for two more and so on through the afternoon until I had read eight novels with two extra for reading after prep that same evening.[16]

As he entered boarding school, he continued his passion for reading but brought several extra talents: he could read very fast; he embraced the stories in his memory; and he loved to retell those stories, holding his school friends spellbound. He would complete his homework at great speed so he could have time left over to read, especially history. [17]

> I can't remember how it started but it was discovered that I had a huge repertoire of stories by heart...I was in a large dormitory divided into individual cubicles...the lights would be put out early and when nobody felt sleepy the boy next to me would call out:

> "Powell will tell a story." Other voices would take it up: "Story! Story!" until the Prefect's voice would be heard magisterially, "All right Powell! Let's have it!" And I would lie back on my bed, my hands behind my head and in a clear voice like my mother's I would tell another man's story in my own way…I was a good narrator. My mother's readings aloud had taught me the value of pauses, of change in voice, of change in speed… I had a photographic memory and knew a lot of poetry by heart…[reciting "Drake's Drum" with the boys drumming along on the partitions, "Drum! Drum! Drum!" all the while thinking about their fathers and older brothers in danger]…the Housemaster would come to the door, saying, "Drake's Drum," eh? They'll drum them in the Channel, eh? Now…no more drumming! Goodnight all!"…And I would lie there staring up into the darkness getting drunk on rhymes, while the dormitory slept.[18]

At the time of finishing Upper School, Powell thought he would seek a scholarship and study history at college. But this was not to be. "That hope was knocked on its head," he acknowledged.[19] "I was told I must leave school and find a job."[20] His mother and father divorced and his father decided that he must go to work. His father found him a job as a bank clerk, where he worked for two years. "I must have been the most unpromising bank clerk!" he later said.[21] But at Christmastime in 1920, his imagination was ignited by a magazine article he had read about film making. He knew at once that a life in movies was for him. [22]

The Mind of an Historian and an Adventurer
His grandfather Corbett was a routine visitor of second-hand bookstores and the library, especially the British Museum Reading Room. Containing a copy of all books and journals published in

England and many of the books published in Western Europe, this library was restricted to pass holders only. Powell writes that his grandfather used this library throughout his life, first as a solicitor and mayor of Worcester, then as a journalist, and then finally, simply for pleasure. Following in his grandfather's footsteps, Powell loved reading of all kinds: newspapers, *The Times Literary Supplement*, fiction, and non-fiction. In *My Life in Movies* Powell made special mention of his Aunt Ethel, who would send on to him *The Times Literary Supplement* after she had finished reading it: "[It became] a necessary part of my life."[23] This exposed him to still wider circles of subject matter.

He credited his other aunt, Aunt Ula, with giving him a book that shaped his thinking as a storyteller interested in history. The book was *The Blazed Trail* by Stewart Edward White. According to Powell, "This mixture of photographic realism and strenuous adventure was very much to my taste, as many rueful actors both dead and alive could testify."[24] He sensed that a non-fiction account could be realistic and yet convey something more.

Love of history, with its details and over-arching story, was part of the way Powell's mind worked. His Latin teacher, Reverend H.V. Tower, was one of his most influential teachers because "he made [Latin] a living language…He made us hear and see the bustle of the Roman market place. He introduced us to Roman slang and proverbs and racy equivalents…he would talk about the Roman invasion of Britain and the Roman walls of Canterbury."[25] This explains why Powell was disappointed in Jacques Cousteau, a man Powell greatly admired, when Cousteau's divers went diving in France at the Fontaine de Vaucluse, at the base of Roman era buildings, and reemerged saying, "There is nothing there."[26] For Powell, there was always something there to be noticed and considered. Thus, Rex

Ingram picked the right person when he sent the young Powell on his first assignment to evaluate a location for a film—a monastery. "Powell, I've got a job for you," he said. "Do you know what a Trappist monk is?...Here's the address of the monastery. They are bound by their rules to receive you for three days. Learn what you can and try to take some stills. Photographers are forbidden but you look like such a fool you'll probably get away with it!"[27]

Maps

Michael Powell loved maps. As he described the preparation for almost every film, he mentioned that he would purchase maps, or locate them in the library and study them. He had little patience for people who did not appreciate maps. When the shooting of *The End of the World* was nearing completion, the people of the island of Foula pooled contributions with the intent of having a farewell dinner. But after long delays caused by two weeks of unrelenting violent storms, the film company was ordered off the island. Michael Powell delayed this departure by one day to allow for the shooting of one final sequence. Time had run out for a proper goodbye. The men of Foula gathered to say good bye and handed Powell the money. He later wrote,

> The appreciation of the men of Foula and the fellowship that had grown between us, the memories that would always be shared; this deep feeling more than anything was the cause of the shock and our instant revolt when asked to pick up and leave as if our long struggle of 18 weeks meant no more to us than an illicit weekend…

As he accepted the gift of money, Powell promised to provide his own gift:

> [I offered] a souvenir map, in color, of Foula with the names of camps and the places where we've worked and pictures of the things we all know, and every man who worked on the film shall have a copy, to frame it and hang it on the wall and show his grandchildren what a tough old bird he is thanks to those days on Foula.[28]

Taken together, these attributes—his quick mind, retentive memory, hunger for reading, appetite for history and scholarship, engagement in current events and the social fabric of Great Britain, and continuing interest in maps—suggest that Michael Powell saw himself as a quick-minded person interested in everything of the past and the present. A more thorough reading of *My Life in Movies* reveals that at the start of every film, he wrote that he would go to a library, many times the British Museum Reading Room. He would carry a box of books with him when he was filming away from a studio, or when he was on a trip to India or Machu Picchu. When he traveled to do research for *49th Parallel* or *The Spy in Black*, he would buy maps and pick up pamphlets and newspapers to learn the details of the place, much as a contemporary historian would. In the book *Edge of the World*, he wrote about his earlier movies: "All these years I had been reading up lighthouses, ship building, dam-construction, fire-assessing, plumbing and housemaid's knee for various pictures, but any spare time I had was devoted to my pet subject, the Islands. I read Seton Gordon, Keaton, Martin, Boswell and Johnson."[29]

In fact, he described himself as an historian and an explorer. As he contrasted his developing way of making a shot of a waterfall with Rex Ingram's approach, he said, "My methods are different. Rex couldn't shoot anything that didn't interest him. *I am interested in everything.* In Rex's place I would have vanished with a local guide into the Cuban jungles until I found the waterfall, come back and dragged my reluctant company of actors and technicians to the scene. Heroic stuff..."[30]

Powell experienced his intellectual and creative life as an explorer, studying a map spread out before him, anxious to go directly to the empty places to see what was there. "I look upon my films the way an explorer surveys an empty portion of the map and vows to fill it up" he said.[31] He wrote with great enthusiasm about pontoon airplanes that allowed an explorer to dip into a remote location, unvisited by the outside world for many years, and then leave the society unchanged upon departure:

> I sometimes think and smile of all the obscure corners of the world that were illuminated, held briefly in the spotlight and then allowed to lapse back into obscurity again. Lonely rivers, sacred lakes that had been left to the birds and beasts for hundreds of years, were to hear the thunder of [pontoon plane] engines and a native prince would dream of international airports. Then suddenly one morning a better landing-place would be found, his lake would be down-graded to Emergency Landing Only and the sleep of centuries resumed.[32]

In each of his films up to the time of *AMOLAD*, maps are visible as set decoration or props used by the actors:
- *Edge of the World*—map shown at beginning of film
- *49th Parallel*—maps in Hudson's Bay post and throughout the film
- *Spy in Black*—maps in the submarine
- *One of Our Aircraft is Missing*—maps in the operations room
- *A Canterbury Tale*—map opens during Prologue as well as being visible in Culpepper's office

- *Life and Death of Colonel Blimp*—set decoration in offices at the beginning of Candy's career and consulted as "War begins tonight"
- *I Know Where I'm Going!*—one map in train car and another in Catriona's living room

A Documentary vs. How It Must Have Been

Powell made an important distinction between his way of creating a film with an insistence of accuracy and the approach of a documentarian. In 1933–1934, he had extended discussions with Robert Flaherty, the filmmaker who had just made the first feature-length documentary, *Nanook of the North*.[33] They talked over Powell's plans to make a film of the evacuation of St. Kilda. Flaherty said, "'Tis God's pity that you were not there even with a Kodak on the day the event took place! 'Tis a crime!"

Since Powell and Flaherty were in the same building editing their films, there were many installments of this conversation. Powell maintained that his film of St. Kilda would have a story of the way the islanders' lives would be changed forever. Flaherty continued,

> A story? …Facts are facts. You cannot beat nature. You can't invent the evacuation of an island; you can't ignore the death of a people! Ya' should have been there when it happened! With half a dozen cameras.' By this time half the editing staff had joined the argument fact against fiction, the eternal argument between the liar and the journalist, between 'I was there,' and 'This is how it must have been.

Powell wanted to tell to tell how it must have been.

The only reference I could find to anything that Powell ever feared was having an inaccuracy in his film. Here's what he wrote about accuracy in *Edge of the World*: "I have an anxiety, amounting to morbidity, not to have any serious howler in any film of mine which deals with a technical subject."[34]

Creating a Film

His 1938 book, *The Edge of the World: The making of a film (200,000 Feet on Foula)* provided a glimpse of his intellectual style. Because there were six years between his reading of the first newspaper article concerning the evacuation of St. Kilda and the making of the film, he took time in his book to describe the steps he took. He made a distinction between *the idea of a film*—in this case, the defeat of islanders by an island—and *the story to be told* in the film—of two island families with sons who are best friends but who have opposite assessments of their situation. He also listed the authors and titles of at least five books he read in that time period as well as the reference details of two newspaper articles he read which ignited his thinking. In these details we learn that a) he is a reader; b) he is a researcher who reads widely about this topic; c) he is a scholar who documents his sources; and d) he is an historian who can document the arc of his film from its earliest ingredients. In telling the story of the creation of the film, he could have left all of this material out or summarized it in two or three sentences. But because we know he followed these steps and those steps were as significant to him as telling the stories of obtaining camera angles while perched precariously on a cliff in Foula, we can see that he has an intellectual depth that probably was an integral part of his personality and probably can be seen in his later films. In *A Life in Movies*, he told us that he still went to book stalls and the British Museum Reading Room in the intense days of 1939-1946. While he skipped telling us the titles of some of the books,

I still think that he consulted them as carefully as he told us he did in preparation for his first film.

A Creative Explorer Finds a Medical Map to Explore a New Region

My emphasis on Powell's way of thinking about the world and being a creative force within it explains why he created the medical portions of *AMOLAD*. The idea of the film, shared by both Emeric Pressburger and Michael Powell, was that love is stronger than death or any other force or circumstance. Michael Powell's telling the story of the film was his seeking a scientific explanation for the events of the film.

I believe what might have attracted Michael Powell to neurology was that *the neurological scientists of the time were making a map of the brain, and then surgeons were going to these places on the map to seize a cure from death's grasp.* Through a series of experiments beginning in the 1860s, scientists were determining that the brain had a specific location for each brain function; that location could be deduced by the symptoms of the brain disorder; and a surgeon could be guided by that information to operate successfully to cure the patient's problem and save the patent from death. These brain maps were published in textbooks available to Michael Powell in the British Museum reading room. Michael Powell was capable of reading and understanding this material. *AMOLAD* is a movie to show how neurologists use a map to find a way to the problem and to the solution. In Chapter Seven, I will point out where Michael Powell leaves those maps in plain view as set decoration. In his words, "The gift of curiosity about the world we are born into and in which we grow up is a rare and wonderful one. All artists have it and wish to pass it on to others."[35]

1. Powell, Michael, *A Life in Movies*. (New York: Knopf, 1987), 17.
2. Ibid., 29.
3. Ibid., 163.
4. Ibid., 29.
5. Ibid., 56.
6. Ibid., 57.
7. Ibid., 63–64.
8. Ibid., 65.
9. Ibid., 60.
10. Ibid., 33.
11. Ibid., 163.
12. Ibid., 92.
13. Ibid., 74.
14. Ibid., 76.
15. Ibid., 68.
16. Ibid., 69.
17. Ibid., 106.
18. Ibid., 71–72.
19. Ibid., 106.
20. Ibid., 95.
21. Ibid., 114.
22. Ibid., 92.
23. Ibid., 117.
24. Ibid., 107.
25. Ibid., 69.
26. Ibid., 21.
27. Ibid., 160.
28. Ibid., 322.

29. Powell, Michael, *The Edge of the World: The making of a film (200,000 Feet on Foula),* published 1938. (London: Faber and Faber, 1990), 19.
30. Powell, *A Life in Movies*, 156.
31. Ibid., 242.
32. Ibid., 281.
33. Ibid., 237–38.
34. Powell, *The Edge of the World*, 250.
35. Powell, *A Life in Movies*, 419.

Chapter Two:

Sudden Losses and Medical Hope: The Story of A Matter of Life and Death *and a Reflection of the Era*

One way to think about *AMOLAD* is that it is a story concerning special boundaries of time and space. Powell and Pressburger created a story in which the pilot Peter Carter will move across those boundaries in ways that people usually cannot. A special type of boundary is one that allows movement in only one direction. *AMOLAD* has many of these one-way boundaries: time, knowledge, death, and movement from Earth to Heaven. While it seems simple-minded to say that once an event has occurred, we will always be aware of it and cannot go back to erase that awareness, there is an example of that one-way boundary within the first few moments of *AMOLAD*. The narrator says, "Hello! There's a nova! A whole solar system exploded. Someone must have been messing about with the uranium atom. No, it's not our solar system, I'm glad to say!"

The narrator suggests that this movie straddles the boundary of knowledge about the atom bomb. Peter, in the cockpit of the burning plane in May 1945, knows nothing about the atom bomb and how future history will be transformed. The audience, eighteen months later, knows a new fear from the atomic bomb. They immediately grasp this reference, while mere months earlier they would not have. The audience is reminded right away that the boundaries of knowledge, time, and space cannot be traveled in a reverse direction. Yet Powell and Pressburger are going to do that very thing in this film by having Peter travel between Heaven and Earth for the next three days.

The film begins on the night of May 2, 1945. Peter Carter (David Niven) has flown his Lancaster on a bombing mission to Berlin and is returning to England. En route, his plane is hit by anti-aircraft fire. While his other crewmen have either parachuted to safety or have been killed, Peter is stuck because his parachute has been destroyed. He speaks on the radio with June (Kim Hunter), an American radio operator based in England, expecting that it will be the last conversation of his life before he chooses to die quickly by jumping from the plane into the fog. He awakens on a beach and learns to his great surprise that he is not in Heaven but rather on Earth, and in fact very near June's lodgings. He finds June, and they fall completely in love.

But Peter was supposed to die, and the angel sent to pick him up, Conductor 71 (Marius Goring), is in hot water for his poor performance. His supervisor angel sends him back to Earth to pick up Peter. Learning this from Conductor 71 in an encounter that evening, Peter refuses to go, saying it was not his fault and he wants to appeal this decision. June, worried that Peter is suddenly convinced that he has had a conversation with an angel, goes the next morning to her English friend Dr. Frank Reeves (Roger Livesey) for help.

Luckily, Dr. Reeves is a neurology expert and, after interviewing Peter that afternoon, invites him to come to his home for further observation. At Dr. Reeves' house, Peter has several more encounters with Conductor 71, who informs him that his appeal will be taken up by a tribunal in which a Boston Yankee who was killed in the Revolutionary War (Raymond Massey) will bring the case against Peter. Peter's encounters with Conductor 71 become more intense, and Peter travels closer and closer to the other world in each encounter.

By the next morning, Dr. Reeves is convinced of the cause of Peter's brain problem and, furthermore, that Peter must have emergency brain surgery before the end of the day or Peter will die. That evening, during a torrential rain storm, Peter is transported by ambulance to the American military hospital. Dr. Reeves rides ahead on his motorcycle, but is killed in an accident. While Peter is on the operating table, the trial takes place in Heaven with Dr. Reeves now acting as his defending counsel. June is called as a witness in the trial. June's proof of her everlasting love, unaltered by circumstance of illness or difference in country, persuades the Heavenly Court to allow Peter to live a long and happy life with her. Peter awakens from successful surgery in June's embrace, declaring, "We've won."

A 1946 film audience would be aware of the explosion of important medical advances in the first half of the twentieth century. Major advances were being made in every aspect of medicine and surgery. One primary development was that it was finally conceivable to survive brain surgery and recover from some brain illnesses and trauma. This was the cumulative effect of the work of neurologists, neurosurgeons, and researchers from the 1860s onward. We will trace some of these achievements with the intent that they can help the reader understand the neurologic elements present in *AMOLAD*.

Even without the details of medical history, an audience member in 1946 would be aware of several prominent people who had suffered significant neurological problems in the 1930s. The injuries and deaths of these prominent people would resonate with audience members as they watched *AMOLAD*, because *AMOLAD* achieves a different, modern solution to problems caused by brain trauma.

While there were many practicing neurosurgeons by 1939, the work of pioneering surgeons Joseph Lister (Scotland, 1827–1912), William Macewen (Scotland, 1848–1924), Victor Horsley (England, 1857–1916), Harvey Cushing (America, 1869–1939), Hugh Cairns (Australia, 1896–1952), and Herbert Olivecrona (Sweden, 1891–1980) is echoed in *AMOLAD*, and several of their famous patients would probably come to mind if we were to ask an audience member of 1946. Specifically, some audience members very likely could recount the end-of-life medical problems of T.E. Lawrence, Frigyes Karinthy, George Gershwin, and General George Patton. When these prominent people were in medical trouble, prominent surgeons were called to try to save their lives. Their medical problems intensified over several days, and daily updates were reported in the newspapers of the day. These well-known public figures were experiencing intensifying medical difficulty, and that true-to-life suspense was a commonly shared experience.

T.E. Lawrence, Lawrence of Arabia (1888–1935)

Thomas Edward Lawrence was a dramatic figure of WWI and the following decade. He had traveled widely in the Middle East as an archeologist in the years before 1914. The British Foreign Service enlisted his help as WWI began to help organize the Arab tribes to engage the Turks in battle with the hopes of diverting some of the military resources of the Turks and their allies, the Germans.

A Matter of Life and Death

Lawrence was very comfortable with the customs and culture of the Arab world and dressed in Arabian garb. His handsome face and dramatic story made him a popular hero after the war, his reputation enhanced by the films of Lowell Thomas.

Lawrence loved fast travel. Returning to England, he owned several powerful motorcycles, his favorite—"a Brough Superior, given to him by his friend George Bernard Shaw—having power and acceleration that outstripped its handling and braking characteristics." He routinely rode without wearing a helmet.[1]

On May 13, 1935, he was riding at high speed on the twisting, hilly roads near his home in Cloud's Hill, Dorset, when he encountered two boys in the road. He swerved to avoid them and flipped over the handlebars, suffering a fractured skull. Neurosurgical specialists were called try to save his life, among them Hugh Cairns. Lawrence died five days later without regaining consciousness at age 47.[2]

This was a defining moment in Cairns's neurosurgical career. He wrote that as a result of that experience among others, he wanted to reduce the number of head injuries caused by motorcycle accidents. Using the careful descriptive and statistical methods he learned while training under Dr. Harvey Cushing in Boston, Cairns began to collect data on head trauma associated with motorcycle accidents. He was able to demonstrate that the incidence of head injury and death was markedly reduced with wearing helmets. Cairns was single-minded in pushing relentlessly for wearing of motorcycle helmets to be compulsory for British army cyclists. Motor cyclist fatalities were reduced by more than 50% after helmets became compulsory in late 1942. The importance of wearing a helmet while riding a motorcycle will be an important detail of plot within *AMOLAD*. (See appendix I)

T.E. Lawrence was an important figure for Michael Powell. There is a picture of Lawrence visible in his short film from 1941, *An Airman's Letter to his Mother.* Later in his career, he considered making a film about Lawrence.

George Gershwin (1898–1937)

In 1936, at the age of 38, George Gershwin had already written a number of significant longer pieces including *Concerto in F, American in Paris, Rhapsody in Blue, Cuban Overture,* and *Porgy and Bess,* as well as a large number of popular songs. He was handsome, vigorous, and very physically fit, walking six miles daily. He told one reporter that he felt he had a hundred unwritten songs inside of himself. He was the life of the party and played the piano into the night at the many gatherings to which he was invited.

But then in February 1937, he faltered briefly while performing *Concerto in F* at the piano at the Hollywood Bowl. Oscar Levant took note of this very brief pause while the conductor Alexander Smallens finessed the lapse so that it was hardly noticeable. Levant later wrote that after the concert, he joked with Gershwin that George must have been nervous because he was in the audience.[3] Gershwin told his private physician and later his psychiatrist that he had smelled an odor of burning rubber just before he briefly blacked out. His first episode of smelling burning rubber had occurred in 1934.[4] He also experienced headaches and dizzy spells. The doctors attributed these symptoms to overwork or difficulties in his personal life.

The results of a physical exam performed in early 1937 were normal. But then the headaches, blackouts, and episodes of smelling burning rubber became more frequent. He had two episodes of strange behavior that were interpreted as being caused by a possible unconscious psychological conflict. He also had symptoms of an odd stomach sensation which he called his "composers stomach."

He played the piano for the last time in his bungalow in Los Angeles on July 9, 1937. By evening he fell into a coma from which he never awakened. He had pupilary changes and asymmetric responses to pain and reflex testing. Although he had refused a spinal tap in the week before his death, a tap performed after he lapsed into coma revealed an abnormally high cerebro-spinal fluid pressure. He was then diagnosed as having a rapidly expanding brain tumor. The pressure of the tumor on other brain structures was causing his lapses of consciousness and unusual behavior. He was having complex partial seizures whose presenting symptoms were olfactory (burning rubber), and epigastric, and also exhibited confused behavior with loss of consciousness. These seizures are called uncinate seizures because of the origin of the symptoms in the uncinate gyrus of the temporal lobe. This will be discussed more fully in the next chapter.

Urgently, Dr, Harvey Cushing was called to operate, but Dr. Cushing refused, saying that he had retired and feared that his abilities were not as acute as they had been. At the behest of Gershwin's friends contacting the Governor of Maryland, the U.S. Coast Guard was sent to find prominent neurosurgeon Walter Dandy, a visitor on the DuPont yacht, sailing on the Chesapeake Bay. Arrangements were made to fly him to California, but neurosurgeon Howard Nafziger of the University of California Medical School, Berkeley, was flown from Lake Tahoe to operate on Gershwin. The composer had an advanced glioblastoma and despite surgery, he died on July 11.[5,6,7]

Funeral services were held concurrently in New York City and in Hollywood. In New York, four thousand people attended his funeral at Temple Emanu-el. Fifth Avenue was closed because thousands of people stood outside the synagogue in the street in the rain. *The*

New York Times listed many notables attending, including Fiorello LaGuardia, DuBose Hayward, Cole Porter, and Charlie Chaplin.[8] A film of the life and death of George Gershwin, *Rhapsody in Blue,* was made in 1945.

Frigyes Karinthy (1887—1938)

Frigyes Karinthy was a popular Hungarian satirist, who wrote numerous plays, short essays, and poems. In March 1936, he began to have short episodes of hearing loud sounds resembling locomotives as well as episodes of altered consciousness. Sometimes he heard a musical phrase, the same one, over and over. He was evaluated by a series of physicians in Budapest, and eventually a diagnosis of brain tumor was made. The tumor was causing complex seizures whose first symptom was auditory.

He was sent to Stockholm to be treated by one of most prominent neurosurgeons of Europe, Herbert Olivecrona. The surgical procedure was successful, and he was able to return home. He wrote about his experiences in *A Journey 'Round My Skull*, which was published in 1937 and translated into English in 1939.[9] Reviewers found it a remarkable book that offered unique insights into the workings of the human mind. Reviewers and physicians indicated they had never read a book where the author was able to reflect on his thoughts as he tried to determine what was real and what was a seizure symptom.[10] In an amusing, everyday way, this book allowed readers to think about hallucinations, imagination, psychiatry, and brain surgery. In the first chapter of the book before any neurological symptoms have occurred, Karinthy describes attending a medical lecture where revolutionary brain surgical techniques were being shown in a movie. The surgeon in the film was Harvey Cushing. His trainee, Herbert Olivecrona, would soon save Karinthy's life.

George Patton (1885–1945)
George Patton was the commander of the Third US Army in Europe during WWII. On December 9, 1945, near Mannheim, Germany, one day before he was due to return to the United States, Patton was injured in a car accident.[12] He had been out on a hunting trip shooting pheasants when his Cadillac was struck by an army truck in the fog. The General was thrown forward, striking his head on a metal partition in the car. He was paralyzed from the neck down. Newspaper reports indicated that he was having some neurological recovery, but in fact it was minimal. Among the specialists called to treat the General was Hugh Cairns. Cairns determined that surgery could not remedy the fracture of his fourth cervical vertebrae. Cairns wrote, "What the next week will bring forth is uncertain…The General is in good spirits and is an excellent patient. He is clearly regarded with the greatest affection by his fellow generals. I liked him very much and felt privileged to help a little."[11] Patton died December 21, 1945, of a pulmonary embolism.[12]

The Filmmakers and Audience of 1946
As shown above, the moviegoing audience of 1946 would have shared common memories of these prominent people having serious neurologic problems and seeking expert help for a potential reprieve. Additionally, Michael Powell had his own experience of sudden illness and cataclysmic loss when his beloved older brother died at age fifteen of a ruptured appendix; and later on the same day his grandmother died of a heart attack.[13] The moviemaker and the audience shared the common experience of having the same urgent, painful questions: What is happening? What should we do? Why is the person acting strangely? Is the person cracked? Or done for? Can they survive? Is it my fault? What does it mean? How will their future be affected?

Shouldn't we hurry and do something? Can't we do something better? Why did they have to die? Do they know how much we miss them?

By 1946, Michael Powell and Emeric Pressburger had already created ten films in a very fruitful partnership that began in 1937. One consistent aspect of their work was factually accurate portrayal of technical and historical details. One reason why *AMOLAD* is so compelling is because in its medical reality, it touches the real experiences and feelings of the audience. In his revisions of the script, Michael Powell wanted the medical part of the story be completely realistic. To achieve that result, Powell would harness the strength of medical scholarship. In the next chapter, we will explore facts about the workings of the brain available to the neuroscientists of 1945 and then trace how that scholarship is woven into the dialogue, the set decoration, the movements of the actors, and even in the point of view of the camera.

1. Maartens, N.F., Wills, A.D., Adams, C.B.T., "Lawrence of Arabia, Sir Hugh Cairns and the origin of motor cycle helmets," *Neurosurgery* 50 no. 1 (Jan 2002): 176–180, quote on 177.

2. Kuhn, Ferdinand, "Lawrence of Arabia Dying," *The New York Times* (May 14, 1935).

3. Rosenberg, Deena, *Fascinating Rhythm: the Collaboration of George and Ira Gershwin,* (New York: Dutton, 1991), 366.

4. Sloop, Gregory, "What caused George Gershwin's untimely death?" *Journal of Medical Biography* 9 (2001): 28–30, quote on 28.

5. Teive, H.A.G., Germiniani, F.M.B., et al., "The Uncinate Crisis of George Gershwin," *Arq Neuropsiquiatr* 60, no. 2-B(2002): 505–8.

6. Carp, L., "George Gershwin: Illustrious American Composer: his fatal glioblastoma," *American Journal of Surgical Pathology* 3 No. 5 (Oct. 1979): 473–78.

7. Silverstein, Allen, "The brain tumor of George Gershwin and the legs of Cole Porter," *Seminars in Neurology* 19, suppl. 1 (1999): 3–9.

8. "Thousands attend Gershwin funeral," *The New York Times,* (July 16, 1937).

9. Karinthy, Frigyes, *A Journey 'Round My Skull*, translated from the Hungarian by Vernon Duckworth Barker (London: Faber and Faber, 1939).

10. Thompson, Ralph, "Books of the Times," *The New York Times* (Aug. 10, 1939).

11. Fraenkel, G.J. *Hugh Cairns: First Nuffield Professor of Surgery* (Oxford: Oxford University Press, 1991), 173–74.

12. McLaughlin, Kathleen "Patton seriously injured as auto hits army truck," *The New York Times* (Dec.10, 1945). See also Dec. 12, 1945, and Dec. 22, 1945.

13. Powell, Michael, *A Life in Movies.* (New York: Knopf, 1987), 78–79.

Chapter Three:

"Dr. Cushing, Have You Ever Seen the Soul?" An Introduction to the Workings of the Brain

This chapter begins with the history of one important idea in the field of neuroscience: the brain has discrete locations for various functions, and those locations are in the same place in every person. Then we will take a little time to review some important aspects of how the brain works. Before you yawn and turn the page, entertain this argument: By understanding a little about how scientists understand the brain, you will be traveling the same intellectual path that Michael Powell did. If you familiarize yourself with some of the basic ideas of neuroscience, you will be able to more fully appreciate the brain science woven into *AMOLAD* by Michael Powell.

From the early 1800s scientists, surgeons, and physicians—many of them from England, Scotland, Ireland, and Australia— pressed on to make sense of what they observed in a patient's symptoms and how that somehow connected with what they saw at the time of surgery.

The mechanism of the brain's function began to reveal its secrets. Even today, the evaluation and diagnosis of a person with a brain problem begins with the skilled investigation of the neurological exam. It is my belief that by the time Michael Powell finished the final draft of *AMOLAD* in his cabin of the ship *Queen Elizabeth*, he had taught himself and thoroughly understood those details of the neurologic exam and the workings of the brain and the eye. He wove those details throughout the entire story. Specifically, Michael Powell carefully included accurate, subtle details about complex partial seizures in portraying Peter Carter's hallucinations and impending death.

If you prefer, you can proceed directly to my analysis. As an alternative, you might like to read my brief mini-tutorial of how the brain works. If you take the time to learn those details as Powell did, you will be rewarded with seeing the film's embedded riches. While my mentioning the names of surgeons and neurologists may seem tedious right now, you will see how all the pieces fit together as Michael Powell crafted a film of the intellectual heritage of Britain.

Mini-Tutorial:
What Michael Powell Learned about
How the Brain Works

In 1930, Harvey Cushing, the neurosurgeon mentioned in the previous chapter, was asked, "During your surgery, have you ever seen the soul?" This question implies that the soul is a special function of the brain and there is a special location for it.

Eighty years earlier, in 1850, that question would not have been possible. At that time, the brain was not well understood, beyond the fact that it is a three pound, soft, pink, apparently uniform mound of tissue appearing on its surface as indistinct as liver. Proposals concerning how the brain worked had begun with Hippocrates. But in the early 1800s, very gradually and then with more intensity, a combination of ideas from philosophy, experiments from physiologists, and observations during surgery began to emerge, allowing some proposals to demonstrate real validity. No one knew for sure what functions the brain performed, if there were significant locations in the brain for each of those functions, or even if those functions were located in the same place from person to person; but a path towards that understanding was starting to take shape.

Because the primary purpose of this book is to analyze a movie, I cannot take too much time to chart the antecedents of these ideas. An interested reader might enjoy learning more, such as how the ideas of Franz Josef Gaul connecting functions of the brain with phrenology led Paul Broca to correctly predict that a patient who had lost speech from a stroke would have a particular location of damage, which itself subsequently influenced experimenters Gustav Fritsch and Eduard Hitzig to experimentally evaluate brain lesions.[1, 10]

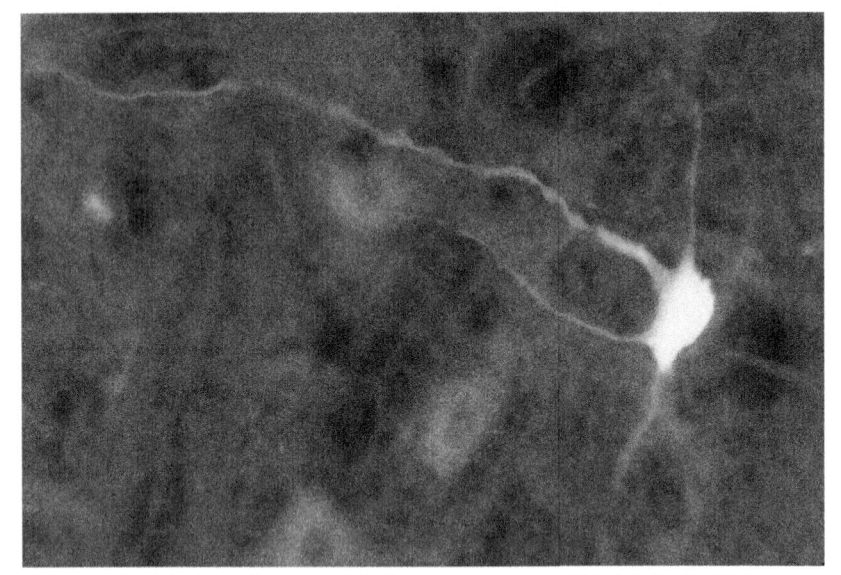

Neuron (1991). Photograph by kind permission of Ralph Lydic PhD.

The Origin of a Way To See

The period from 1850 to 1945 was the blossoming of a significant understanding of the brain. This understanding was made possible by breakthroughs in the understanding of one particular brain condition, seizures. Seizures are the events that David Niven's character Peter Carter experiences in *AMOLAD*.

In 1850, the philosopher Herbert Spencer was developing a new science of psychology separate from philosophy. He was asking questions about how the mind works; how we sense time and space; and how we speak, remember, and move. He published his ideas in 1855 in *Principles of Psychology*.[2]

In the 1860s, a young British physician, John Hughlings Jackson (1835-1911), was influenced by Spencer's ideas. He had special interest in patients with brain problems, especially epilepsy, the condition of having recurrent seizures. He developed two fundamental findings in neuroscience. First, he made careful observations of persons with seizures, realizing that a patient tended to have the same characteristics in seizure after seizure. While one person's seizures might be different from the next person's, one patient's seizures all tended to resemble each other. When autopsies were permitted, he recorded the location of brain lesions—caused by tumor, stroke, infection, abnormal blood vessels, or trauma—and made the important connection that brain lesions in one location tended to produce similar appearing seizures. The second important finding followed: John Hughlings Jackson concluded that it was likely that each location in the brain had a discrete function, and that location was in the same place from person to person. He also proposed that the brain had many locations of other discrete functions yet to be uncovered.[3,4,5,6,7]

How Seizures Occur

Neurons

Today we understand that the brain is a complex network of millions of neurons that make formal communications pathways through the release of discrete and specific brain chemicals called neurotransmitters. When one neuron releases a neurotransmitter and when that chemical transmitter touches the receptors of an adjacent neuron, an electrical charge moves down the exterior of the second cell's membrane to the terminal end, where another neurotransmitter is released. This transfer of chemical information takes place in fractions of a second and over distances stretching from the top of the head to the base of the spine. This chemical communications system creates tiny electrical gradients that can be detected with electrodes placed on the scalp—the electroencephalogram (EEG).

Diane Broadbent Friedman

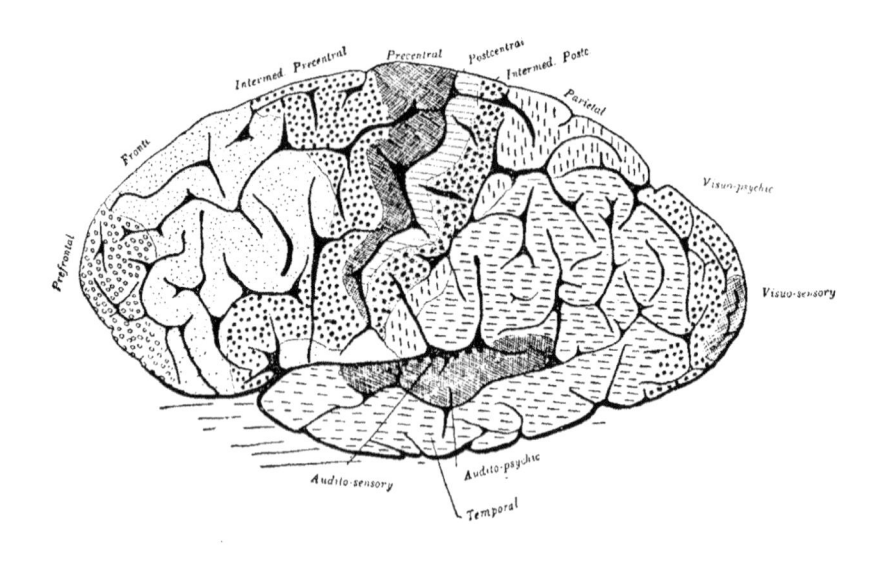

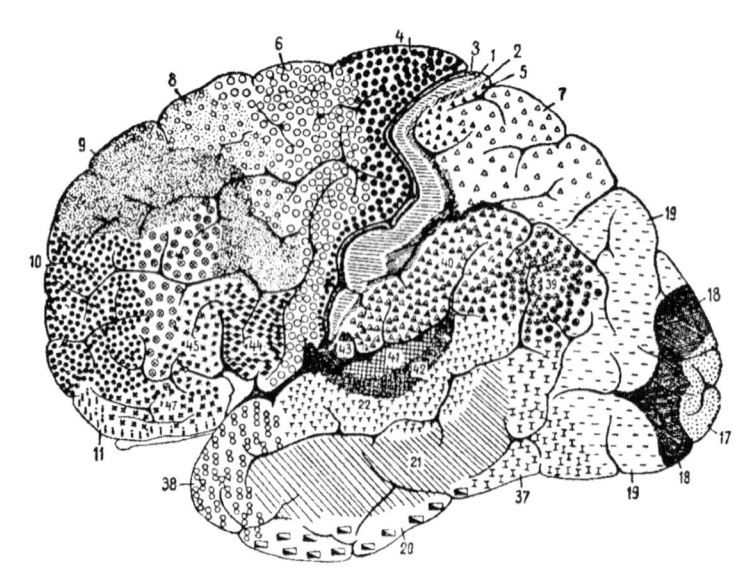

Campbell's cytoarchitectural map, Brodman's areas and localization of brain function. Figure 68 (p.327) from "Physiology of the Nervous System" by Fulton, John F. © (1938) By permission of Oxford University Press.

Activation and inhibition

When brain cells send chemical signals to adjacent cells, those signals may be to *activate* a second cell or to *inhibit* that cell. Think of the example of threading a needle: your brain is sending signals to allow you to use some muscles while inhibiting others, so that your hand does not shake as you coordinate your hands and eyes to accomplish the task.

Normal brain function

Usually the cells of the brain are in various states of activity and inhibition to allow us to think and to perform voluntary actions while suppressing other actions. The brain is organized by locations of activity. There are discrete locations for vision, movement, sensation, memory, smell, thinking, hearing, speech, and emotion, among many other functions. Some of these locations are inter- connected by complex sets of neuronal pathways from one side of the brain to the other and from front to back, as well as pathways running down the spinal cord (and returning, which bring information from the outside world!)

Seizure

A seizure occurs when groups of brain cells are suddenly and unpredictably recruited to an active state. They all fire synchronously and release their neurotransmitters at the same time. The seizure stops just as unpredictably when the brain somehow inhibits this recruitment of neurons and restores the usual balance of activity and inhibition of the cells. No one yet knows exactly why this happens. If there is some damage to a cell, why does it begin a seizure at one moment and not another? What helps the brain stop its own seizure? What can we do to keep the cells functioning normally all the time? Contemporary researchers are working on these questions.

In the classification of seizures, there are two broad subtypes: those that affect part of the brain—partial seizures—and those that affect the entire brain—generalized seizures. *Generalized seizures* affect consciousness and the movement of all the body's muscles at the onset. These seizures are recognized when a person loses consciousness, falls, and begins rhythmic jerking movements of arms and legs. The person sleeps afterwards and frequently does not remember what happened, since consciousness and memory areas were affected. *Partial seizures* begin with only a part of the brain being affected. In this case, the person may continue to be conscious and may be able to talk and remember if the seizure is beginning in a movement or sensory or visual area. There are times when the seizure starts in one place but then recruits all the cells of the brain. This is termed a *partial seizure with secondary generalization*.[8]

For instance, John Hughlings Jackson determined that when a seizure's first symptom was a tingling sensation in the right hand, the neurons of the left parietal lobe were responsible. He could then recommend to the surgeon, Victor Horsley, where to make the incision to find a possible tumor. Until Jackson made those conclusions, brain surgeons sometimes operated on both sides of the head, looking for possible treatable lesions. While this seems simple now, it is important to know that in 1886 it was revolutionary.[9]

Jackson's observations were so powerful that partial seizures were named after him. When seizures show a *Jacksonian march*, it means that the visible symptom begins in one place, such as the twitching of the muscles in the left hand, and then progresses up the arm, indicating that a recruitment of adjacent brain cells is taking place in the right motor strip of the frontal lobe.

The understanding and treatment of epilepsy has made significant gains.[10] If you would like to know about the most up-to-

A Matter of Life and Death

date information concerning diagnosis and treatment of seizures and living well with epilepsy please see the web sites of the Epilepsy Foundation of America (http://www.epilepsyfoundation.org/) or the British Epilepsy Association (http://www.epilepsy.org.uk/).

● ●

Diane Broadbent Friedman

June lost from Peter's view in the rhododendron grove. *A Matter of Life and Death* (1946). "Stairway to Heaven"© 1946,1974,1996. Carlton Film Distributors Limited. All Rights Reserved. Courtesy of Columbia Pictures.

Peter Carter Experiences Partial Seizures Arising from the Temporal Lobe

A series of observations

If we look carefully at the *AMOLAD* scene in the garden using the information from the preceding paragraphs, we can consider my proposition: that Peter Carter is experiencing complex partial seizures that are affecting his consciousness.

Let's trace the events of Peter's spell in the garden as a neurologist would, from the first event onward:

We first observe that Peter is speaking with June. All seems well. He then reaches for a cup to pour a drink. This cup disappears from his view. Then a second cup also disappears.

He smells something and sniffs his flask to see if that is the source of the smell. Peter seems to think that something is not working properly in his head because he reaches back and taps it

He looks up and sees Conductor 71, a French man dressed in a late eighteenth-century aristocratic outfit. While June seems to be asleep, Peter has an extended conversation with this man who seems real to him. They discuss whether Peter is dead and should follow the Conductor to Heaven. We see the Conductor tease Peter by waving his cane in front of Peter's face. Peter recovers the cups, which have been held by the Conductor. Peter disputes the claim that he should go to Heaven at that moment and tells the Conductor that he wants an appeal of the decision. Conductor 71 says he will return again in his own time and leaves.

Then June speaks, and we learn that only a few moments have actually passed. Peter remembers the strange conversation with Conductor 71 and realizes that it is so unusual that he worries about "being cracked." He then jumps up in confusion and agitation, calling out for the Conductor. He claps his hands to his face and exclaims that he has an awful headache.

He looks back and is unable to see June. This deeply upsets him. His field of vision is partially obscured. She moves into a clear portion of his visual field and he sees her. He feels a little reassured and exclaims, "I thought I'd lost you!"

A neurologic interpretation

Powell has shown us carefully and deliberately all the elements of a partial seizure, and we can guess where Peter's brain lesion is. Here are the elements in the order they occur:

- o Peter experiences a sudden onset of symptoms.

- He smells an unusual odor.
- He loses sight of objects (the cups) in the lower visual field.
- He has a dreamy vision (a person in eighteenth-century French clothing).
- His dream has thematic elements of death.
- The dream seems to last several minutes, although it is only a moment in real time.
- Afterwards he can speak and remember and move without problems. The odor is gone.
- He seems agitated and says he has a headache.
- He has a loss of the lower-left visual field, which Michael Powell shows us through the lens of the camera.

My analysis: Peter is having a complex partial seizure—one that affects his consciousness but does not generalize to his entire brain. The seizure begins in the innermost, mesial basal part of the temporal lobe on the right side. There are three lines of evidence for this.

First: His aura, the smell of fried onions. Damage to the inner temporal lobe produces auras of smell and of stomach sensations (recall my comments in the previous chapter concerning George Gershwin smelling burned rubber).

Second: His loss of the lower-left part of his visual field. The visual pathway travels through the temporal lobes on its way from the eyes to the back of the brain, where the information is processed by the occipital lobe. The contour of his lower-left visual field loss corresponds to the right temporal lobe.

Third: His hallucination. Temporal lobe seizures can present as dreamy states where the person has a hallucination or dream. It is not simply seeing an indistinct shape but rather a complex vision—possibly because the memory areas are also located in the inner parts of the temporal lobe.

When a complex partial seizure concludes, the person often has a headache and feels confused and agitated. We see Peter going through this experience. John Hughlings Jackson wrote several papers on complex partial seizures that included hallucinations which seemed to threaten death; this aspect is also present in Peter's experience.[11] The detail that Peter's heavenly messenger is wearing an eighteenth-century outfit may also be an element that weaves into the neurological details of the complex partial seizure. This will be discussed more fully in the next chapter.

Aura

Sometimes there is a signal of an impending seizure which is called an aura. This word comes from the observation by the ancient Greek physician Galen, who noticed a boy having repeated seizures. The boy's friend told Galen that every time a seizure happened, the boy would mention that he felt a cold breeze blowing on his cheek. The word *aura* comes from the Greek meaning "breeze." This boy was having a partial seizure, and the seizure symptom indicated that the brain cells associated with the sensory area of the face were the location of this boy's seizure focus.[12]

Can you now recall the appearance of the wind blowing through various scenes of *AMOLAD*? At first there is just a simple breath of wind as Conductor 71 arrives in the garden to have his first conversation with Peter. As the conductor leaves, the bushes are moved by a breath of wind once again. When he next arrives during the Ping Pong game in Dr. Reeves' study, the Conductor makes a joke of causing a brief heavy storm with more intensely blowing wind.

Peter even remarks, "Warn me when you are going to do that again." As Peter's condition grows more grave, storms rage outside with more intensity. I think that Michael Powell is using the wind to suggest an aura, the symptom of onset of a seizure. The aura's intensity grows as Peter's situation worsens.

I believe that Michael Powell has presented all the information we need to diagnose and localize the origin of Peter's complex partial seizure. We have not yet determined why Peter is having seizures and what needs to be done. That can wait for the next chapter.

Peter and Conductor 71, holding his cane and the missing cups. *A Matter of Life and Death* (1946). Photograph by kind permission of Granada International.

The cane

The inner part of the brain's temporal lobe is called the hippocampus. It curls under the brain resembling the curling tail of a seahorse—also known as a hippocampus. But these complex partial seizures having a dreamy presentation are also called by another name—uncinate seizures, referring to the uncinate gyrus, another name for the hippocampus. Uncinate comes from the Greek word meaning hook or crook, which is what Conductor 71 waves in front of Peter's face at the beginning of his first spell. Was this a purposeful neurologic connection on Michael Powell's part? I cannot say for sure, but the cane surely is waved purposefully in this *AMOLAD* scene.

How Could Michael Powell Possibly Know about Complex Partial Seizures?

I hope that my interpretation of the garden scene with the heavenly messenger persuades you to further consider my two conclusions: 1) that Michael Powell deliberately imbedded significant neuroscience within *AMOLAD*, something that perhaps you sensed but did not fully appreciate; and 2) that Powell developed significant neurological expertise in order to accomplish this feat. Not only did Powell provide the information necessary to identify Peter's problem, but he additionally described the entire evaluation process. We will look at that diagnostic process in Chapter Four. In Chapter Six we will learn about the neurological resources available to Michael Powell at the time that he created the script. He had direct connections to at least two surgeons and indirect connections to the neurosurgeon Hugh Cairns. He copied dialogue from medical papers he found or was given. We will use those resources to probe more deeply into the film.

1. Rose, F. Clifford, *A Short History of Neurology: the British Contribution 1660–1910* (Oxford: Butterworth-Heinemann, 1999).

2. Spencer, Herbert, *The Principles of Psychology* (New York: Appleton Press, 1873).

3. Hughlings-Jackson, J. "On a particular variety of epilepsy ("Intellectual aura"), one case with symptoms of organic brain disease" *Brain* (1888–89): 190–207.

4. Buzzard, Farquhar, "Hughlings Jackson and his influence on neurology," *The Lancet* (Oct. 27, 1934): 909–13.

5. Hogan, R. Edward, Kaiboriboon, Kitti, "The 'dreamy state': John Hughlings-Jackson's ideas of epilepsy and consciousness," *American Journal of Psychiatry* 160 (October 2003): 1740–47.

6. Khalsa, Sahib S., Moore, Steven; Van Hoesen, Gary W., "Hughlings Jackson and the role of the entorhinal cortex in temporal lobe epilepsy: From Patient A to Doctor Z" *Epilepsy and Behavior* 9 no. 3 (November 2006): 524–31.

7. Hogan, R. Edward, Kaiboriboon, Kitti, "John Hughlings-Jackson's writing on the auditory aura and localization of the auditory cortex," *Epilepsia* 45 no.7 (2004): 834–37.

8. Leppik Ilo E., *Managing your Epilepsy: A Guide to Balancing Your Life* (New York: Demos Medical Publishing, 2005).

9. Horsley, Victor, "Brain-surgery," *The British Medical Journal* (Oct. 9, 1886): 670–75.

10. Wyllie, Elaine; Gupta, Ajay; Lachhwani, Deepak, *The Treatment of Epilepsy: Principles and Practice* fourth ed. (Philadelphia: Lippincott, Williams and Wilkins, 2005).

11. Greenberg, D., Hochberg, F., and Murray, G., "The theme of death in complex partial seizures," *American Journal of Psychiatry* 141 (1984): 1587–89.

12. Temkin, Oswei, *The Falling Sickness: A history of epilepsy from the Greeks to the beginnings of modern neurology* (Baltimore: Johns Hopkins Press, 1945), 36.

Chapter Four:

"Do You Think I'm Cracked?"
The Neurological Evaluation of Peter Carter

Why did Michael Powell portray Peter Carter as having complex partial seizures? Powell described his thinking process in *A Life in Movies*. Foremost, he valued realism and accuracy. Realism in every film was a deliberate artistic decision, even in his earliest "Quota Quickies." Quota Quickies developed as a response to marketing of British and American films. By 1925, profitable American films were being shown in Britain and were overwhelming the British film industry's ability to make a profit on their own productions. In response, a new British law was enacted: Quota Quickies, shorter British-made films, needed to be shown during the same screening if an American film was to be shown in a British theater. To fulfill this definition of Quota Quickie, at least 75% of the movie's payroll had to go to British subjects, and a British writer must have written it. They were of uneven quality, although some films had lasting impact—but the law had the unintended result of allowing British film-makers like Michael Powell to learn to make films economically, creatively, and very efficiently.

These lines were written in the section of his autobiography devoted to *AMOLAD*:

> The sequence in [*I Know Where I'm Going!*] is obviously based on a real experience and of course it was. Even some of the dialogue is stolen verbatim from our hostess [at the Castle of Sound]. It was the authenticity of our eccentric characters which endeared them to our audiences...
>
> [talking about *Red Ensign* (1934) in a conversation in 1935] ...Joan Maude [who would later be the supervisor angel in *AMOLAD*] said that there was something serious in it, something that she couldn't quite put her finger on which had impressed her. It was a first reaction by my puzzled public to a Powell film. And probably it was the first time that Michael Powell realized that there was something special about a Powell film, something going on on the screen, something intriguing, aloof, but in the long run, memorable. Perhaps it is the tendency to take things seriously: a passion for getting my facts right; and a habit of verifying my quotations...[1]

In *The Edge of the World: The making of a film (200,000 Feet on Foula)* in 1938 he referred to the plot details in earlier Quota Quickies as he wrote, "All these years I had been reading up lighthouses, ship-building, dam-construction, fire-assessing, plumbing and housemaid's knee for various pictures, but in my spare time I was devoted to my pet subject." [The Hebrides and St. Kilda][2] It seems right to repeat his statement: "I have an anxiety, amounting to a morbidity, not to have any serious howler in any film of mine which deals with a technical subject."[3]

In writing about the blending of fantasy and reality in *AMOLAD*, he wrote,

> I realized that the whole idea of a trial in heaven had to have a solid base in reality, medical reality and that the appearance and disappearance of the heavenly messenger would have to be matter-of-fact and realistic if we were to get away with such fantasies at the end of a great war to end all wars. It was the firm acceptance by all the principals of the solid medical reason for the operation on the pilot's brain that made the rest of the plot so satisfying to the audience. When the Americans wanted to rename our film "Stairway to Heaven" we knew at once that they hadn't understood at all what we had succeeded in doing. They saw it all as a fairy tale. I saw it as a surgical operation.[4]

In an interview with Kevin Gough-Yates in 1970 he said the same thing:

> For me, *A Matter of Life and Death* was the most perfect film—the technical perfection, the fact that it is a wonderful conjuring trick to get handed. It is the most fascinating to me because all of this fantasy is taking place in a medical case, inside somebody's damaged head, so there is a good reason for every fantasy image on the screen. This appeals to me for I like to have my fantasy based on something real because life is more fantastic than fantasy…Emeric had sequences where people appeared and disappeared, where you saw shots where the window curtain was moving and he was gone. I simply said, "I can't do it." But I started reading medical textbooks. Out of those

> I got the facts that hallucinations can take place in space not in time. That was a turning point because that meant I could stop time. And then there were all the other things like the pressure on the eyes and the smell of fried onions which all came from textbooks. I rewrote the script entirely and everything came out of natural ideas.[5]

The Challenge of the Story of *AMOLAD*

In 1944, the head of the Films Division of the British Ministry of Information, Jack Beddington, had challenged Michael Powell and Emeric Pressburger to write a story which would emphasize the common heritage of American and England as WWII was drawing to a close. Emeric Pressburger took this idea and expanded it to a far more complex concept. Powell later wrote, "It can be seen that Emeric's interpretation of Jack Beddington's original brief—'Can't you fellows think up a good idea to improve Anglo-American relations?'—created plenty of scope for the director."[6] Then Powell added his ideas of medical realism as a plausible way for a normal man to be experiencing Heaven and Earth as he stated, "…[W]hile the American brain specialist fights for his life in this world, Dr. Reeves fights for his life in the Other World…(in the Heavenly court). Every issue between the two countries, important or trivial, is brought up and examined…"[7]

Emeric Pressburger wrote the original script. Powell wrote, "Emeric's first draft was full of fantasy, light-hearted miracles, mysterious appearances and disappearances. I decided my job was to make each world as real as the other…"[8]

Reality Becomes Medical

Work on the *AMOLAD* story began in 1944 while *A Canterbury Tale* was being edited. Powell and Pressburger decided that they

A Matter of Life and Death

wanted to use color film, but Technicolor would not be available until the war was over. So instead, they made *I Know Where I'm Going!* while continuing research on the structure of *AMOLAD*. One day, when they were both working in the British Museum Reading Room, Emeric Pressburger shared with Powell his findings concerning the first battle in the American Revolution [see Appendix V]. Then Powell asked Pressburger, "Do you know that the olfactory nerve is one of the signals that the brain uses to predict a hallucination, by recalling some smell to the owner of the nerve, a familiar, easily identifiable smell, like fried onions, for instance" [9]

Michael Powell was able to say this because he had consulted with his brother-in-law, Joe Reidy, a plastic surgeon whose specialty was to repair the faces of WWII pilots burned in crashes. Mr. Reidy suggested medical textbooks which, Powell said, "gave me the idea of staging hallucinations in space, not in time. I copied out chunks from medical reports."[10] Powell went on to elaborate on this concept:

> During the next few weeks while we were waiting for the answer print of *A Canterbury Tale*, we both did research in our various ways. Frankie's brother, Joe Reidy, is a plastic surgeon and went through the war as one of McIndoe's team of plastic surgeons who were giving burnt pilots back their faces. "Hallucinations," he said. "You don't need drugs to have hallucinations. Pressure on the brain will do it, if the brain is good enough. Here! Take this pamphlet." I read that, "pressure on the brain can produce highly organized hallucinations, comparable to an experience of real life and which took place in space but not in time."[11]

Powell also went on rounds with an unknown surgeon:

> I use this phrase [highly organized hallucinations] because it was quoted to me by the surgeon who did

> the job in the particular case I was studying. And then he uttered another marvelous phrase which really altered the whole conception of the film. He said, "And this illusion can take place in space but *not* in time." [12]

On the *Queen Elizabeth* in March of 1945, Powell wrote the final draft. He had been filming the final scenes for *IKWIG* when they received the call that their standby tickets for America were available, but only for one person. Powell decided to travel to New York, and Pressburger would follow quickly at the next opportunity. He traveled on a ship which packed eight Americans to each room, with a total of 12,000 soldiers on the ship, traveling 24 knots and making the crossing in 4 1/2 days to avoid German U-Boats. Powell and Pressburger had been working on the script for several months.

> …Emeric and I had had numerous conferences while he was writing the script, and I was working from his final draft. The next one—mine—had to be our definitive version…Emeric had done the historical research and written the story and most of the jokes. I had my medical notes and brought to the script all that I knew and loved about England…[13]

Pressburger reviewed Powell's final draft when Emeric arrived in New York. "He liked slashing straight into the love scene after the prologue," Powell wrote, "and he liked the quotations I had chosen for David to spout, and the medical scenes and the new jokes."[14]

The Neurologic Evaluation of Peter Carter
We can see that finding a medical condition which produces hallucinations was a conscious artistic decision, and that Powell did not invent medical details. Rather, he spent time learning about brain

functioning and how neurologists evaluate patients. That evaluative process is present in several scenes of *AMOLAD* as we watch Dr. Reeves do his work. I will share that analysis now. At the end of this chapter, I will describe more of the neurologic evaluation which is available to the audience even before Peter Carter is examined by Dr. Reeves.

Dr. Reeves' attic
The evaluative process begins in the scene where June speaks with Dr. Reeves as they work with the camera obscura, which is described more fully in Chapter Five. Dr. Reeves reviews what he knows about Peter: 1) Peter believes that he bailed out of an airplane without a parachute; 2) Peter has headaches localized to the right side of the head as Dr. Reeves points to the right side of June's forehead; 3) Peter maintains that he hears and sees things which he believes are "not rubbish." Peter has had a serious recent head trauma with a period of unconsciousness, he has a worsening headache, and he has a fixed belief in the reality of recent hallucinations, although he also realizes that this is a little fantastic. We see that Dr. Reeves is beginning to establish Peter's medical history, which consists of a series of significant events, Peter's state of mind, the length of his amnesia after the fall, his ability to tell reality from fantasy, and the location and duration of his headaches. We learn that Dr. Reeves has taken the time to speak with Peter's commanders to get more information about his mental status prior to the accident.

Lee Wood House
From the 1880s to the present day, a standard neurological exam is conducted in a systematic fashion. First the patient's level of consciousness is determined as well as mood and orientation to time and place. Then information is gathered about the patient's age, level

of education, occupation, and personal and family medical history. The patient is asked to describe the symptoms, when they started, and how severe they are. Then, a physical examination is conducted assessing the function of the nerves of the face (cranial nerve exam); symmetry of facial muscles; facility of speech; visual field examination; balance, evaluation of coordination, muscle bulk and strength, and sensation in upper and lower extremities comparing right to left. This exam assesses deficits in various brain regions and determines if the symptoms and problems detected in the exam indicate possible neurological disorders. A neurologist begins the patient evaluation from the first minute he sees the patient. How the patient sits, walks, converses, and the degree of interest in the environment are all part of the analysis.

You will recall that Dr. Reeves tells the dogs up in his attic that he has formed many diagnoses from his vantage point through the camera obscura; that is, using his disciplined powers of observation. As Dr. Reeves walks across the Great Room in Lee Wood House, we see Dr. Reeves looking carefully at Peter before Peter sees him.

They shake hands and Dr. Reeves continues to study him as they exchange pleasantries. We learn that Peter is a published poet and teaches European History at Oxford. Peter demonstrates some irony as he answers questions about his family medical history and reports that he shares a cause of death with his father—from war.

Next, Dr. Reeves inquires about Peter's extensive flight experience. Peter confirms his medical officer's report that he is having a worsening problem with headaches in a frontal and temporal location as Dr. Reeves summarizes. Dr. Reeves proposes trauma as an explanation, but Peter dismisses that.

A Matter of Life and Death

Visual field exam of Peter Carter by Dr. Reeves. *A Matter of Life and Death* (1946). Photograph by kind permission of Granada International.

Then Dr. Reeves conducts a visual field examination. He stands behind Peter so he can compare his visual field with Peter's. He asks Peter to look straight ahead and then asks questions about his central vision and peripheral vision. Michael Powell is careful to show us that Peter has difficulty with his left peripheral vision, and we sense that Peter is making up his answer, a confabulation which Dr. Reeves detects. Peter cannot see the curtains and he guesses at their color. We also learn that Peter realizes that he cannot see that area clearly; he checks his response with a direct gaze towards the windows. Peter is clearly worried, probably because he realizes that this could interfere with his continued flight status.

Peter then answers questions about his appetite, thirst, and weight, all of which had some disturbance dating before Peter's fall from the plane. Then the question of Peter's hallucinations arises. Peter discusses them calmly and states that he sees the Conductor clearly. He recognizes that they are strange but he does not feel that he is mentally unstable.

Finally Dr. Reeves poses the unusual question about the possibility of Peter smelling something that could not possibly be there. Peter smiles and expresses relief that Dr. Reeves seems to understand the nature of Peter's experiences.

It is interesting to reflect that all of this medical information is gathered by Dr. Reeves within about ten minutes. We in the audience also learn more information about the three protagonists: Peter doesn't brag about his accomplishments; June loves Peter for himself, not his status; and Frank continues to think about his patients, even after their deaths.

The Differential Diagnosis

Because you have read the preceding chapter you can understand Dr. Reeves' thought process. When Dr. Reeves first heard from June that Peter had suddenly started to have hallucinations, and that he believed that he had survived a fall from a plane without a parachute, Dr. Reeves developed a mental list of possible medical explanations for those symptoms. What disorders could account for all of these symptoms? That list is called the differential diagnosis.

What is in the differential diagnosis for Peter's set of symptoms? Is it a psychiatric problem stemming from combat stress and loss of close compatriots? Or could it be a psychosis, post-traumatic stress disorder, or bipolar mania and depression? All are possible.

However there are other explanations. A fall and resulting loss of consciousness fits the definition of concussion. Is the set of symptoms the result of a concussion and exposure to lying in the ocean for three hours? (From 04:00 to 07:30, as Powell tells us in the film.) Brain

A Matter of Life and Death

trauma could lead to a bruise, brain contusion, or a bleeding torn brain artery that is slowly building pressure in Peter's brain.

Dr. Reeves inquires of Peter's Medical Officer and then confirms with Peter that symptoms of headache, hunger, and thirst *predate* the fall, while the hallucination began about twelve hours *after* the fall. A brain problem that slowly develops over a period of time suggests a possible tumor or something blocking the flow of cerebrospinal fluid. Both problems could slowly but relentlessly build pressure on the brain. From Dr. Reeves' questions in Lee Wood House, we can determine that he has already decided that Peter has a problem that has been developing slowly over time. The fall from the plane may be playing a role, but Peter would be having a problem even if he had never jumped from the plane.

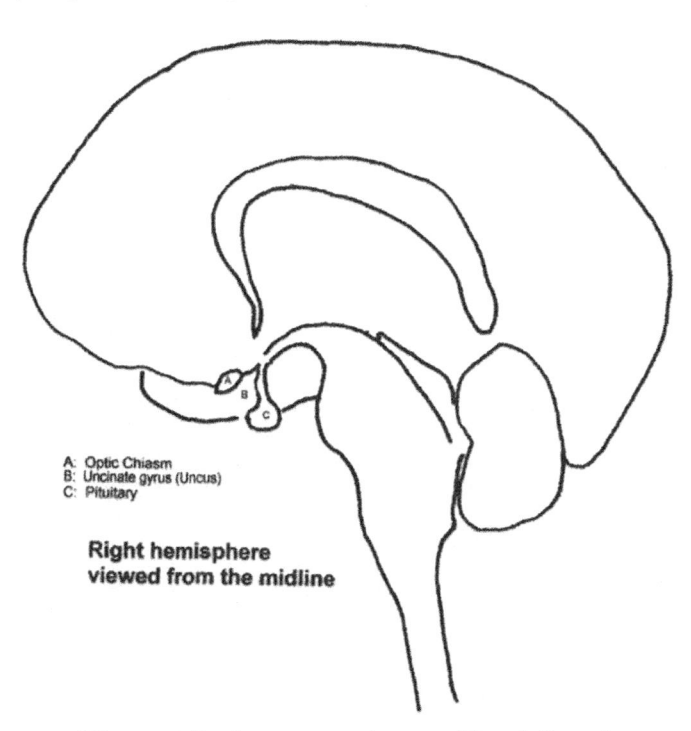

A: Optic Chiasm
B: Uncinate gyrus (Uncus)
C: Pituitary

Right hemisphere viewed from the midline

Diagram of brain structures in area of Peter's Carter's brain lesion. Author's illustration.

Diane Broadbent Friedman

When Dr. Reeves conducts the visual field exam and finds a deficit, that information suggests a specific location in the brain. As you can see from the illustration in Chapter V, the deficit in Peter's visual field corresponds with the visual field fibers as they course through the right temporal lobe. Dr. Reeves then adds his knowledge of the location of the pituitary gland, located very close to the temporal lobe area corresponding to the deficit. The pituitary gland is responsible for regulation of thirst and satiety. Finally, Dr. Reeves wonders if the hallucinations could result from involvement of the inner portion of the right temporal lobe—which would produce uncinate seizures—beginning with smelling an unusual odor and sometimes involving visual hallucinations. So in this scene, we see that Dr. Reeves suspects a gradually developing process—a tumor or obstruction of cerebrospinal fluid— affecting the right temporal lobe and involving the pituitary gland. This developing process is causing Peter to experience headaches, changes in appetite and thirst, visual field disturbances, and now complex partial seizures.

So Dr. Reeves does not pull these questions out of a hat. They are not poetic or fanciful, as Raymond Durgnat wrote in 1965: "In each film of Powell's, this romantic urge sports a different livery—coexisting with the everyday and with only a mildly pusillanimous humour (the Heavenly Messenger is always heralded by the smell of fried onions.)[15] Steve Crook, the webmaster of the Powell and Pressburger Pages, helpfully reminded me that Durgnat was one of the first serious film scholars to analyze Powell and Pressburger films, and he did so without the benefit of being able to watch them several times because the prints lapsed into obscurity. As other audience members of Powell and Pressburger films have experienced, Durgnat noticed something and was drawn in, although not completely understanding why.

A Matter of Life and Death

Instead, these details are a realistic depiction of a neurologic evaluation. At the end of this scene, we also learn from Dr. Reeves that this information is incomplete. There is some information that he lacks to be sure of his diagnosis. Dr. Reeves arranges for Peter to come to his home, hoping he can witness Peter's next visitation/hallucination to be sure that it is a seizure. Peter has a wonderful description of the unpredictability of a seizure. He says that his visitor "picks his own time and stops it." Dr. Reeves wants to exclude the possibility of a psychiatric problem, which is also in the list of differential diagnoses. He also seeks additional historical information that could support and strengthen his hypothesis that Peter has had a problem that began well before the fall.

Dr. Reeves' study

Peter has a visit from Conductor 71 while Peter is sleeping. Peter sniffs as if he smells something, and then he awakens to his hallucination. Seizures happen in sleep as well as during wakefulness. In fact, sleep and sleep deprivation can enhance seizure activity. The audience realizes that the sequence of symptoms experienced by Peter in the study is similar to the sequence in the garden when Peter meets Conductor 71 for the first time.

After the Conductor leaves, the audience witnesses a series of events similar to those in the Garden after the Conductor left. Again we see Peter showing some confusion and agitation, and again he has a headache. He is unable to ring his bedside bell because the seizure affected him too quickly. Although Peter is confused, he responds to Dr. Reeves' firm command to sit down. We see his agitation start to resolve. Dr. Reeves ascertains that this spell was similar to the first in the initial symptom of smelling fried onions.

Dr Reeves checks Peter's right eye (probably for pupil dilation) and the sole of his left foot for his Babinski reflex. (Do you recall that Gershwin had pupilary changes and reflex abnormalities?) In real life, a neurologist would always check both sides, but in Peter's condition, which affects the region of the right temporal lobe and area of the pituitary gland, the neurologist would expect to find abnormalities of the right pupil and possibly an abnormal left Babinski reflex. Those are the actions that Dr. Reeves demonstrates, eliciting the Babinski reflex by using an object from his pocket to stroke the bottom of Peter's foot. Using a handy sharp object, like a key or the end of a pen, would be very typical of a neurologist working on the spot. In Chapter Seven, we will see that the choice of these actions may also suggest the identity of a particular British neurologist, James Collier.

<u>The operating room of U.S. Base Hospital 56</u>
Dr. Reeves talks to the neurosurgeon Dr. McEwen. He has learned that Peter had a slight concussion two years earlier with no after effects at that time. Dr. Reeves concludes that the results of Peter's neurological exam and history point to a progressive process which Dr. Reeves believes are post-traumatic arachnoid adhesions involving the olfactory nerve and the brain. Adhesions (fibrous scar tissue from the arachnoid cell layer covering of the brain) could cause obstruction of the brain channels in which cerebrospinal fluid normally circulates. That accumulation of fluid would cause pressure on the brain. Relieving that adhesion could allow the cerebrospinal fluid to once again flow freely and the brain pressure would return to normal. His seizures would likely resolve and Peter would be restored to health.

In summary, Michael Powell's inclusion of medical details is consistent throughout the film. He never confuses the details of the

A Matter of Life and Death

right and left side of the brain. During the operative procedure, in a later scene, the incision is made on the right side of Peter's head.

Medical Information Available to the Audience but not to Dr. Reeves

An analysis of the medical portions of the film might begin with the scenes of Dr. Reeves, but in fact, relevant medical information is apparent from the beginning of the film. There is medical information available to the audience that Dr. Reeves does not know. We know something more about Peter's neurologic condition from what we see during the time beginning with his conversation with June on the radio while he is in the burning airplane and extending to their meeting on the beach three and one half hours later. Moreover, medical papers written by contemporary neurologists touched on some of these factors, including survival after prolonged water immersion[16] and behavior immediately post-concussion.[17, 18, 19]

In the cockpit of the burning plane, we know that Peter expresses himself well and has a very good memory for poetry. He is bright, quick, calm, and insightful. He is friendly and good-humored even at the moments before his death when he speaks to his dead friend, Flying Officer Trubshaw, just before he chooses to die by falling rather than burning.

Next, we see that he is unconscious and floating in the water. We can determine that this lasted for about three hours—from the time he jumped to the time established that June cycles back to Lee Wood House after breakfast. Once he awakens, he appears unhurt. His gait is normal and he is able to coordinate the removal of his wet clothes with both hands. We also see that he can stand on one foot. While this appears to be performed for humorous purposes, standing on one foot at a time is a standard part of the neurological exam to test

Peter stands on one foot after awakening on the beach. *A Matter of Life and Death* (1946). "Stairway to Heaven"© 1946,1974,1996. Carlton Film Distributors Limited. All Rights Reserved. Courtesy of Columbia Pictures.

both coordination and the sensory information coming from each foot that allows balance to be maintained.

Then Peter looks about and concludes that he must be in Heaven. The neurologist C.P. Symonds wrote in 1937 that a patient with a concussion goes through a series of recovery stages, emerging from stupor and then experiencing disorientation in space and time "…with a tendency to interpret the immediate surroundings in terms of long-past experience. Recovery of consciousness might be extremely rapid but however rapid there was a transition from deep stupor to a state of dazed bewilderment before full consciousness was regained."[17]

Believing he is in Heaven implies that he recalls his circumstances immediately before the jump. He sees the naked goatherd and assumes him to be a heavenly figure. Michael Powell mentioned that

A Matter of Life and Death

he specifically intended a visual reference to Theocritus, a Greek poet who wrote about the idyllic life of shepherds and shepherdesses, in developing this scene.[20] Peter's supposition would be consistent with his background in poetry and European history, as well as his religious background. The audience also thinks he is in Heaven, partly because we might assume that no one suffers from lingering injuries there! We see that his speech is normal and fluent. When he sees a sign on the beach, the audience determines that his vision and his sense of irony and humor are all intact when he reads, considers, and follows the command, "Keep Out". We are as startled as Peter to find such an odd "Welcome" sign! This small moment has a dual purpose, because reading and performing a command written by an examiner is also part of the standard neurological exam.

Peter quickly adjusts his perception of reality when he understands that he is not in Heaven but rather that he survived his fall and is in England. We also see that he quickly makes a connection between "the Yank girl" riding the bike and June on the radio. Therefore he has very little retrograde amnesia, except for the moments of the fall itself and the time spent in the sea. He is able to run fast and in a coordinated way in sand, without a limp or hesitation. His strength, sensation, balance, coordination, vision, orientation to time and space, memory, and personality are all restored to normal by the time of his conversation with the goatherd.

The audience concludes that Peter is neurologically normal except for brief retrograde amnesia following three hours of unconsciousness and floating in the sea with possible mild hypothermia. While Dr. Reeves cannot know for sure about Peter's neurological and psychological condition before or directly after the fall, we, the audience, know it and therefore we can accept Peter as his dashing, handsome self. Once again, Michael Powell has inserted accurate neurological details within the film without drawing attention to them.

The audience knows how charming, brave, and intelligent Peter is. We see these qualities completely intact throughout the film, although gradually these qualities are only present in Peter's mind. From Dr. Reeves' point of view, he knows Peter as a person he met only a few hours earlier and who is having increasingly severe neurological problems. June encountered Peter briefly on the radio before the difficulties commenced. While the audience believes Peter to still be his wonderful self, June has given her heart and a commitment to someone who is in great difficulty and becoming more ill by the minute.

This film is not a true medical mystery, because Powell and Pressburger allow the audience to have all of the information in this world and the other world. The audience has more information than any of the characters in the film, and yet we are still in suspense. Since most audience members are not neurologists, we do not recognize the real meaning of the medical information before us. And since none of us audience members have visited Heaven, we cannot know how that realm really operates!

Powell and Pressburger commented on this process of allowing the audience to have more information than the figures in the film in a 1985 interview with Ian Christie, in reference to *The Life and Death of Colonel Blimp*:

> Pressburger: Only the audience understands [why Colonel Blimp is interested in the three girls of the film]—*only* the audience knows …she never knows why, we never tell why, but—
>
> Powell: But *we* know—
>
> Pressburger: Only the audience understands. Now I think without knowing it at that time when we were

making the film…I'm sure that you, Michael, know what I am trying to say—

Powell: I think it gives something special to the film and other films too, if the audience knows things that the people on the screen don't. As in *I Know Where I'm Going!*, for instance.[21]

Why Does Michael Powell Give Peter Carter Complex Partial Seizures?

The preceding discussion answers this question. Complex partial seizures represent a condition where a psychiatrically normal man may have hallucinations. This type of seizure suggests a specific brain localization. These seizures may be from a stable condition, but they can also arise from a worsening condition—a helpful dramatic thread for the film. The hallucinations having the thematic element of death make a believable transition between Heaven and Earth. Using arachnoid adhesions as the cause for the seizures allows brain surgery to be performed to treat the life-threatening problem, and it provides a condition from which a patient can fully and definitively recover and survive. A happy ending can be an honest resolution to this story, whereas a brain problem caused by trauma, stroke, infection or tumor would not have as certain a result. So when Peter asks, "Do you think I'm cracked?" we now can see how complex a question that is, and in what a skillful way Michael Powell unfolds the answer.

I hope I have persuaded you that the medical evaluation of Peter Carter is thorough and informative, realistic and complete. In Chapter Six I will review the medical literature that I believe Michael Powell consulted in preparing the relevant portions of this movie script. But our evaluation of the medical physiology within *AMOLAD* is not complete. In addition to information about the function of the brain, there is an equal abundance of information about a parallel and interconnected system of vision and the eye. Our analysis will next turn to learn more about Michael Powell's study of the eye.

1. Powell, Michael, *A Life in Movies*. (New York: Knopf, 1987), 539.

2. Powell, Michael. *The Edge of the World: The making of a film (200,000 Feet on Foula)*, published 1938. (London: Faber and Faber, 1990), 19.

3. Ibid., 250.

4. Powell, Michael, *Million Dollar Movie*. (London: Heinemann, 1992), 418.

5. Gough-Yates, Kevin, "Interview with Kevin Gough-Yates" in *Michael Powell in Collaboration with Emeric Pressburger* (London: John Player and Sons 1971), 7.

6. Powell, *A Life in Movies*, 497.

7. Ibid., 497.

8. Ibid., 497.

9. Ibid., 459.

10. Ibid., 498.

11. Ibid., 458.

12. Badder, David, "Powell and Pressburger: The War Years," *Sight and Sound* 48, no.1 (1978/1979 Winter): 8.

13. Powell, *A Life in Movies*, 502.

14. Ibid., 514.

15. Durgnat, Raymond, "Durgnat on Powell and Pressburger" in *Powell, Pressburger and Others,* edited by Ian Christie. (London: British Film Institute, 1978), 65--78, quote on 68.

16. Critchley, Macdonald, "Problems of naval warfare under climatic extremes," *British Medical Journal* (Aug 18 1945): 208–12.

17. Symonds, C. P. "Mental disorder following head injury," *British Medical Journal* (1937): 879–81, quote on 879.

18. Symonds, C. P. "Disturbance of cerebral function in concussion," *The Lancet* 1 (March 2, 1935): 486–88.

19. Symonds, C. P. and Russell, W. Richie, "Accidental head injuries: prognosis in service patients," *The Lancet* 1 (January 2, 1943): 7–10.

20. Powell, *A Life in Movies*, 543.

21. Christie, Ian, "Powell and Pressburger," in *Michael Powell Interviews,* edited by David Lazar (Jackson: University of Mississippi Press, 2003), 115.

CHAPTER FIVE:

"I Discovered I Had an Eye."
References to Normal and Abnormal Vision

I find an abundance of information concerning the workings of the eye in this film. We know that Michael Powell was very interested in the eye as a metaphor as well as the fundamental organ of his work. He makes a reference to it as a painting on the bow of a ship in the opening scene of *The Thief of Bagdad*, for instance. Pressburger and Powell chose a bull's eye target as the symbol for their production company, The Archers. In the next chapter, I will show that Powell took dialogue for *AMOLAD* from a medical paper published in a British ophthalmology journal. In *AMOLAD*, he makes a many-layered reference to vision: in hallucination; in color vision differentiating the character of two separate worlds; and seeing into someone's heart. I want to show you that there is an additional layer where he interweaves the story with the physiology of vision.

In a nutshell, the visual system of the eye and brain allows us to detect and focus on an object, track its movement, see its color and contour in a three-dimensional representation, change our focus from the object to its surrounding field, and collect all of these impressions in an environment which might be sunny or star-lit. Within the texture of the film, Michael Powell displays the physiology of the eye, the examination of the functions of the eye, and evaluation of an intact visual pathway; as well as revealing how the deficits experienced by Peter Carter point to the location and treatment of his brain problem. What follows is my ophthalmologic analysis of the film. I would encourage the reader to read the accompanying brief summary of vision physiology to gain a better appreciation of what Michael Powell must have understood in order to use concepts of vision in plot, dialogue, and action on the screen. You can also refer to this summary if you encounter any unfamiliar concepts.

A Matter of Life and Death

• •

Mini-Tutorial: What Michael Powell Learned about Vision

Humans have three-dimensional color vision. We see a visual field shaped like a circular panorama. Our central vision is the most acute while we are able to see movement, although with less detail, at the periphery of the field. We move our eyes in tandem to see something of interest, hold our focus as we turn our heads, and hold our gaze steady as long as necessary.

The Anatomy of the Visual Pathway

These attributes of vision are a result of the anatomy of the visual system. Light enters the pupil and passes through the lens, striking the retina at the back of each eye. The visual information is upside down with respect to the outside environment. The photons of light excite the rods and cones of the retina. The rods and cones are perpendicular to the retina, sticking out like the pile of a carpet, and they are excited by discrete wavelengths of light. These nerve cells send their axons to a central collecting point where the nerve bundle becomes the optic nerve. In the retina, the optic nerve's exit point is bare; there are no rods or cones in that spot. That nerve leaves the eye and approaches a meeting point with the optic nerve from the other eye called the optic chiasma.

At the optic chiasma, the fibers of the two eyes are joined, so that some of the fibers from one eye are intermixed with those of the other. Half of the set of newly intermixed fibers then course though each temporal lobe in a pathway called Meyer's loop. The fibers reach the occipital lobe at the back of the brain. The fibers containing information about the bottom of the visual field terminate in the upper region of the occipital lobe. At this point the visual information

Diane Broadbent Friedman

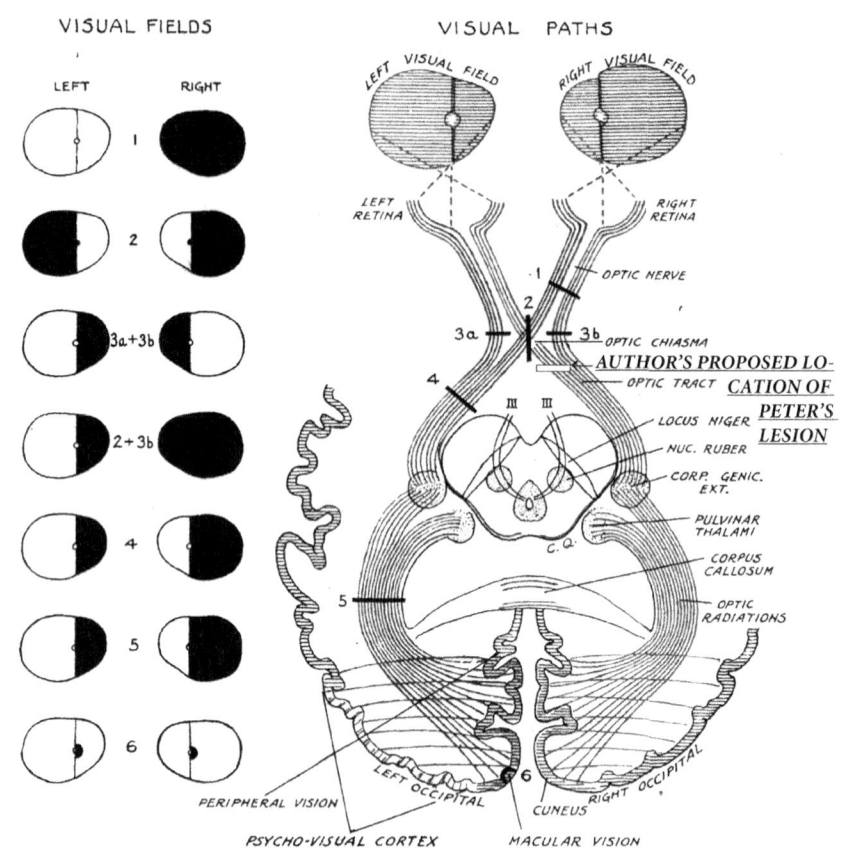

Fig. 41.—Diagram of Visual path.

Lesion at 1 produces blindness of R. eye with loss of direct light reflex.
,, ,, 2 ,, bi-temporal hemianopia.
,, ,, 3a + 3b ,, bi-nasal hemianopia.
,, ,, 2 + 3b ,, blindness of R. eye with nasal hemianopia of L. eye.
,, ,, 4 ,, R. homonymous hemianopia with hemiopic pupillary light-reaction.
,, ,, 5 ,, R. homonymous hemianopia with normal pupillary reaction.
,, ,, 6 ,, R. homonymous central hemi-scotoma.

Anatomy of the visual pathway with the author's proposed location of Peter's visual deficit. Purves-Stewart: *The Diagnosis of Nervous diseases*, 9th ed. 1945 , Figure 41 pg.81; The Williams and Wilkins Company, Baltimore. © Lippincott Williams and Wilkins, 2008.

is then communicated to and interpreted by the frontal lobe, which reorganizes the view—the orientation of right and left as well as down and up is restored—so that the person interprets the information as a representation of the outside world.

Coordination of Eye Movement

The ability of eyes to focus on an object and track its movement arises from a portion of visual fibers leaving the optic chiasma as well as additional fibers leaving from the occipital lobe. Both sets of fibers arrive in specialized regions of the the brain stem. Fibers then return to automatically control the muscles of the iris and the three pairs of muscles attached to each eyeball. The visual information returning to the iris allows the pupils to widen just the right amount to automatically regulate the intensity of light entering the retina. The information to the outer muscles of the eye allows the eyes to move and to work in perfect tandem. This allows the brain to track objects of interest—in smooth pursuit, rapid tracking, and continued attention—without jerks or loss of the target.

The Visual Exam

Once again, as when conducting the neurological exam, a physician can detect damage to a specific part of this complex system by asking a patient to perform certain visual tasks and then observing the results. In the visual exam, the patient is asked to identify objects at close range and then distantly. The patient may be asked to read a written instruction and perform that instruction (for example, "close your eyes") to check for comprehension. Then the visual field is tested—the extent of the peripheral limitations and any segment or quadrant of the 360-degree field of vision that is deficient. The person is asked to look to each quadrant of the field as the examiner watches to see if the eyes move properly in tandem. The ability to follow a moving object is tested in the lateral fields. This lateral eye tracking is called *saccadic* movement. Eyes should move when they are following a moving target and then should be still when the target is still. Vertical movement is also examined. Each aspect, the size and shape, and the reactivity of the pupilary muscles is assessed. A difference in the size of the pupils can suggest a location of a brain lesion. Then the ophthalmoscope is used to see inside the eye. This is like looking though a small window into a curved room. The size and shape of the optic nerve, as well as the appearance of the retina, is assessed.

The Complete Loop of the Visual Pathway
The physiology of the visual system allows for *automatic* function as well as *purposeful*, attentive gaze. As you have deduced, the exam allows the examiner to know about the health of each part of the pathway as it travels from the eye to the back of the brain and to the brainstem and then either up to the eye fields for interpretation of the visual image or back to the eyes themselves to produce eye reflexes. In other words, the functioning of the complete pathway is necessary for a person to correctly identify and interpret what an image is. This also provides the final connection for a feedback loop to produce reflexes for automatic behavior of the eye—for blinking, detecting and avoiding a threat, and regulating the amount of light entering the pupil so that people can continue to see as they move after dinner from the cozy light of a kitchen into the moonlit darkness of the garden in the back yard.

• •

A Matter of Life and Death

The Eye in *AMOLAD*

There are a number of accurate references to normal and abnormal vision, crucial to the development of the story of *AMOLAD*.

Distance vision

In the first scene, neither June or Peter can see because of darkness and fog. As Peter awakens on the beach, Michael Powell shows us the blue sky, the first of several shots from Peter's point of view. We can surmise that Peter's visual system is working well because he can see and draw conclusions from what he sees. Peter reads a lettered sign that instructs "Keep Out," and he shows by his facial expression that he not only comprehends the words but also is confused by it since he, and we in the audience, believe that he is in Heaven and therefore expect he would be coming to a welcoming place. Then Peter sees a dog, the goatherd, and finally June cycling by at a distance. Peter's distance vision is intact.

Visual field deficit

In the nighttime garden scene we observe Peter lose a portion of his visual field when he cannot see the cups. That loss is confirmed when we look through Peter's field of vision and realize that he cannot see something important—June—in the lower-left quadrant of his visual field.

Normal visual field

In the next scene we see the camera obscura in an attic room of Dr. Reeves' house. I believe that Michael Powell is showing us a very large model of an eye and how it works. The room is like the interior of an eye. The image projected on the table top is showing us an intact visual field created by the light coming through the lens, mounted in the roof, and projected onto the retina-like table top. He also shows

Diane Broadbent Friedman

The Camera Obscura, two blocks from John Laurie's home. (www.dumgal.gov.uk/museums) Reprinted with kind permission from Dumfries Museum and Camera Obscura, The Observatory, Rotchell Road, Dumfries DG2 7SW.

A Matter of Life and Death

Hand controls of the camera obscura in AMOLAD. *A Matter of Life and Death* (1946). Photograph by kind permission of Granada International.

how he can track a moving object by moving the camera obscura apparatus. You will see that the visual information is upside down with respect to Dr. Reeves. We also see him following the bicyclists with his "eye," using his arm muscles to coordinate the view. Later, when June arrives, the visual scene is now oriented to be right-side up with respect to June and Dr. Reeves. (In Appendix I, the camera obscura is described more fully. We will see that Michael Powell could have visited a very similar camera obscura in the town of Dumfries, Scotland, actor John Laurie's home town.)

Color vision

In Lee Wood House, Dr. Reeves formally examines Peter's visual field and confirms his visual field deficit. In the novelization of the film, we also learn that Peter has lost his color vision for red and green, although that is not made clear in the film.

Visual saccades
Then at Dr. Reeves' house. we watch a game of ping-pong. I think that the back and forth movement of the camera is meant to suggest the saccadic movements of the eye—the side-to-side tracking of the eyes made possible by an intact visual coordination system. (This is described more fully in the eye physiology section.)

Dilated pupil after a seizure
In Dr. Reeves' study, after Peter sees Conductor 71 and collapses back in the chair, Dr. Reeves checks Peter's right pupil. While a true neurologist would check both eyes, the pupilary deficit would appear on the right in Peter's condition. This finding helps Dr. Reeves to build his hypothesis that if there is a localized increase of intracranial pressure near the inner portion of the right temporal lobe at the optic chiasma, one dilated pupil would be found on the same side as a result of the intensifying intracranial pressure.

Visual field
A more obvious visual reference in the film is the closing of the eyelid in surgery as the anesthesia takes effect. Once again we see through Peter's point of view as his visual field changes from an outer focus to an inner one.

Color vision
Michael Powell wrote that he purposefully used very little color in the operating rooms as a way to suggest a transition between the color of the earthly realm and the black and white of Heaven.

A Matter of Life and Death

View of the heavenly court. *A Matter of Life and Death* (1946). "Stairway to Heaven"© 1946,1974,1996. Carlton Film Distributors Limited. All Rights Reserved. Courtesy of Columbia Pictures.

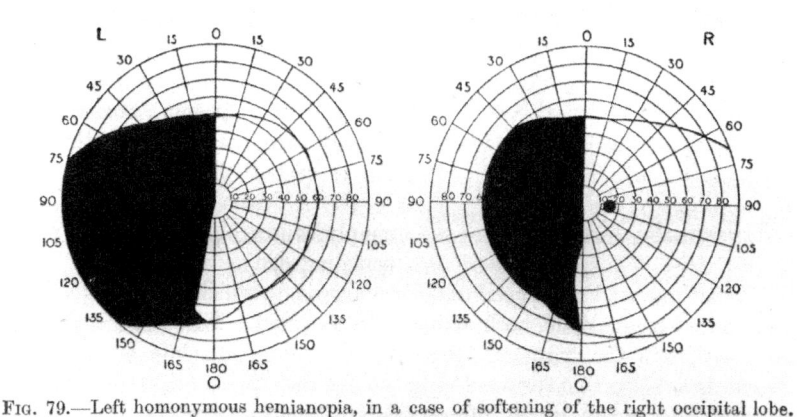

Fig. 79.—Left homonymous hemianopia, in a case of softening of the right occipital lobe.

Ocular report of homonymous hemianopsia. Purves-Stewart: *The Diagnosis of Nervous diseases*, 9th ed. 1945 , Figure 79, pg.241; The Williams and Wilkins Company, Baltimore. © Lippincott Williams and Wilkins, 2008.

Diane Broadbent Friedman

Other Visual References That May Be Deliberate

An eye
The heavenly court reminds me of the curved retina at the back of the eye. The legions of observers in the heavenly courts might also resemble the vertical orientation of rods and cones. The elevated, bare spot in the middle where the court and jury are seated is the entry point of the optic nerve. As the camera pulls away from the heavenly court, the layout of the bowl-shaped courtroom looks very much like an eye chart used to record the visual field deficit.

A pupil
In Heaven, when Bob Trubshaw and the Registration Officer look down into the records office through the round opening in the floor, it reminds me of looking with an ophthalmoscope through a pupil into the back of the eye. A medical professional in training who is learning the use of an ophthalmoscope is told to imagine that one is looking through a window or a porthole (the pupil) into a room beyond.

Seeing when no sight is possible
Dr. Reeves rides his motorcycle in the rain. He cannot see. The novelization of the film described the scene: "Soon he was drenched with the rain which lashed at his face and streamed over the blurred glasses of his goggles. Between the lightning flashes it was pitch dark and his headlight, reflected back from the drenched surface of the road was of very limited service...*by his great familiarity with the route he could have almost covered blindfolded...* [emphasis added]"[1]

Another reference to being blindfolded may lie in the chess masters mentioned by Conductor 71. In Dr. Reeves' study, both Alexander Alekhine and Francois-Andre Philidor are mentioned.

Philidor was the first chess player to win multiple matches playing blindfolded. Alekhine at his peak had played thirty-nine and forty-two players simultaneously while blindfolded. (See Appendix I for more information about chess in *AMOLAD*.)

A Clue Suggesting Medical Input in the Development of *AMOLAD*

The book of the film changes Peter's visual field deficit. In the film we see that Peter can see June clearly in the center of his field but has a reduction in vision in the left-lower quadrant. The description in the book is different:

> "June, you're there aren't you?" The same splitting pain that he had felt on the beach pierced his skull and his vision suddenly seemed to become narrowed down so that his field of sight was reduced to a jagged slit, straight ahead of him, a narrow patch of bright moonlight with complete darkness on either side. He put out his hands gropingly as he called to June.[2]

This description of Peter's visual field deficit, combined with his color blindness, places the lesion directly at the optic chiasma. In the film, the combination of pituitary symptoms, left-lower quadrant deficit, and visual hallucinations plus olfactory symptoms places the lesion slightly farther back, nearer the right temporal lobe. This change, equally neurologically plausible, also suggests that someone knowledgeable about neurology was involved in the editing of the novelization of the film.

In sum, the fact that all of these details are present in the film, purposefully included, supports Michael Powell's self-description that he found everything interesting. Complex technical information did not scare him away. He found creative inspiration in neuroscience. He thought an audience could grasp this or, at least, sense the authenticity. In this chapter, as we have paid attention to the technical details, we realize he didn't fake the authenticity, even though he could have. Now we also have a greater appreciation for the medical information he mastered and then used artistically.

1. Warman, Eric, *A Matter of Life and Death: The book of the Michael Powell and Emeric Pressburger film* (London: World Film Publications Ltd., 1946), 74.

2. Ibid., 34.

CHAPTER SIX:

How Did Michael Powell Acquire this Medical Information?

If you have been following this analysis closely, you may have been asking yourself, "This is all very nice, but how do you know that Michael Powell put in these subtle, accurate neurological details on purpose?" This chapter will describe the evidence I have found in the literature of the day, my correspondence with his brother-in-law surgeon Joseph P. Reidy, and hints from a passage in Michael Powell's date book from 1945. I will differentiate information that I know for sure and ideas that are my speculation. Taking all of these data together, I hope to demonstrate that Michael Powell indeed did consult neurological texts in the development of the script. In the next chapter, I will outline medical literature of the time which strongly suggests to me the possibility of having influenced Michael Powell, but of which I cannot be sure. In this chapter, I will present only that information of which I am certain.

Diane Broadbent Friedman

What Medical Literature Did Michael Powell Read?

I have found one article that contains language identical to dialogue from the film. Because I found that article by reading a prominent and popular neurology textbook of the time, I am including that book as a highly likely source as described in the following paragraphs.

Diagnosis of Nervous Diseases (1945)

I found my way to the article that was the source of several passages of dialogue as I looked through a British textbook for medical students, *The Diagnosis of Nervous Diseases* by Sir James Purves-Stewart (the ninth edition, published in 1945).[1] This textbook has sections which are suggestive of visual aspects of *AMOLAD* and possibly *Black Narcissus* as well.

At the time of the publication of this edition, this textbook was described as one of the most popular books for British medical students of the day. The first edition was written in 1906. In the introduction to the ninth edition, Purves-Stewart reviewed the work of the scientists of the previous generation, including Hughlings Jackson, Horsley, and Cushing, all of whom were introduced in Chapter Two of this book. The visual field deficits diagnostic of specific brain lesions is discussed in detail. The diagnostic significance of hemianopsia, a partial field loss, is discussed. The reader will recall that Peter Carter develops a loss of the left side of the lower visual field. A drawing reproduced here shows the effect on a visual field in Figure 78 of the textbook, which resembles the visual field deficit of Peter Carter seen through the lens of the camera in the Garden, and later elicited during visual field testing in Lee Wood House.[2] While the caption indicates that the patient has an occipital lobe injury, the deficit is somewhat similar to Peter Carter's deficit.

A Matter of Life and Death

A section on the previous page of the Purves-Stewart book describing transient blindness experienced by aviators is of interest:

> Transient bilateral blindness lasting only a second or so sometimes occurs in aviators—the so-called "black-out." The pilot doing a steep turn at high speed, or pulling abruptly out of a steep dive, may have a sudden dimness of vision, amounting to a sensation of intense blackness. This is due to sudden anaemia of the head, including the retinae, the blood being driven by centrifugal force into the abdomen and legs. Recovery is equally sudden, snapping away like a camera shutter. In addition to the visual symptoms, there may be a transient loss of consciousness.
>
> In other air manoeuvers, especially inverted spins, outside loops, etc., the converse condition occurs, i.e. the blood is driven centrifugally *into* the head and upper parts of the body. In such cases objects in the field of vision suddenly appear red- so called "red-out." *Red-out symptoms are of little practical importance, since they are not likely to occur except when the "plane is out of control."*[3] [emphasis added]

When I read this section I thought of the moment in *Back Narcissus* when Sister Ruth, rejected by Mr. Dean, sees red and loses consciousness. How interesting it is to speculate that these textbook words might have given Michael Powell the idea of visual field turning red when a character is out of control!

In the section discussing brain tumor, there is a section on the causes of pseudo-tumor cerebri. *Pseudo tumor* is a term applied to a set of conditions which produce symptoms suggestive of tumor, because each condition puts pressure on the brain. One of those conditions is described on page 844 as chronic localized serous arachnoiditis. Arachnoiditis in the area of the optic chiasma, also near the location of the olfactory nerve, could cause visual field impairment. (In *AMOLAD*, this is the diagnosis given by Dr. Reeves as he speaks with Dr. McEwen in the anteroom of the American operating theater: "Everything points to arachnoid adhesions involving the olfactory nerve and the brain.") The textbook then states that "the most certain mode of diagnosis is by a decompressive operation at which the meningeal adhesions are freely divided. This usually cures the symptoms."[4]

"Chiasmal Arachnoiditis" (1943)
Then the reader of this section of the Purves-Stewart textbook is referred in a footnote to a journal article written by A. J. B. Goldsmith, "Chiasmal Arachnoiditis," in *Proceedings of the Royal Society of Medicine* 1943.[5] When I read that article, I found passages which are identical to the dialogue in *AMOLAD*. The film contains language which is identical to passages in this article which could describe Peter Carter's condition. (See full article in Appendix IV.)

Dialogue in the film. Here are the sections of the film which are pertinent. All emphasis is mine:

> Examination in Lee Wood house:
> [Frank asked] "These headaches…when did they start?"
> "About six months ago."
> "Where mostly?"
> Peter indicated two places, one on his forehead and one on the side of his head. "*Frontal and temporal,*"
> Frank commented, "Any loss of appetite…Nor of thirst?"
> "No fear!"

"In fact if anything, you've been *eating and drinking more than usual.*"

<u>In the anteroom of the surgical theatre:</u>

"Hullo Frank! Anything new?"

"Deterioration all around," Frank said quietly. "We ought to operate tonight."

"That's impossible. We're swamped. You're sure of your diagnosis?"

"Certain. I've discovered the missing fact. *He had slight concussion two years ago with no after effects. X-Ray is inconclusive.* You've seen the *ocular reports.* You know about these highly-organized hallucinations. Everything points to *arachnoid adhesions involving the olfactory nerve and the brain.*"

"It's an interesting operation…I've never seen one."

"I have…several…at the l'*Hôpital de la Pitié in Paris.*"

<u>As Frank Reeves stands on the stairway at the end of the film:</u>

"My diagnosis was right. *Fine avascular meningeal adhesions binding the optic nerve to the brain, the internal carotid and the chiasm. Similar adhesions between the chiasm and the brain…*"

Excerpts from "Chiasmal arachnoiditis"

Here are excerpts of the article "Chiasmal arachnoiditis" which are pertinent. Again, all emphasis is mine:

"… [Discussing a review of literature from the French Ophthalmologic Society in 1937] 63 cases were collected from the literature and a further 66 were added which had been operated on by Clovis Vincent and his assistants at the *l'Hôpital de la Pitié*.

"I shall describe the three cases which we have dealt with…The first patient was a woman, M. H., admitted to hospital in 1942. She was aged 32…formerly a worker in an aircraft factory. There was nothing in her family history nor in her personal history except for *a motor cycle accident fourteen years ago following which she was unconscious for twelve hours, but suffered no sequelae* [a concussion defined as a head trauma with resulting unconsciousness]. In 1939 she began to have attacks of violent *frontal and temporal headaches…* She noted deterioration of vision in her right and left eye also. Other symptoms elicited by questioning were that for several months se had noticed *increased appetite and thirst*, polyuria and lack of energy.

"*The ocular findings* suggested a pituitary lesion…but no space occupying lesion was found [by air pneumo-encephalogram]…We therefore considered the possibility of arachnoiditis as a cause of the symptoms, and in view of the progressive loss of vision it was felt that an exploratory operation was justified…A right frontal osteoplastic flap was turned down…

"It was found that the nerves and chiasm were much pinker than normal and that masses of *fine avascular meningeal adhesions were present binding the optic nerves to the overlying brain, to the internal carotid*, to the diaphragma sellae and *to the anterior part of the chiasm*. In addition a thick band of *avascular adhesions stretched between the chiasm and the brain…*

"I did colour fields in these cases and while there was contraction of the fields to red and green…"

[And from the legends of drawings accompanying the article] "…*Arachnoid adhesions involving the dorsum sellae, optic and the olfactory nerves, chiasm and the brain…*"

A Matter of Life and Death

I want to be clear that for me this does not constitute plagiarism. Instead I think this is simply the extension of Powell's use of people's actual words to add validity to dialogue. Use of words from this article adds a significant degree of accuracy to a character who would have likely read this article. Using this article implies that Michael Powell understood the concepts fully, as he included them in several places, and that he did not simply throw in several technical terms for effect. (The reader might find it interesting to know that the l'Hôpital de la Pitié was where Sigmund Freud trained in neurology. This was also the institution where Jean-Martin Charcot evaluated the techniques of hypnotism.)

Who Did Michael Powell Consult?

I have determined that there were at least four people whom I am sure that he consulted: plastic surgeon and brother- in- law Joseph P. Reidy; his technical advisor for the film, anesthesiologist Bernard Kaplan; and general surgeons Niall MacGinnis and MacGinnis's father-in-law William George Macdonald. In a 1978 interview with David Badder, Michael Powell stated that he went on rounds with a doctor, but I have not been able to determine who that person was.[6]

Mr. Joseph Reidy

When I read the following passage n Michael Powell's autobiography, I knew I wanted to know more about how the film was created:

> Frankie's brother Joe Reidy is a plastic surgeon and went right through the war as one of McIndoo's team [of plastic surgeons who were giving burnt pilots back their faces]. "Hallucinations," he said. You don't need drugs to have hallucinations. Pressure on the brain will do it, if the brain is good enough. Here! Take this pamphlet. I read that "pressure on the brain can

> produce highly organized hallucinations, comparable to an experience of actual life and which took place in space not in time [7]

When he mentions a pamphlet, I suspect that Powell was given a reprint of a medical journal article. I decided to find Mr. Reidy and that article. I was successful in corresponding with Mr. Reidy in the spring and fall of 1990. I had hopes of learning more about his contribution and whether he had specifically mentioned seizures. Dr. Reidy wrote to me, "I was [stationed] at Stoke Mandeville Hospital. Dr. Cairns [Hugh Cairns, neurosurgeon] took care of the brain injuries and I took care of the external cover."[8] He told me that he contributed ideas for the film but could not recollect them clearly for me. When I asked him, he could not recall specifically about seizures as a dramatic device. He could not recall any specific articles that Powell might have read, saying that his memories of long ago were not as clear. He passed away about six months after our last correspondence.

Joseph P. Reidy (1907-1991) was a significant clinician, teacher, researcher and author. He was described in his obituary as a surgeon held in great affection by his colleagues and patients and as "he was built like a [rugby] line backer, he always commanded respect."[9] In 1949 his surgical abilities were recognized by the British Association of Plastic Surgery by making him secretary of the two- year-old organization. He became president in 1962. During his career at Stoke Mandeville, Westminster Hospital and the London Hospital, he received many national and international honors. He wrote a book, *Physical Methods in Plastic Surgery* (1956)[10] and over 25 scientific articles concerning a variety of problems including cleft lip and palate, congenital uro-genital malformations and burns.[11] In his article summarizing the development of plastic surgery as a surgical specialty he pointed out, "World War II came in September

A Matter of Life and Death

1939 and at that time in the United Kingdom there were only four senior plastic surgeons and two junior surgeons. Plastic surgery units were considered a necessity not only to cope with possible casualties requiring repair but also to train more plastic surgeons."[12] He can be seen sitting in the midst of 91 other plastic surgeons at the 1948 Clinical Congress of the British Association of Plastic Surgeons at Stoke Mandeville.[13]

Having an effective team approach to the treatment and rehabilitation of burned aviators had a major impact in outcome, scientific development and evaluation of new approaches, and the application of those techniques in the civilian population. Readers might be interested in learning more about the development of wartime plastic surgery through the efforts of the four lead plastic surgeons, Sir Harold Gillies (Park Prewitt), T.Pomfret Kilner (Stoke Mandeville), Rainsford Mowlem (St. Albans) and Archibald McIndoe (East Grinstead), especially in the stories of the Guinea Pig Club.[12,14,15]

Bernard Kaplan

Dr. Kaplan was an anesthesiologist who was listed in Eric Warman's book of *AMOLAD* from 1946 as the film's technical advisor. A section in the book, referring to the making of the film stated

> "In order to ensure absolute accuracy in the operation scenes, Captain Bernard Kaplan R.A.M.C. was called in to give expert advice on the equipment and procedure of the operating theatre. He also advised on the intricate brain operation by which Peter Carter was cured of his hallucinations."[16]

This suggests that possibly Dr. Kaplan gave information to Michael Powell before the final script was complete. The following is the information I located on Dr. Kaplan: In 1937 he lived in Essex, having graduated from medical school in 1926. He practiced at Guy's Hospital and in South Africa, and by 1954 had privileges at East Hampstead Memorial Hospital, London Jewish Hospital, and Upney Ilford and East End maternity hospitals. He was a fellow of the Royal Society of Medicine.[17] I was able to find two scholarly articles written by him. "Music with nitrous oxide-oxygen" was published in *Anaesthesia* 1956, suggesting that the patient could have a more comfortable and effective anesthesia induction if he or she selected from a large musical palette ranging from Clair de Lune to Nat King Cole's piano solos.[18]

More compelling for our purpose was an earlier article that Michael Powell could have read. In 1936, Kaplan published an article in *The Journal of the British Institute of Cinematography*.[19] (This journal was published from 1934 to 1938 and there is only one library in the U.S. that has the collection—The George Eastman Library in Rochester, New York.) Dr. Kaplan's article appears in the Medical and Scientific Section and is entitled "Cinema-radiography." In the article, Dr. Kaplan reviews ground-breaking efforts by radiologists to capture the dynamic action of a fluoroscope on film. Unfortunately this is the extent of the information I could locate concerning Dr. Kaplan.

I have not been able to look through the volumes of this journal, but I was able to read one editorial from March 1936 which might be of interest to film scholars concerned with the 1930s.

LET BRITAIN LEAD!

> The British film industry occasionally shows with quite startling suddenness the heights to which it can reach. Honor is due to those pioneers who have proved to the world the possibilities that lie dormant in this country for the production of really great films. Surely the time is rushing upon us when this country will

A Matter of Life and Death

take hold of what fate is offering it, namely, the chance of becoming the greatest film production country in the world. There lies the possibility of a great new industry, of employment for thousands, of great export potentialities, and of a medium through which the great artistic and literary genius of our race can be exploited. We are—and will remain—the centre of the literary world; it is but a small step to change the medium of expression from paper to film. But courage and imagination are required. It is here, and to our own people, that we must preach the gospel of our future in the films. Action and vision are wanted, and there are risks to be taken, but the British people will not, I know, found to be wanting; but the time is now ripe to go ahead. Let Britain lead![20]

Niall MacGinnis and William G. Macdonald

Michael Powell wrote in *A Life in Movies* about the process of developing the ideas for *AMOLAD*: "During the next few weeks while we were waiting for the answer print of *A Canterbury Tale*, we both did research in our various ways. Joe Reidy is a plastic surgeon…"[7]

From Michael Powell's date book:

April 14, 1944
Print of CT. 3PM
Reidy concert 6:15
Beddington dinner

April 19, 1944
Ernest Betts lunch
Niall and Sheila 7 dine

July 15, 1945
Niall. Boxmoor Station 5 miles this side of Berkhamsted Green End House. Dr. Macdonald. The Swan 12.30.

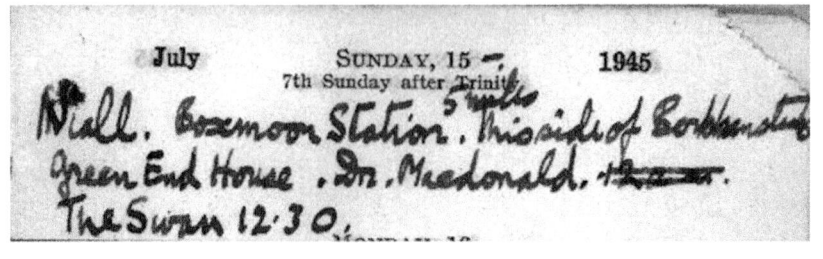

Entries from Michael Powell's date books (April 1944, July 1945), reproduced with kind permission of Thelma Schoonmaker Powell.

"Mr. Macdonald" was a general surgeon living outside of London in Boxmoore, Hertfordshire. He attended Aberdeen Medical School, graduating in 1904, and practiced at West Hertfordshire Hospital and Charing Cross Hospital. He published an article concerning abdominal surgery in 1921: "Two cases of congenital hypertrophic pyloric stenosis."[21]

"Niall" refers to Niall MacGinnis, an actor and close friend of Michael Powell. MacGinnis appeared in *The Edge of the World* (1937), and *49th Parallel* (1941) before completing his medical education and enlisting in the Navy, where he served in 1941 as a surgeon-lieutenant on the H.M.S. Hogue and H.M.S. Barfleur. Mr. MacGinnis also practiced at Charing Cross Hospital in 1944 and was stationed at the evacuation hospital for Charing Cross at Ashridge. MacGinnis was married to Sheila Macdonald, Mr. Macdonald's daughter.

Shooting on *AMOLAD* began on August 14, 1945, the day of the Japanese surrender.[22] By the time of the Powell, MacGinnis, and Macdonald meeting on July 15, the script must have been completed, since Powell wrote that Pressburger had accepted the final draft in April 1945 while they were in America seeking the actress who would play June, Kim Hunter. There is no indication concerning the topic of meetings in the date book. Could they have talked about the medical basis of *AMOLAD*?

The first diary entry for April 14, 1944, parallels with the paragraph in *A Life in Movies* because "CT" refers to *Canterbury Tale*. Possibly the conversation occurred with Mr. Reidy on that day as well. I'm guessing that Mr. Powell obtained some of his medical information from Niall MacGinnis, because it appears they met a week later, April 19, 1944, after Mr. Powell met with Mr. Reidy. Possibly he was the one who helped arrange for Mr. Powell to follow a surgeon. Perhaps Powell followed a doctor at Ashridge, a college two miles north of

Berkhamsted and a few miles from Boxmoore, which had turned over its grounds to Charing Cross Hospital during the war. They saw large numbers of patients there including many French and English evacuated from Dunkirk. Possibly the doctor Powell followed was either Macdonald or MacGinnis himself!

Located in Hertfordshire, Ashridge was first established as a monastery in the late thirteenth century. In World Wars I and II, its grounds were turned over to St. Albans and Charing Cross Hospitals, respectively, to shelter patients.[23] In 1946 there were 1,200 patient beds. Hospital huts built on the grounds were used as surgical theatres, a dispensary, sites for occupational and physical therapy, and a chapel. More than 20,000 patients were treated from 1939 to 1946, and 12,000 surgical operations were performed.[24] During this period, three bombs, a mine on a parachute, a V1 rocket, and a V2 rocket fell upon Ashridge, and both an American bomber and an English bomber crashed.[25] Ashridge is now a prominent international business school.[26]

In reviewing information from Mick Thompson, archivist for Ashridge Business School, I learned that Ashridge has a beautiful long promenade of huge rhododendron bushes, planted in the 1870s.[27]

A reunion of Ashridge/Charing Cross medical and nursing personnel in 2000 was organized by the National Trust. Mr. Thompson helped me to correspond with several attendees including Ms. Ruth Buckingham, Ms. Rosemary Biggs, Dr. J. Warner and Dr. Peter King, from whom I received very kind letters. Two other people remembered Niall MacGinnis clearly. Ms. Irene Spruce, a junior nurse at Ashridge in 1944, recalled MacGinnis as "a film-star" working at Ashridge. She wrote to me, "Yes, I recall Mr. MacGinnis as a houseman because he rode a motor cycle in the grounds."[28]

A Matter of Life and Death

Dr. Vivian Edwards wrote several detailed letters to me containing his memories (Ashridge 1944-45 and then Burma from mid 1945 to 1947) and those of his wife (a nurse at Ashridge 1939-1946):[29]

> Ashridge was an emergency medical hospital during the war. About 30 Nissen huts were built, comprising wards and two operating theatres. General surgery, orthopaedics, gynaecology and basic medicine were done. My wife and I knew MacGinnis well professionally but not socially. We do not recall Mr. Macdonald. No neurosurgery or neurology was done at Ashridge. MacGinnis was just a senior house surgeon and I was his junior house surgeon 1944-1945 on a surgical firm. He supervised my first operating session.
>
> During Christmas 1944, he became rather unpopular with some people as he insisted on giving German prisoners of war a festive meal of turkey etc. on Christmas Day. Today of course such action would be applauded but things were different in 1944. He was older than most medical students and did not talk about his private and social life.
>
> The scene [in AMOLAD] that takes place in a garden with very large rhododendrons is very likely to be Ashridge. The main feature of the garden being a grassy drive flanked by large rhododendron bushes with small alcoves where much courting was done between nurses and medical students and in the summer the students would study their medical textbooks there. The building in the background I think is Ashridge.
>
> Niall MacGinnis was not the kind to wear a helmet when he rode his motorcycle. He would wear a cloth cap. I should imagine he would be a very fast driver.

Diane Broadbent Friedman

Grove of rhododendrons, Ashridge, Berkhamsted, England, reproduced with kind permission of Ashridge Business School (Ashridge.org.uk).

Conductor 71 in the grove of rhododendrons. *A Matter of Life and Death* (1946). "Stairway to Heaven"© 1946,1974,1996. Carlton Film Distributors Limited. All Rights Reserved. Courtesy of Columbia Pictures.

Petrol was very short during the war and severely rationed. Doctors would get priority. There was a bar down in the crypt at Ashridge. The beer was very weak but it never ran out. There were no spirits. MacGinnis was a frequent visitor there and sometimes would serve behind the bar.

Prior to the advent of penicillin, sulfonamides were the wonder drug. I well remember the arrival of penicillin at the hospital. It was given by injection only. The medical staff put on gowns and masks and scrubbed up as for a major operation. It was quite a ritual.[29]

As far as I have been able to determine, Mr. Macdonald did not perform neurosurgery, but even in the 1940s some general surgeons performed neurosurgical procedures. Because MacGinnis lived in

Ballycullen, Ashford, County Wicklow, Ireland, from 1958 until his death in Wales in 1977, I contacted people in Ashford to see if any one recalled Mr. MacGinnis's surgical specialties. (Part of the 1960 film *Sword of Sherwood Forrest* was filmed in the woods of Ballycullen) I was able to see a copy of a book describing the history of Ashford. A passage describes Mr. Macdonald as "a nerve specialist in Charing Cross Hospital."[30] It also says that Mr. MacGinnis had "an interest in brain function." Could Mr. Macdonald and/or Niall MacGinnis have provided information about brain function or medical aspects of the film? It is possible, but I can not make any further connection.

Small but Valid Neurologic Details within *AMOLAD*

<u>An unnamed neurologist/neurosurgeon</u>
In an interview with David Badder, Michael Powell stated that "I went on rounds,"[6] but I have not been able to determine who that doctor was. When I watch *AMOLAD*, there are small details which seem to me could have only been gathered during a visit to a neurological hospital wing. They are not details that would appear in a textbook or article. They are passed on as a trainee observes his mentor.

The scene in Dr. Reeves' study is especially eloquent for me, an advanced practice nurse who has experience caring for people with epilepsy. I have observed many people having complex partial seizures while they were admitted to our hospital's special epilepsy monitoring unit. Patients would be admitted there if we had tried, over months and years, all of the medications available to us but had not been able to bring the seizures under control. We wanted to observe a seizure and to record the brain electrical activity with the electroencephalogram (EEG) from the very first moment of the seizure to determine in what part of the brain the seizure began. If the seizure began in a surgically favorable part of the brain, surgeons could remove that portion, eliminating the seizure focus without impairing the person.

Peter tries to tell Dr. Reeves and June about Conductor 71's visit. *A Matter of Life and Death* (1946). Photograph by kind permission of Granada International.

In Dr. Reeves' study, we see Peter sleeping, a bell on a small table close at hand. In our hospital unit, we would have a similar device near to each patient. We would ask each person to press the call bell or signal if he or she felt a seizure coming on. Often times the seizure would happen so fast that they could not signal, but it was a reasonable thing to have available.

After Peter finishes his conversation with Conductor 71, he calls for Dr. Reeves and June. We see him looking a little confused, and he pushes the books off the small table. We know that Peter is trying to describe Conductor 71's actions, but from Dr. Reeves' perspective, he simply observes someone who is confused and a little agitated. Confusion and agitation can sometimes, although not always, occur after a complex partial seizure. So Dr. Reeves says in a stronger, very directive voice, "Peter! Sit down." This also has authenticity for me because sometimes a stronger tone and a simple command can help to direct someone who is confused after a seizure.

After Dr. Reeves checks Peter's right eye, the doctor reaches into his pocket and fishes out something. I think Dr. Reeves is pulling a key or a coin out of his pocket to check Peter's left Babinski reflex. This small gesture is something many physicians perform. All of these aspects—the bell, the command, the reflex check with a key—are not details Michael Powell would find in a neurology textbook. He must have visited a hospital wing where people with epilepsy were evaluated and where he could watch a neurologist at work. These details may not only represent the actions of a neurologist but also may reflect the work of a British neurologist, Dr. James Collier, who will be discussed more fully in the next chapter.

What Else Did Michael Powell Read?

A Journey 'Round My Skull (1937)[31]
It has been reported in several sources that Michael Powell and Emeric Pressburger were influenced by the autobiographical account of Frigyes Karinthy facing the diagnosis of a brain tumor in the 1937 book *A Journey 'Round My Skull*.[32] I will first discuss the book and then show how details from it are present in *AMOLAD*.

When the English translation by Vernon Duckworth Barker, Hungarian Scholar at University of London, was published in 1939, it made a significant impact on the general reading public and on the medical community. The book was reviewed twice in *The New York Times* in August 1939. One article began by listing the praise from British reviews: "*The London Evening Standard*…extraordinary; …*The New Statesman and Nation*…remarkable; *The Spectator*…

unusual and extremely interesting; *The Glasgow Hearald*...literary achievement; *John O'London's Weekly*...terrible and marvelous; and the *British Medical Journal*...a book of the highest value."[33]. A second review written two weeks later captured the many-layered ironies of Karinthy's situation: "A satirist writing an account of his progressive changes in thought and perception as he seeks to hold on to his life, his everyday activities and pleasures; his attempts to outwit his doctors and avoid their diagnoses; his confusion and fear and his funny and fearful reactions to his situation; and yet he faithfully and accurately records the entire process as he falls ill and then recovers."[34]

At a neurology conference concerning the significance of auditory and visual hallucinations sponsored by the British Medical Association July 26–28, 1939, the neurologist Macdonald Critchley mentioned Karinthy: "...various neurological conditions, for example brain tumor, migraine, epilepsy, and narcolepsy, could cause hallucinations. Hallucinations sometimes occurred in the sane...Karinthy, in *A Journey 'Round My Skull*, referred to the hallucinatory noises during the early development of a cerebellar hemangioblastoma." [35]

The 1941 book *Neuro-Ophthalmology* discussed visual hallucinations caused by temporal lobe tumors at length. "In connection with the above the reader might turn in his leisure moments to Karinthy's *A Journey 'Round My Skull* in which the writer has described in a most entertaining form his own symptoms of a tumor in the brain."[36]

Surely Emeric Pressburger would have been aware of Karinthy since they were both Hungarian and living in Budapest, and because Karinthy had already received acclaim in 1912 for his satirical book *That's How You Write*. Karinthy had been writing for at least ten years when Pressburger's career began. Another connection is that Frigyes Karinthy worked as a story editor for the filmmaker Sandor Korda in 1910. Mr. Korda would later move to England and change his first name to Alexander. In 1937, at a script writing meeting for *The Spy in Black*, Mr. Korda would introduce the director of the film Michael Powell to the new scriptwriter, Emeric Pressburger.[37]

Frigyes Karinthy was a social humorist and satirist after leaving his training as a medical student. Frequently he wrote articles for the Budapest newspapers satirizing the government and daily life. In translation, the works I have read remind me of James Thurber and Mark Twain. He said that his own model was Jonathan Swift. He kept a notebook as daily images struck him. He had a stimulating intellectual life of witty friends who met in cafes for conversation. His first wife passed away in the flu epidemic of 1917. He then married Aranka Böhm, a psychiatrist. His son, Ferenc Karinthy, known by the nickname Cini in the book, became a filmmaker in adult life. His grandson Marton is a director of theater in Budapest.

Karinthy's powers of observation, satire, philosophical reflection, plain speaking, and irony faced their greatest challenge in 1936, when Karinthy was 49. On the afternoon of March 10, 1936, he was sitting in a café thinking over his next story, when he heard the sound of a rumbling train, coming closer and closer. He looked around, although certain there were no trains in the area and that this was impossible. From that moment, he began to experience the symptoms of the rapidly intensifying threat to his life—a brain tumor in his cerebellum. The book chronicles the onset of his symptoms, his process of diagnosis, his everyday life, and the interlocking lives and personalities of his family, friends and physicians. It also is a saga of Karinthy's interior, mental life.

In this book he accomplished something unique: allowing the reader to follow his experience and his analysis, all while he is having hallucinations which he sometimes believes might be real, as he becomes more unsteady in his balance, and as he has more

A Matter of Life and Death

difficulty seeing and making himself understood. Karinthy allows the reader to experience his reality in his amusing, ironic voice. It is a challenge to describe a process of confusion with clarity.

As the tumor growth places steadily more pressure in important areas of the brain, Karinthy loses his ability to see and stand. He begins to make a separation between the part of his brain that has stopped functioning properly—causing seizures, confusion, blindness—and the part he calls "Little Me," the place where his personality, creative spirit, sense of irony, and love of life reside and persist.

In the first half of the book, he cannot believe that he has such a serious condition where action needs to be taken immediately. Eventually he travels to Stockholm, where his evaluation and surgery is performed by Herbert Olivecrona, a student of Harvey Cushing and Hugh Cairns. The location of Karinthy's lesion is in the cerebellum at the back of his brain, but the pressure from the expanding mass is causing seizures from the temporal lobe at the front of the brain. This surgery takes place with Karinthy lying on his stomach, awake and looking at the floor. Karinthy believes that to survive the surgery mentally intact, it is essential that he remain alert and focused. He fights to remain conscious and calm while Olivecrona operates at the base of his skull. True to his personality and soul of a writer, Karinthy describes the details of his experience during surgery and in the drama of recovery that followed.

A Journey 'Round My Skull **and AMOLAD**
There are many echoes of *A Journey 'Round My Skull* in *AMOLAD*, and some are easy to list:

1. Karinthy hears a hurdy-gurdy playing as an auditory aura[38] similar to the piano theme heard by Peter Carter in Lee Wood House in *AMOLAD*.

2. Karinthy has a hallucination or a dream described in the chapter, "Death Comes To Visit."[39] In this vivid dream, a doctor comes to his house and proposes to do a spinal tap to remove the cerebrospinal fluid in which the brain is suspended. In reality, this procedure would cause rapidly fatal brain herniation. This visit is reminiscent of the visit by Conductor 71, in which an imaginary figure portends death in the next few moments.
3. During surgery, Karinthy imagines himself getting up from the operating table and watching his surgeon proceed,[40] which is similar to Peter Carter leaving the operating table.
4. At the beginning of the book, before Karinthy begins to experience symptoms, he describes seeing a documentary of Harvey Cushing in the operating room performing brain surgery.[41]

Stairways

But there are other, more subtle concepts in *Journey 'Round My Skull* which have an echo in *AMOLAD* as well. Karinthy describes stairways on several occasions.[42] These are locations where he pauses to reflect. The stairway represents a boundary that, in crossing, will reveal knowledge about his future that he will not be able to ignore for long. These stairways lead to the offices of neurologists or ophthalmologists who will announce his fate. One important insight took place in the moments before he would climb the steps, enter the office of his doctor, and learn his diagnosis

> At ten o'clock I found myself on the doorstep of Maria-Ucca eye hospital. Just look at yourself! You're

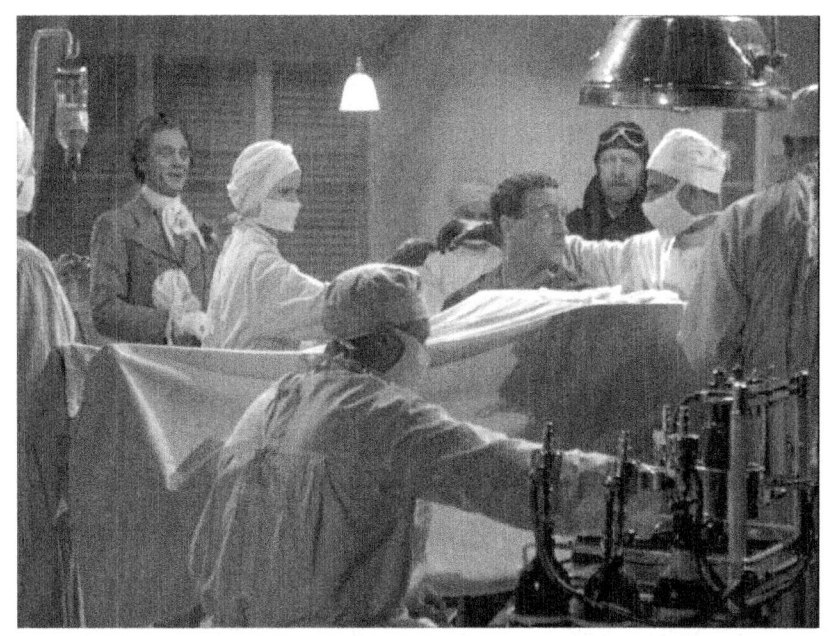

Peter observes his own surgery. *A Matter of Life and Death* (1946). "Stairway to Heaven"© 1946,1974,1996. Carlton Film Distributors Limited. All Rights Reserved. Courtesy of Columbia Pictures.

> becoming an old hypochondriac...And then I smiled for an idea had suddenly occurred to me. I would write a sketch in 20 scenes on the "Calvary and Ascension into Heaven of a patient suffering from an itch in the ear," as he drags himself from specialist to specialist... I was still playing with the idea when I reached the first floor of the hospital. This staircase was to be the last stage of my childish life which I thought would go on for six thousand years. It was to ring down the curtain on my carefree arrogant existence...[43]

He also traces the changes he sees in his analytical ability and the awareness of his creative process:

> Yes I talk to myself theatrically—you needn't be afraid of saying it—using dramatic gestures as if I were on

> the stage. It seemed absurd and yet it was true that my outward carelessness and cynicism, even my cheery, imperturbable manner, have been made possible by these inner theatricals…This secret theater has made it possible to bear with life…That afternoon I could find my stage no longer. I looked in vain in my heart for the fine words and the talking images…Something had gone from me that afternoon—something I had never missed before since I was capable of thinking at all….my self-dramatizing instinct…[44]

I cannot prove it, but I sense that Michael Powell and Emeric Pressburger would have found this description of the storyteller threatened with the loss—not only of his life, but also his inner eye and inner voice (Karinthy calls that inner voice "Little Me")—very compelling. Karinthy strives to stay true to the story rather than improving on the truth, but ultimately he cannot resist:

> As I write, Little Me has come butting in again, stopping my pen and upsetting my train of thought. He insists that I must break off at once before the "writer'—the other part of me who produces the imaginative works—tries to go one better than reality. The writer in me sometimes entertains an arrogant belief that he could improve upon the truth by a little deliberate artifice…[45]

If a writer or a filmmaker is skillful and lucky and honest, something more emerges. This would be the most fundamental commonality between Karinthy and Powell and Pressburger.

Fortunately, not only did Karinthy survive but, almost miraculously, his vision was restored. The vigor and tone of the book imply that his neurological deficits were resolved for a time. He published his book and was completing a book of poetry when

A Matter of Life and Death

he died from a recurrence of his brain tumor two years later on August 29, 1938, while on vacation in the Hungarian lakeside town of Siofok. His book, *A Journey 'Round My Skull*, has as much to say to thoughtful people and physicians today as it did seventy years ago. In March 2008, it has just been reprinted in English for a new generation of readers.

The Oxford Book of English Verse[46]

Michael Powell valued this book. He took it with him on the *Queen Elizabeth* and consulted it as he made the final changes to *AMOLAD*:

> "The opening of the film with Niven spouting poetry and the bomber roaring down, that's all Powell. I took with me to America—as well as my medical notes—the *Oxford Book of English Verse*, so that I could pick out some good bits for Niven to declaim as the bomber fell."[6]

While some film reviewers found it contrived for Peter Carter to quote poetry as he came to his death, Michael Powell had personal experience with poetry as an integral part of his life. He had a prodigious memory for poetry and could recite very long poems late into his life. Poetry is part of the intellectual fabric of England. It is also an expression of the workings of the brain and the mind. Rather than being an odd ingredient in the film, I think British poetry fully belongs there alongside the physiology and the representation of British neuroscience to complete a presentation of the workings of the life of the mind.

It is instructive to look through this book. Because it is English verse, some American poets are included. I have counted twenty-two poets in the film and novelization of *AMOLAD* whose work is found in the 1940 volume of the *Oxford Book of English Verse*. Robert Bridges' "My Delight and Thy Delight," among many poems of the following poets, is reminiscent of the emotions and situations in *AMOLAD*. Below is the list of poets whose work appears in *AMOLAD*:

Robert Bridges
Sir Thomas Brown
Lord Byron
John Bunyan
Geoffrey Chaucer
Samuel Taylor Coleridge
John Donne
John Dryden
T.S. Eliot
John Keats
Henry King
Cecil Day Lewis
Andrew Marvell
George Meredith
John Swinnerton Phillimore
Alexander Pope
Sir Walter Raleigh
Sir Walter Scott
Percy Bysshe Shelley
Stephen Spender
Lord Tennyson
William Wordsworth

The topic of poetry makes a good bridge into the next chapter, for in it I will describe details of the film which suggest to me associations with literature or neuroscience. For instance, I believe that the lives

A Matter of Life and Death

of the Georgian poets Rupert Brooke, Walter de la Mare, Siegfried Sassoon and Wilfrid Owen—whose work is also present in the *Oxford Book of English Verse*—are mirrored in the situation of Peter Carter. I have collected my speculations in the next chapter so the reader can evaluate my interpretations, realizing that I have no conclusive proof, only strong suggestions of further connections.

1. Purves-Stewart, James, *The Diagnosis of Nervous Diseases*, ninth ed. 1945 (Baltimore: Williams and Wilkins Co., 1945).

2. Ibid., 241.

3. Ibid., 239.

4. Ibid., 845.

5. Goldsmith, A. J. B., "Chiasmal Arachnoiditis," *Proceedings of the Royal Society of Medicine* (1943): 163.

6. Badder, David, "Powell and Pressburger: The War Years," *Sight and Sound* 48, no. 1 (1978/1979 Winter): 8.

7. Powell, Michael, *A Life in Movies*, 458–59.

8. Joseph P. Reidy, personal correspondence, 1990.

9. Bailey, B.N. "Obituary: Joseph Patrick Irwin Reidy," *British Journal of Plastic Surgery* 45 (1992): 253.

10. Reidy, J.P., *Physical Methods in Plastic Surgery* (London: Actinic Press, 1956).

11. Reidy, J.P., "Burns II: Skin cover for full-thickness skin loss," *British Journal of Medicine* (Nov. 4, 1950): 1030–33.

12. Reidy, J.P., "Formation and early history of the Stoke-Mandeville plastic surgery unit," *British Journal of Plastic Surgery* 39 (1986): 85–95.

13. McIndoe, A.H., "Editorial," *British Journal of Plastic Surgery* 2 (1949):1-3.

14. Andrew, D.R., "The Guinea Pig Club," *Aviation, Space and Environmental Medicine* 65(1994):428-31.

15. Davies, R.M. "Relationships: Archibald McIndoe, his times, society, and hospital," *Annals of the Royal College of Surgeons of England* 59(1977):359-367.

16. Warman, Eric, adaptation of Michael Powell and Emeric Pressburger's *A Matter of Life and Death: The book of the film* (London: World Film Publications, 1946), 117.

17. *The Medical Directory* (London: J and A. Churchill, 1937 and 1954).

18. Kaplan, Bernard, "Music with nitrous oxide" *Anaesthesia* 11, no.2 (April 1956): 160—63.

19. Kaplan, Bernard, "Cinema-radiography," *The Journal of the British Institute of Cinematography* 4, no. 3 (March 1936): 26.

20. "Editorial," *The Journal of the British Institute of Cinematography* 4, no. 3 (March 1936): 3.

21. Macdonald, William G., " Two cases of congenital hypertrophic pyloric stenosis," *Lancet* vol.1 (February 26, 1921): 428.

22. Christie, Ian, *A Matter of Life and Death*, (London: British Film Institute Publishing, 2000), 29.

23. Sanecki, Kay, Thompson M., *Ashridge*, (Norwich: Jarrold Publishing, 1998), 5.

24. Edmonds R., *Ashridge in World War II* (The National Trust),18.

25. Ibid., 14.

26. Ashridge Business School, Berkhamsted, England.

27. Mr. Mick Thompson, historian, Ashridge Business School, personal correspondence, March 2008.

28. Ms. Irene Spruce, personal correspondence, March, 2008.

29. Dr. Vivian Edwards and his wife, personal correspondence, March, June, July 2008.

30. Clarke, Shelia, *Ashford, a Journey Through Time*. (Dublin: Martello Press, 2003), 191.

31. Karinthy, Frigyes, *A Journey 'Round My Skull*, translated from the Hungarian by Vernon Duckworth Barker, (London: Faber and Faber, 1939).

32. Christie, Ian, *A Matter of Life and Death*, (London: BFI Publishing, 2000), 20.

33. Thompson, Ralph, "Books of the Times," *The New York Times*, August 10, 1939.

34. Cornos, John, "A strange adventure of the mind," *The New York Times*, (August 27, 1939).

35. *The Lancet* (August 19, 1939): 426–27.

36. Rea, R.L., *Neuro-ophthalmology*, second ed. (St. Louis: Mosby, 1941), 559.

37. Powell, *A Life in Films*, 301.

38. Karinthy, *A Journey 'Round My Skull*, 74, 127.

39. Ibid., 144.

40. Ibid., 241.

41. Ibid., 21.

42. Ibid., 58, 62, 67, 121.

43. Ibid., 62.

44. Ibid., 208.

45. Ibid., 200.

46. Quiller-Couch Arthur, ed. *The Oxford Book of English Verse 1250–1918*, New edition, (London: Oxford University Press, 1940).

Chapter Seven:

Neurologic Hints, Echoes, and Possibilities

In 1952, Michael Powell read Chaim Weizmann's autobiography *Trial and Error* and after a few pages, he wanted to make a movie about his life and the founding of Israel. What was his first step in preparation of that script? "As soon as I finished the book," Powell said, "I was off to Charing Cross to buy a beginner's handbook to organic chemistry (second-hand of course), for Chaim Weizmann was a chemist, and thereby hangs a tale."[1] When Michael Powell prepared to make a film, clearly he was unafraid of technical topics and felt a need to understand them as part of the artistic process of developing a script and a film. With regards to *AMOLAD*, Powell had carefully researched the technical aspects of the film "even with the spectacular opening sequence in space, which we had discussed with Arthur Clarke." [2].

Michael Powell had a mind that not only relished information but also absorbed that information and synthesized it, sometimes years after having read it, all in the service of creating a compelling story. When Powell wrote his autobiography, he wove important details throughout that structure as well, sometimes reflecting about *AMOLAD* within the first few pages and then again many pages and years removed from the making of that film.

Powell's habit of mind to interweave his ideas makes it a challenge for a researcher to tease those ideas apart for discussion. In his book, *The Edge of the World*, he touched on that aspect of the creative process—namely, looking at the final creative product and detecting the components which led to its creation:

> I have always been fascinated by bare bones, but now that I return to the beginning of my own adventure I find that I have a nervous horror of being tedious. Frankenstein would feel very much as I do. I can imagine him, surrounded by reporters: "Now please tell us, Mr. Frankenstein, how did you first get your idea of the monster? Please give us an outline of your experiments!" I am sure that the inventor, shaken and astonished by triumph after a hundred failures, faced with the supreme fact of the fulfillment of his dream, would look back with weariness on his first struggles.[3]

While I emphasize Powell's scholarship, I make the assumption that Pressbruger at least ratified and supported that medical scholarship, partially on the strength that *AMOLAD* is not the first Powell and Pressburger film that contains subtle technical details supporting the greater artistic work. As Ian Christie pointed out in his essay on *A Canterbury Tale*, "Within this [Colpeper's] house, the film offers a cluster of visual and graphic clues to Colpeper's values that can take us beyond, or behind, the rhetoric of his various speeches to the pilgrims."[4] Christie then explains the meaning behind the details of the agricultural and hiking books on Colpeper's desk, pictures on the wall, and other details seen in the room. Christie makes the case that each detail is an artistic judgment to amplify our understanding of the character. I make the assumption that this same artistic technique is present in AMOLAD, and that these details are present within the film because *both Powell and Pressburger wanted them there.*

As I watch AMOLAD, I experience a flood of associations with aspects of neuroscience. A moment, a phrase, or a gesture will remind me of a person in the history of neurology or neurosurgery, a discovery, a paragraph of an historical scientific paper, a belief held at the time, or a neurological anecdote. I want to tell the reader about my impressions in the full richness of detail that I think Michael Powell mastered so that he could use these details creatively and with subtlety.

What follows is a collection of interpretations I have developed from my study of AMOLAD. I think that they will bring deeper appreciation of Michael Powell's scholarship. The difficulty is that in some of the movie's scenes, the neurological basis is clear, while in other scenes neurological details are just as likely coincidental as they might be purposeful. For all the details that follow, I have found references in the medical literature of the time. Because the notes of the film are not available, I cannot be sure that Michael Powell actually read any of the materials listed below.

All of this information was available to him—in the British Museum Reading Room, from secondhand booksellers' stalls, or from medical people with whom he conversed. We know he sought out those resources, and we know he was not intimidated by technical materials. To my mind, therefore, the following details probably reflect purposeful insertion by Michael Powell following purposeful scholarship. I present this information for your review. You can draw your own conclusion about the intentionality of each. I know he was capable of understanding this material and inserting it into the story. In the historical novel *The Devil in the White City*, Erik Larson confronted the same dilemma of interpretation from incomplete information. He phrased his approach this way, "...I document my reasoning and my approach and cite the facts upon which I relied. The citations that follow constitute a map. Anyone retracing my steps ought to reach the same conclusion as I..."[5]

A Brief Summary of My Interpretations

To help the reader understand the scope of these interpretations, I will very briefly summarize my impressions. Each impression is more fully developed in a separate essay in the Appendix.

> 1. *"In space, not in time"*: The experience of space and time are jointly necessary to be conscious. With a sense of time missing, the person is no longer conscious. Despite Peter Carter hallucinating that a conversation is transpiring in real time, Conductor 71 is telling Peter that he is not conscious.

> 2. *A poet treated by a neurologist during war*: Henry Head, M.D., one of the foremost British neurologists of the first half of the twentieth century, cared for several poets injured during service in World War I. Head also lived in a country village and wrote poetry himself, as well as serving for a time as editor of the neurology journal *Brain*.

> 3. *Music heard in Lee Wood House*: The two pieces heard during the afternoon play rehearsal—*A Midsummer Night's Dream* played on the record player and then a foreboding piano theme—can be seen variously as a musical aura, a precipitant of seizure, and/or emblematic of Sir Victor Horsley, considered by some to be the first neurosurgeon and the first to perform epilepsy surgery.

A Matter of Life and Death

Peter hears music in the common room of Lee Wood House. *A Matter of Life and Death* (1946). Photograph by kind permission of Granada International.

4. *The man who jumped and lived*: Nicholas Alkemade did jump without a parachute and lived to tell about it. When he first awoke, he thought he was in Heaven.

5. *An experienced pilot who seems pretty calm after escaping death twice, first from a burning plane and then from drowning*: During World War II, two British neurologists, Macdonald Critchley and C. P. Symonds, published several research papers on survival during extreme situations such as prolonged immersion in sea water, as well as on the psychological stress experienced by pilots.

6. *Literature and neurology*: Peter Carter quotes poetry, but so do British neurologists. In the medical literature of the 1900s, the neurological experiences of poets and writers are analyzed by neuroscientists.

7. *Why fried onions?*: A number of contemporary neurologists published detailed accounts of patients having "dreamy states" in which they saw complex figures, heard conversations, music or identifiable sounds, and/or smelled a variety of specific odors.

8. *The staircase and the statues*: Peter Carter's dream of the big statues and big staircase could be a neurological distortion of the small statues and piles of books seen in Dr. Reeves' study. Additionally, many of the statues represent historical figures that were thought to have epilepsy.

Dr. Reeves does not wear a helmet when he rides his motorcycle. *A Matter of Life and Death* (1946). "Stairway to Heaven"© 1946,1974,1996. Carlton Film Distributors Limited. All Rights Reserved. Courtesy of Columbia Pictures.

9. *Motorcycles and head injury*: Hugh Cairns, a prominent British neurosurgeon, examined Lawrence of Arabia after his motorcycle accident but could not save him. After this experience, Cairns single-mindedly pushed for mandatory motorcycle helmets and demonstrated that the fatality rate among army

motorcyclists was significantly reduced when this rule went into effect.

Dr. Reeves did not follow that advice.

10. *The camera obscura*: Michael Powell was a frequent visitor to John Laurie's home, two blocks from a camera obscura in Dumfries, Scotland, which very closely resembles the one used by Dr. Reeves in the movie.

11. *After Peter sees Conductor 71 for a second time, Dr. Reeves checks the reflexes in Peter's left foot and the condition of his right eye; the next morning, the doctor rides to the American hospital where he urges that the surgery must take place that night*: Dr. James Collier, a British neurologist popular with patients, colleagues, and students, had published articles on gauging the imminent danger of increasing intracranial pressure resulting from expanding brain lesions, by assessing the Babinski reflex and pupilary responses.

12. *Peter is cared for by Dr. McEwen, Dr. Leiser, and Dr. Reeves*: Could these names reflect real surgeons with neurological expertise as well as expertise with brain maps—William Macewen, John Lizars, and Langdon Rives?

13. *A neurological joke that did not appear in the film*: A joke written in but then crossed out of the script is almost identical to a joke told by John Hughlings Jackson to the neurophysiologist David Ferrier at the completion of the first epilepsy surgery performed by Victor Horsley.

14. *Why chess?* There are several anecdotes concerning chess and neurology.

15. *Who was Abraham Farlan?* This is one detail that does not match with the research I have done. His name does not appear on the lists I have seen. Maybe there is significance beyond what I could determine.

Diane Broadbent Friedman

ANATOMY

of

THE BRAIN,

from

THE CELEBRATED DISSECTIONS

of

JOHN LIZARS, M. D., ETC., OF LONDON,

comprising

FIFTEEN ENGRAVINGS (COLORED AFTER NATURE,)

with

ACCOMPANYING EXPLANATIONS.

EDITED BY

LANDON RIVES, M. D.

CINCINNATI:
PUBLISHED BY H. W. DERBY, MAIN STREET.
1854.

Title page from <u>Anatomy of the brain from the celebrated dissections of John Lizars M.D.</u> comprising fifteen engravings (colored after nature) with accompanying explanations. Ed. by Landon Rives, M.D. Cincinnati, H.W. Derby, 1854. Courtesy of the Galter Health Sciences Library, Special Collections, Northwestern University, Chicago, IL.

A Matter of Life and Death

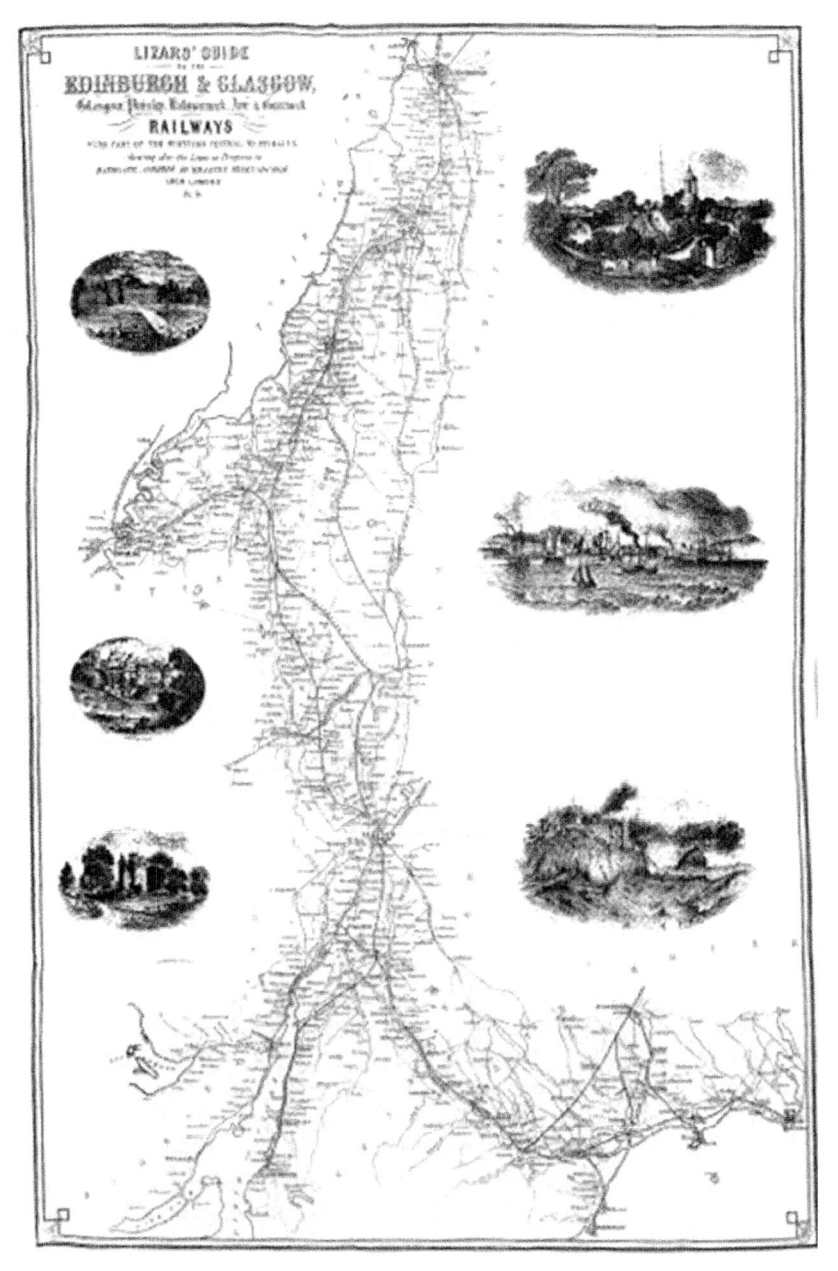

Lizars' Guide to the Edinburgh and Glasgow Railway,
W.H. Lizars Edinburgh, circa 1860.

Diane Broadbent Friedman

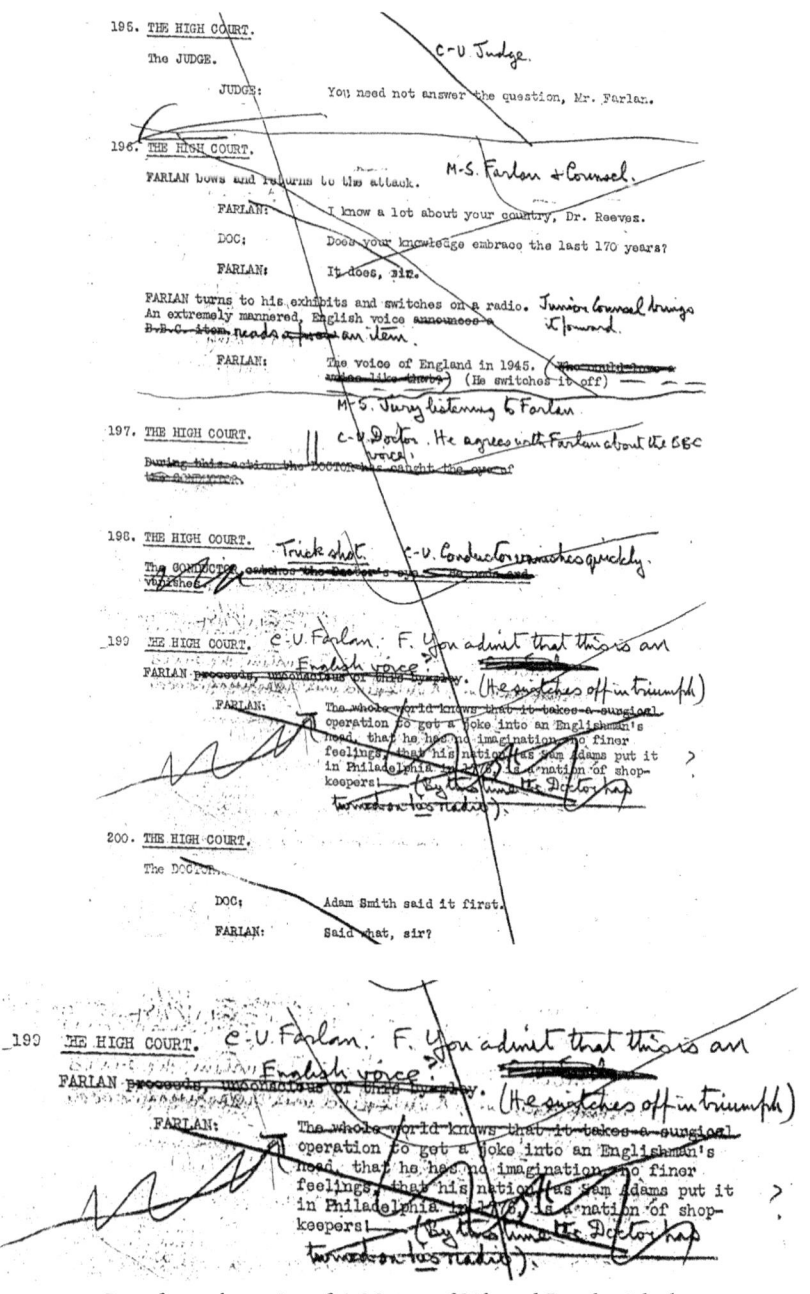

195. THE HIGH COURT.

The JUDGE.   C-U Judge.

    JUDGE: You need not answer the question, Mr. Farlan.

196. THE HIGH COURT.
                                              M-S Farlan + Counsel.
    FARLAN bows and returns to the attack. Junior Counsel brings
    An extremely mannered, English voice announces a   it forward.
    B.B.C. item reads from an item
        FARLAN: I know a lot about your country, Dr. Reeves.
        DOC: Does your knowledge embrace the last 170 years?
        FARLAN: It does, sir.
    FARLAN turns to his exhibits and switches on a radio.
        FARLAN: The voice of England in 1945.
                    (He switches it off)
                                        M-S Jury listening to Farlan.

197. THE HIGH COURT.   C-U Doctor. He agrees with Farlan about the BBC
                          voice.

198. THE HIGH COURT. Truck shot.   C-U Conductor — watches quickly.

199. THE HIGH COURT. C-U Farlan. F. You admit that this is an
    FARLAN   English voice.   (He switches off in triumph)
        FARLAN: The whole world knows that it takes a surgical
                    operation to get a joke into an Englishman's
                    head, that he has no imagination, no finer
                    feelings, that his nation as Sam Adams put it
                    in Philadelphia in 1776 is a nation of shop-
                    keepers! (By this time the Doctor has
                    turned on his radio.)

200. THE HIGH COURT.
    The DOCTOR.
        DOC: Adam Smith said it first.
        FARLAN: Said what, sir?

199. THE HIGH COURT. C-U Farlan. F. You admit that this is an
    FARLAN   English voice.   (He switches off in triumph)
        FARLAN: The whole world knows that it takes a surgical
                    operation to get a joke into an Englishman's
                    head, that he has no imagination, no finer
                    feelings, that his nation as Sam Adams put it
                    in Philadelphia in 1776 is a nation of shop-
                    keepers! (By this time the Doctor has
                    turned on his radio.)

Page from the script of *A Matter of Life and Death* with the passage of the surgical implantation of a joke. Reprinted with the kind permission of Thelma Schoonmaker Powell.

A Matter of Life and Death

The Objects in Dr. Reeves' Study

A number of objects in Dr. Reeves' study have neurological importance: objects on his desk; the books in a pile by Peter as he lays on the day bed; the pictures on the wall; and a large book on the floor. One difficulty in fully exploring these objects is that I have a DVD which does not allow me to clearly see many titles of books fully in view. As the camera pans around the study at the beginning of the scene, and when it shows June looking at the desk, there are books whose titles might be readable if they were in sharper focus.

The objects on Dr. Reeves' desk

There is a book open to drawings of brain anatomy. I have not been able to locate the specific book nor can I be positively sure of the content of the drawings, but my best guess is that the top drawing is of the underside of the temporal lobe and the second drawing is of the brain from the side. A drawing, such as the one appearing on page 34, is typically found in most of the neurology textbooks of the time. One large book in the upper-left corner of the desk resembles in size and color *Gray's Anatomy*. The twenty-fourth edition from 1942 is red with lateral gold stripes on the spine, and it is three inches thick.[6]

A model of the brain is evident, turned upside down, with the brain stem removed to allow for study of the floor of the brain where Peter's lesion is located. There are a variety of other books and magazines on the desk, possibly medicine or poetry, some positioned so that we would be able to read the titles, but the film is exposed to the point that they cannot be read.

Although we cannot make out many of the books on the desk, these two main details—the drawing of the brain localizations and the model of the brain, represent maps which will lead Dr. Reeves to the location of the brain lesion.

Diane Broadbent Friedman

June looks at Dr/ Reeves desk. *A Matter of Life and Death* (1946). "Stairway to Heaven"© 1946,1974,1996. Carlton Film Distributors Limited. All Rights Reserved. Courtesy of Columbia Pictures.

Piles of books

There are many piles of books throughout the study, as well as on a table next to Peter. On close inspection of the stills from Dr. Reeves' study, a number of the piled up books are volumes of the *Encyclopedia Britannica*. The inclusion of these books makes a perfect visual metaphor for the uniting of British and American efforts. The *Encyclopedia* was first written in 1768 in Edinburgh. Leading scholars of the day were invited to write articles for it beginning in 1815.

The eleventh edition was produced with the support of Cambridge University, but by that time the ownership of the work was held by Sears, Roebuck and Co. of Chicago. The University of Chicago took ownership as a gift to the University by Sears President and University trustee Julius Rosenwald in 1941.

Did Michael Powell refer to these books as he wrote his script? I reviewed volumes of the eleventh and fourteenth editions for topics including "Camera Obscura," "Neurology," and "Neuroanatomy," but I did not find any sources of dialogue. It is interesting to review the "Hallucinations" article from the fourteenth edition written by William McDougal, professor of psychology at Oxford. He devotes a page to the work of The Society for Psychical Research:

> Is there any sufficient justification for the belief in a causal relation between the apparition of a person at a place distant from his body and his death or other exceptional and momentous event in his experience? The Problem was attacked in a thoroughly scientific spirit in *Phantasms of the Living* using statistics to demonstrate…that such telepathic phenomena are true.[7]

This is the same body of research to which Ian Christie referred in his book of *AMOLAD*, and it reminds us of Dr. Reeves' comment that he has thought too much about the survival of human personality after death.[8] This article is a snapshot in scientific time, reflecting not only the robust era of scientific growth but also the dynamics of evaluating competing scientific theories, where some older hypotheses were replaced with newer, more accurate ones. Hans Berger's EEG was invented in 1929 in his attempt to demonstrate the existence of telepathy. He came to realize that it did not serve this purpose, but meanwhile it proved to be an invaluable tool in the determination of a location in the underlying brain that was the source of a seizure. By the late 1930s, neurologists were being sent from Montreal to Cambridge and from London to Boston to learn the most recent techniques of its use.

Diane Broadbent Friedman

The edges of the books and the little statue mimics the staircase and the statues. (close up) *A Matter of Life and Death* (1946). Photograph by kind permission of Granada International.

The books next to Peter Carter

The book at the top of the stack is *The International Library of Famous Literature*.[9] The first story in this anthology is 'The Gorgon's Head' by Nathaniel Hawthorne. I cannot make any connections between this book and the film, although this title reminds me of the series of books that Powell's mother owned. Powell noted, "I would hate to part with the pocket libraries that crowded her shelves. I have them still: the Canterbury Poets; Everyman's; little red Nelsons; the World's Classics; *The Rubaiyat*, George Borrow and Maurice Hewletts…I have twice sold my books and pictures. I have never sold hers."[10]

The second book is turned away from the camera.

The third book is *Physiology of the Eye*, by J. Grandson Byrne.[11] Written by Joseph Grandson Byrne, the president of Fordham University Medical School (New York City, 1917–1921) and a member

A Matter of Life and Death

of the Royal College of Surgeons, the complete title of the book is *Studies on the Physiology of the Eye: Still Reaction, Sleep, Dreams, Hibernation, Repression, Hypnosis, Narcosis, Coma and Allied Conditions*. Some of Dr. Byrne's laboratory research summarized in this book was performed in England. Clearly this title is a listing of all the various states and levels of consciousness, focused on research of the function of the eye—Michael Powell's favorite image.

The fourth book is *The Prevention of Malaria*, by Ronald Ross.[12] This book was written by the prominent British physician and Georgian poet, who was the second Nobel Prize winner in Medicine in 1902 for his work to discover the mechanism for the transmission, infection, and prevention of malaria. Malaria was a significant problem, not only in countries like Egypt, India, and Panama, but also in the marshy areas of Kent in England. Also known in England as "marsh fever" and "tertiary or quaternary ague," it was the cause of death of Andrew Marvell, the poet quoted by Peter Carter at the beginning of the film. This book represented the conquering of a public health menace and the application of mathematics to the understanding of infectious disease, and it would have been as significant in its day as *The Double Helix* was in the 1970s. Ronald Ross lived from 1851 to 1932 and was indefatigable in his efforts to overcome official resistance and apply simple methods to prevent malaria. While this book does not refer to a neurological problem, it does reflect the ingenuity and sheer tenacity of British medicine in overcoming heretofore insolvable problems.

Statues

There are several small statues in the room. One is visible in the same photograph in which Grandson Byrne's book is visible. The pose of the statue is reminiscent of the statues later seen along the stairway leading to Heaven. I think these statues and the books are transformed in Peter Carter's hallucination to produce an illusion of stairs and large statues in a macropsia effect, possibly even a repetitive effect which echoes Macdonald Critchley's visual perseveration in time and space.

Large book on the floor at the back-right corner of the study
I cannot determine the writing on the book. However by its shape and size, it reminds me of the typical size and shape of a brain atlas—typically an oversized book containing drawings of significant details of anatomy which is consulted by surgeons and physiologists. Neurosurgeon Sir William Macewen created a significant brain atlas, *Atlas of Head sections: Fifty-three Engraved Copperplates of Frozen Sections of the Head, and Fifty-three Key Plates with Descriptive Texts*, in 1893.[13] John Lizars also produced a brain atlas, *A System of Anatomical Plates of the Human Body*, printed by his father's publishing firm, W. H. Lizars and Daniel Lizars, in Edinburgh , in 1822 and later republished in Cincinnati in 1856.[14]

Pictures on the wall
I have tried to identify these pictures, but I have not succeeded.

How It Could Have Been:
Since this is a chapter on speculations, I would also like to speculate about how I imagine Michael Powell learning the details I have just summarized. I imagine Michael Powell speaking to a friendly, enthusiastic young British neurologist, neurosurgeon, or possibly a neuro-ophthalmologist. I imagine this person to have completed his training within the previous five to ten years. Why? Because a physician or surgeon still close to his training days could communicate a strong feeling of both the contribution of the giants of neurology who were

A Matter of Life and Death

still living or had just passed away recently combined with the spirit of new discovery and new power over injury and disease. This person would be full of the excitement of new discoveries and with the glow of being trained by some of the neurologic giants, or perhaps their trainees. I imagine this because such a person would have been trained by medical school faculty who themselves were probably taught by the giants of the late nineteenth and early twentieth century such as Joseph Lister, William Macewen, John Hughlings Jackson, Victor Horsley, Henry Head, James Crichton-Brown, Gordon Holmes, and Harvey Cushing. That admiration for their early work, passed on by their students to the next generation of physicians and surgeons, combined with the newly realized power of contemporary scientific discovery engineered by C. S. Sherrington, Macdonald Critchley, Archibald McIndoe, Hugh Cairns, James Collier, and William Adie, must have created an infectious excitement that would have gripped Michael Powell's imagination. Memories of this legacy would be vivid and empowering.

This person would be good at explaining, enthusiastic, and open to sharing the details so Michael Powell could understand. That sharing would include the sharing of books, reprints, and journals. It would probably also include allowing Powell to go on rounds, with this person explaining the details of the neurologic exam and the compelling features of someone having a complex partial seizure. Why do I think this? Because the film does not focus just on the brilliance of the physician or on the personal drama of the patient but intermixes them equally.

Medical students sometimes play the game of proposing who they would like to have as their physician should they become ill. In the 1930s, neurology professors James Collier and William Adie were both greatly admired for medical knowledge and for kindness with patients and students. Both died in 1935. Possibly one of their trainees helped Michael Powell understand the nuances of neurology. The legacy and impact of a teacher who is both knowledgeable and kind is long and profound.

As you review my interpretations, see if you can imagine a physician or surgeon, recently completing his training, telling these stories to Michael Powell as they were told to that physician during his training years.

That admiration for the founders of British neurology is summarized by Macdonald Critchley, who described his feelings as a young neurology trainee:

> It must have been 1923 when I first met Gordon Holmes. Our first meeting was on the occasion of my joining the house staff of the National Hospital, Queen Square, which I found to be something like entering the Valley of the Kings at Luxor. I seemed to be surrounded by the ghosts of such monumental figures as Brown-Sequard, David Ferrier, Bastian, Beevor, Batten, Marcus Gunn…and yet some of the dead seemed still to be alive, for example Hughlings Jackson, Gowers and Victor Horsley. It was an eerie awesome feeling as though they were looking over one's shoulder.[15]

Critchley also wrote this about his education:

> At Queen Square I came under the spell of not one guru but several, all of whom had worked cheek by jowl with those legendary pioneers that still, spook-like, waited around the corner…The wards were cozy, with their caged birds and blazing coal-fires; the ward sisters autocratic, imperious, Junoesque. Like Agag one had to tread warily. "Sir William Gowers would never approve," they would mutter to me or

"Dr. Jackson never said anything like that." In those days after passing through the swing doors into the entrance hall, one was assailed by a strong and evocative aroma made up of a blending of biological ammonia with stale, coarse-cut tobacco. This smell of tobacco has vanished but in the Twenties, it was very much there, piquant and compelling...[16]

As you can see, this film has so many neurological echoes for me. As with any good work in science, it generates more questions: I wonder if Dr. Goldsmith ever saw this film and, if so, recognized his dialogue in the film? I wonder if Roger Livesey observed a neurologist to develop his understanding of his character. I wonder what Niall MacGinnis or William Macdonald thought about the film? Alas, I do not know. Since I don't know, then I choose to believe that they found it as satisfying and wonderful as I do!

1. Powell, Michael, *Million Dollar Movie* (London: Heinemann, 1992), 225.

2. Powell, Michael, *A Life in Movies* (New York: Knopf, 1986), 591.

3. Powell, Michael, *The Edge of the World: The making of a film (200,000 Feet on Foula),* published 1938. (London: Faber and Faber, 1990), 11.

4. Christie, Ian, "'History is now and England:' *A Canterbury Tale* in its contexts" in *The Cinema of Michael Powell*, edited by Ian Christie and Andrew Moor (London: BFI, 2005), 85–86.

5. Larson, Erik, *The Devil in the White City*, (New York: Vintage Books, 2003), 396.

6. Gray, Henry, *Anatomy of the Human Body*, edited by Warren H. Lewis,
24th ed. (Philadelphia: Lea and Febiger, 1942).

7. McDougal, William, "Hallucinations" in *The Encyclopedia Britannica* 14th ed., 11 (London: Encyclopedia Britannica Pub., 1929), 105–9, quote on 108.

8. Christie, Ian, *A Matter of Life and Death* (London: BFI, 2000), 26.

9. *The International Library of Famous Literature* vol. II, Edited by Richard Garnett, (London: Edward Lloyd publisher, 1900).

10. Powell, *A Life in Movies*, 30.

11. Byrne, J. Grandson, *Studies on the physiology of the eye: still reaction, sleep, dreams, hibernation, repression, hypnosis, narcosis, coma and allied conditions* (London: H.K. Lewis and Co. Ltd., 1933).

12. Ross, Ronald, *The Prevention of Malaria* (London: John Murray, 1910).

13. Macewen, William, *Atlas of Head sections: Fifty-three Engraved Copperplates of Frozen Sections of the Head, and Fifty-three Key Plates with Descriptive Texts* (Glasgow, Maclehose, 1893).

14. Lizars, John, *A System of Anatomical Plates of the Human body* (Edinburgh, W. H. Lizars and Daniel Lizars, 1822); *Anatomy of the Brain*, edited by Landon Rives (Cincinnati, Derby Publishers, 1856).

15. Critchley, Macdonald, "Gordon Holmes: the man and the neurologist" in *The Divine Banquet of the Brain* (New York: Raven Press, 1979), 228.

16. Critchley, Macdonald, *The Citadel of the Senses and other Essays* (New York: Raven Press, 1986), vii.

Chapter Eight:

Cinematic Equations, Neurologic Maps

A Life Spanning Eras

In 1990, a biographer of the Scottish neurologist and psychiatrist James Crichton-Browne (1840–1938) observed that he was difficult to characterize because his life spanned a time from the mid-Victorian age to the modern age of medical science. His medical career began when some neurologists still believed that phrenology gave valuable information about the diagnosis and treatment of brain problems, especially of those people with mental illnesses. By the end of his career, he had participated in the development of neurological tools we use today, and he was a strong advocate for the understanding and humane treatment of people with mental illness as well as helping children to grow in more mentally healthy circumstances in hopes of preventing some mental illnesses as adults.

Similarly, Michael Powell's life spanned two eras—from the years of making silent films to the late 1980s. I think that intentionally or not, AMOLAD is a film that had the effect of adopting some of

Crichton-Browne's values. Powell made a film where a person with a brain problem could be seen as a whole person. Peter Carter was not a person to be avoided. Peter Carter was destined for a future on Earth of love and happiness, teaching and poetry. Love and future marriage to June seem obvious to a modern audience, but in 1946 there were still laws making it difficult for someone with a mental illness or epilepsy to marry. "Do I seem cracked?" "Not to me, darling," was a moment of dialogue which would have very different meanings to an audience of 1946 and an audience of today.

A Lasting Film

Michael Powell joined two aspects of storytelling—the fanciful and the realistic. He felt that making his script as factually accurate as possible accomplished his artistic goals and made them more powerful. I would add that it has made his work more enduring.

In the analysis accompanying the Criterion DVD of *The Red Shoes*, Ian Christie comments on the sculpture of Pavlova's foot and ballet slipper: "There is a network of associations and references whether the audience knows it or not. We're expected to know what the figures stand for." Michael Powell expected at least some portion of the audience to be very knowledgeable on the matters depicted in his films. There were details in his films that he did not stop to explain. You can sense some moments are important through clues of lighting or the lingering of the camera. Since it was not Michael Powell's or Emeric Pressburger's habit to explain every detail, there are some left to discover.

The reader is aware that I have come to my interest in this film from my neurological nursing background. As I have come upon film criticism of *AMOLAD*, I still have one lingering question. Why didn't Michael Powell make the neurological accuracy of the film more clear

A Matter of Life and Death

to reviewers and film scholars in his interviews? James Chapman, in his article "The true business of the British movie?" points out a typical review, penned by Richard Winnington of *News Chronicle* on November 22, 1946, which stated, "[*AMOLAD*] is even farther away from the essential realism and the true business of the British movie than their recent *I Know Where I'm Going!* and *A Canterbury Tale*."[1] Chapman describes the dissatisfaction by critics in late 1946 and beyond for *AMOLAD*. The critical comments by writers of the time stand in remarkable contrast to the appreciation of the film's richness from today's viewers. I think Mr. Winnington of the *News Chronicle* would have reshaped his opinion had he realized that the drama of British neuroscience was displayed before his eyes!

Not everyone in 1946 thought *AMOLAD* was a departure from excellence or an "intellectual" film. On December 29, 1946, *The New York Times* listed their "Top Ten Best." Bosley Crowther had this to say about the film:

> Stairway to Heaven: For its qualities of imaginative concept and cinematic inventiveness, this delightful romantic fantasy about a flier who has hallucinations of the Beyond deserves the highest recommendations of the year. Sensitive and mature performances by David Niven, Roger Livesey, Kim Hunter and Raymond Massey enhance its incomparable charm.

His selection for the nine other films for best of 1946 included *My Darling Clementine*, *The Best Years of Our Lives*, *The Well-Digger's Daughter*, *Notorious*, *Henry V*, *Brief Encounter*, *The Green Years*, *Road to Utopia*, and *Open City*. "Frank Capra's *It's a Wonderful Life* would have got into the charmed circle if its philosophy had been less candified," the critic wrote.

Diane Broadbent Friedman

Bosley Crowther expanded his views of *It's a Wonderful Life* and *Stairway to Heaven* (the American title of *AMOLAD*) as exemplars of American and British cinema in the *New York Times* on January 12, 1947. While I think he is a little too hard on *It's a Wonderful Life*, he sums up his comparison:

> In every respect, this glittering fantasy which Michael Powell and Emeric Pressburger wrote, directed, and produced, has maturity and fascination. Its romance is credibly advanced and its bright and exciting disputation—is love between and English Boy and an American girl an admissible plea?—reveals the plausible thinking of a cultivated English mind. Its quality is in its freshness. And that we'd say is the distinction of better British Films."

Michael Powell hinted that the accuracy in a film is the sensed but unspoken connection between the director and the audience. In his autobiography, he stated, "I was determined to make the film (*IKWIG*) as authentic as possible in every detail," [2] and scholars of Michael Powell know that when he said he was determined about something he would not let go of it! I feel quite sure that people with a medical background in 1946 and later would have recognized the science within the film immediately, as evidenced in the comments made to me (when I presented this information at the Second International Epilepsy Surgery Symposium in 1990) by Fritz E. Dreifuss M.D., neurologist, epilepsy specialist from The University of Virginia, and past president of the International League Against Epilepsy: "I always thought he had complex partial seizures, too." Why didn't they speak up? I have not been able to find any mention of the film (or any others for that matter) in *The Lancet*, the *British Medical Journal*, *Epilepsia*, or the *Journal of the American Medical Association*. (I did find two sentences mentioning the screening in 1947 of *The Best Years of Our Lives* at Walter Reed Hospital in the *Journal of the American Medical Association*.) In an interview, Michael Powell stated that he felt that many people had bumps and accidents from war injuries so he did not want to state things too plainly. Yet, why didn't a neurologist speak up?

Moreover, what did Dr. Goldsmith think? The reader will recall my finding that some of Dr. Reeves' dialogue was taken directly from Dr. Goldsmith's 1943 paper on chiasmal arachnoiditis. We can imagine him sitting in the audience and hearing Dr. Reeves argue Peter's case using Dr. Goldsmith's words. I can imagine Dr. Goldsmith telling his family, "I helped with that!" I tried to locate family members of Dr. Goldsmith but I was unsuccessful. I just imagine it made Dr. Goldsmith smile.

Why didn't Powell speak up? Too busy? Unseemly? An artistic conviction? I just don't know. Regardless of his reason, Powell clearly spoke through his work, for *AMOLAD* expresses itself clearly today. How inspired it was of him to ask the question, "Can there be a basis in medical reality for these unusual events?" I wish he could have been recognized formally in his lifetime for his scholarship in *AMOLAD*. This book is a belated attempt to achieve that recognition for him. I hope that sometime a neurologist approached him at a film retrospective or at a dinner and confirmed for Powell that he had indeed gotten the story right!

Solving the Neurologic Equations

I mentioned in the introduction to this book that Michael Powell had constructed two neurologic equations in the structure of this film. Now you have the expertise to fully appreciate them.

The first equation: The neurological status of Peter Carter

Recall these scenes from the film in order:

- Peter in the cockpit speaking with June on the radio
- On the beach looking at his shadow while standing on one foot
- Conductor 71 with his hook
- June lost from view in the garden
- The visual test in Lee Wood House
- The wind blows, each time a little harder, as the film progresses

You can look at these pictures as the figures of a cinematic equation that can be added together to determine Peter's diagnosis, the source of the brain lesion, and needed treatment. From the first scene in the cockpit, we know Peter is a neurologically normal man, and then apparently unhurt after being unconscious in the water for three hours. But by nightfall, he is having uncinate seizures (suggested by the visual pun of the "hook" and "uncinate") from a lesion at the optic chiasm producing a left homonymous hemianopsia. This visual problem is confirmed by Dr. Reeves in his examination at Lee Wood House. The situation is growing more serious, as the winds blow harder with each visit from Conductor 71. This equation suggests how knowledge of the map of the brain leads to the diagnosis of the brain problem as well as the location where the surgeon must go to find the problem.

The second equation: revealing the workings of the eye

- Looking at the sky
- The camera obscura
- The ping-pong game

A Matter of Life and Death

- The ride on the motorcycle in the rain
- The onset of anesthesia
- The heavenly courtroom

In this equation we start with a complete, unobstructed view of an entire visual field, comprised of a fresh blue sky. The camera obscura shows us how that round visual field is created by light entering through a lens and being projected on a screen— whether that screen is a table top or the back of a retina. Later we see the ping-pong game where the camera moves back and forth, mimicking the movement of our two eyes in tandem as we follow the movement of the ball, the horizontal saccadic eye movement. When Dr. Reeves rides his motorcycle in the rain, his vision is obscured by the rain on his glasses. In the book of the film, he is described as not needing to see because he knows the road by heart. Unfortunately he is not seen by the ambulance until it is too late, and he perishes. When Peter falls asleep from the anesthesia, the large eyelid closes on his field of vision. This represents an unusual camera angle for Michael Powell, known for perching his camera over waterfalls and ledges of cliffs. Here the camera angle is from within the brain. Finally, the heavenly courtroom resembles the visual field maps created by ophthalmologists. This equation demonstrates the function of vision with two eyes—human, binocular vision.

<u>One final clue</u>
I saved the best for last. A scene that lasts just a moment, very early in the film, contains the map leading to the answer to the neurological puzzle of what is wrong with Peter Carter. When you look at this still picture of the housekeeper answering the phone in Dr. Reeves' home, I think that you see Michael Powell's summation of the neurologic aspect of this film.

Diane Broadbent Friedman

Pictures of cortex (left hemisphere) and midline of right hemisphere from <u>Anatomy of the brain from the celebrated dissections of John Lizars M.D.</u> comprising fifteen engravings (colored after nature) with accompanying explanations. Ed. by Landon Rives, M.D. Cincinnati, H.W. Derby, 1854. Courtesy of the Galter Health Sciences Library, Special Collections, Northwestern University, Chicago, IL.

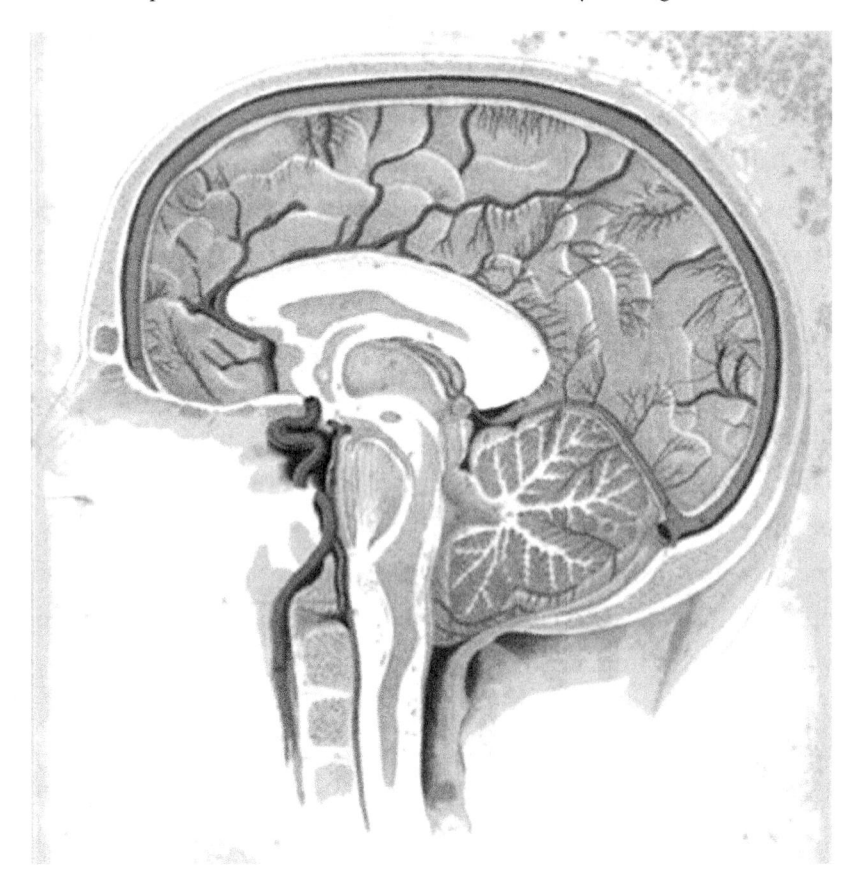

A Matter of Life and Death

These two pictures from Dr. Lizar's atlas are very similar but not identical to those seen on page 148.

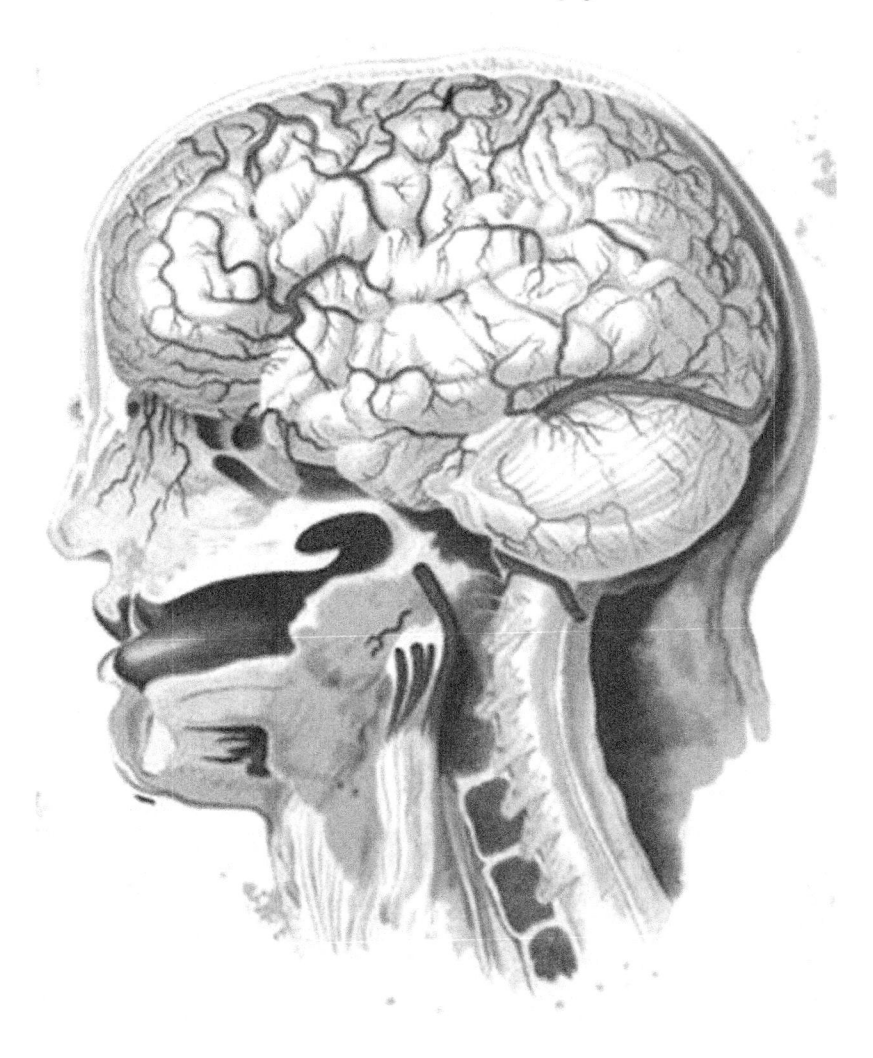

Diane Broadbent Friedman

The housekeeper answers the phone in Dr. Reeves's exam room. *A Matter of Life and Death* (1946). "Stairway to Heaven"© 1946,1974,1996. Carlton Film Distributors Limited. All Rights Reserved. Courtesy of Columbia Pictures.

We see two drawings hanging on the wall and the housekeeper all in one plane. What we are seeing, from right to left:

1. The hairnet on the housekeeper's head, resembling the outside covering of the brain
2. Then the picture on the wall showing outside of the brain with the outer membranes removed
3. Then the next picture to the left showing the brain from a midline view, with the shadow of the cross piece of the window pane running directly through it. The shadow marks the map with the location of Michael Powell's uncharted territory and the route of expedition to the unknown place on the map. The shadow marks the place of Peter's brain lesion and the place where the surgery will take place. This is the site of the lesion (on the right, innermost portion of the brain, the right mesial basal temporal lobe adjacent to the optic chiasma.)

In this briefest of scenes, approximately fifteen minutes into the film, Michael Powell establishes for the most knowledgeable audience member—a neurologist or neurosurgeon—that Powell knows what he is talking about. Emeric Pressburger would likely appreciate the irony—that everything Dr. Reeves needs to know to save Peter is hanging on his wall over his telephone—but of course Dr. Reeves doesn't know that yet!

1. Chapman, James, "The true business of the British movie? *A Matter of Life and Death* and British film culture" *Screen* 46:1 (Spring 2005): 33–49, quote on 37.

2. Powell, Michael, *A Life in Movies.* (New York: Knopf, 1987), 477.

Conclusion:

"We'll Invent the Greatest Lie in Medical History, You and I!"

When I am watching a Michael Powell and Emeric Pressburger film, there will be a moment when I will say to myself, "What was *that*? I think that is supposed to be a big deal, but I don't know why!" As I wrote this book, I kept returning to the image of Lermontov stroking a sculpture of a foot in *The Red Shoes*. In my first viewing, it looked a little odd to me. But then in listening to Ian Christie's commentary on the Criterion DVD where he explained that it was the cast of Pavlova's foot, and additionally that those knowledgeable about ballet would recognize it immediately, it all makes sense.[1] Yet even in realizing Michael Powell's specific choices in specific films, we still have only a partial answer to this question: How did Michael Powell's mind work?

This has been a book of informed speculation where we looked at the finished work of a Michael Powell film and tried to deduce the hidden elements that were brought together to create it, as well as the intellectual process by which the film was developed. My conclusion is that we can find abundant evidence of Powell's creative mind. The finished work of unexplained but sophisticated imagery, interrelating art and medical science suggests a highly intelligent spirit and a highly educated mind. Powell wanted to tell something important but in his own way—telling, but not telling everything to everybody.

Ian Christie also believes that Michael Powell and Emeric Pressburger did not want to reveal too much about their creative process. "Neither Powell nor Pressburger enjoyed talking about the mechanics of their work, believing this should speak for itself, or remain a tantalizing mystery." He reminds us that magicians don't like to tell how their work is done.[2]

At his core, I think Michael Powell was an historian; an explorer with his maps; a researcher in the library, in the book stalls, and in the field; someone with a great memory; someone with the capacity for deep understanding of things which initially seem strange or removed; and still something else—I cannot say what, but these lines don't describe him fully.

I think this was his process of thought, at least through the time of completing *AMOLAD*: He (and, after 1938, Emeric Pressburger) would come upon a book or a newspaper article that captured the imagination. Michael Powell and Emeric Pressburger would then read many other books from related disciplines to more fully understand the dimensions of the situation. I think Powell read widely partly because he enjoyed it, partly because that was simply his nature, and partly because he had success finding details that would resonate in a future project. I think it must have been a pleasure for him, part of his basic nature, to seek out and then to understand more and more, because in *A Life in Movies* he would always mention those steps—coming upon a provocative article in a newspaper, seeking out more books in the library or book stalls, finding and studying maps—as he began each project. Powell and Pressburger would gradually develop a nuanced, deeper, and more original understanding. By the time Michael Powell was done and had added the creativity of "The Regulars"—his trusted band of actors and technicians—The Archers would have produced a unique work. Many readers will know that Michael Powell's first job in silent films was to sweep up the glossy floor of the film set so that the actress Alice Terry's footsteps would not be seen in the next take. It seems that Powell would similarly remove the extra traces in his films so that we could sense that something important was evident, but we could not determine exactly what it was.[3]

Evidence of the same process can be seen in the creation of the *Edge of the World*. In June 1930, he read an article in *The Observer* which described the difficult removal of sheep from St. Kilda during the evacuation of the island. "I tore that paragraph out and placed it in a file, then new, slender and clean, now old, bulging and weather-stained."[4] He then went to *The Observer* and subsequently to *The Times* to read more from their files. When he saw photos of St. Kilda published in *The Sphere*, he wrote, "I said to myself that I would, one day, make a picture of that."[5] In those five years before the creation of the film, he kept on reading—Seaton Gordon, A. A. Macgregor, Boswell, and Johnson—and Powell thought enough of that process of collecting information to document it in his 1938 book *200,000 feet over Foula*.

Recently I found Norman Heathcote's *St. Kilda*, published in 1900.[6] He admires the islanders and their way of life. It has several elements that I can see in *Edge of the World*. Locations in the film look like illustrations in the book; there is no work on the Sabbath and long church services are the norm; islanders use letter boats; the dogs of St. Kilda are workers; young people decide whether they are leaving or staying when coming of age; the island supports many species of birds; and locals race up the cliffs to settle a dispute.[7] But what really struck me was this passage, written in 1898:

> I do not wonder that they (the people of St. Kilda) dislike the foreigners. So many of the tourists treat them as if they were wild animals in the Zoo. They throw sweets at them, openly mock at them, and I have seen them standing at the church door during service, laughing and talking and staring as if at an entertainment got up for their amusement.[8]

This was so surprising to me. I don't think that the islanders are to be stared at like animals in a zoo; nor do you, because we have seen *Edge of the World*. Michael Powell changed the way we think and see, and we didn't even realize that change was happening.

Recall Powell's description of the ongoing debate in 1934 with Robert Flaherty as Flaherty edited *Nanook of the North* and Powell edited another film, two years before he made *Edge of the World*: "the argument [of] fact against fiction, the eternal argument between the liar and the journalist, between 'I was there,' and 'This is how it must have been.'"[9]

I think we are left with the feeling that Michael Powell and Emeric Pressburger have told us how it must have been. Created by Powell nine years earlier in *Edge of the World*, I think we see that process right in front of our noses. The movie starts with visitors (played by Michael and Frankie Powell) who are so separate from the boatman Andrew Gray (played by Niall MacGinnis) that they do not talk much and do not seem to understand him. Through their eyes, we perceive St. Kilda as empty and wild. The visitors cannot see the island as Andrew does. Then the movie quickly breathes life into the deserted island through Andrew Gray's memories, and the island is transformed. We are quickly drawn into lives and hopes and daily ways. The biggest point of the film, that these people are not so different, is interwoven and has the feeling of being obvious. But in 1937, it wasn't obvious. Through his research and creative skill, Michael Powell made the audience come to that conclusion—that these far away people are not so different from the viewer.

That transformation—to make the audience come to believe that what they thought was strange instead makes perfect sense—is at work in *AMOLAD* as well. Michael Powell makes this happen because of his intellectual strengths, love of history, zest for research, and determination for accuracy. He leaves evidence of depth, which he does not explain, to show those with advanced knowledge that he rightfully shares that advanced appreciation of complexity. Once he establishes that evidence of scientific mastery within a fictional story, he can put forward his larger claim—that his point of view has merit. With respect to *AMOLAD*, that larger point is that love, shared between lovers and felt for one's heritage, is stronger than all the weapons, death, time, and space. It endures beyond all attempts to destroy it. After seeing *AMOLAD*, the audience of 1946—with its shared experience of threat, attack, and deprivation; ruined homes, schools, churches, hospitals, and libraries; sudden death of loved ones; and despite all of this, pulling together to save their way of life—knows this is true. We do, too.

1. Powell, Michael, and Pressburger, Emeric, *The Red Shoes*. 1948; The Criterion Collection DVD 1999, Commentary by Ian Christie.

2. Christie, Ian, "Another life in movies: Pressburger and Powell," In *The Cinema of Michael Powell*, edited by Ian Christie and Andrew Moor, (London: British Film Institute, 2005), 171.

3. Powell, Michael, *Edge of the World: The making of a film* [reprint of *200,000 Feet on Foula*, (London: Faber and Faber, 1938)], (London: Faber and Faber, 1990), 13.

4. Powell, *Edge of the World*, 12.

5. Powell, *Edge of the World*, 13.

6. Heathcote, Norman, *St. Kilda*, (London: Longmans, Green and Co., 1900).

7. Heathcote, *St. Kilda*. no work on the Sabbath and long church services:97; letter boats: 84; dogs of St. Kilda: 86; leave or stay: 201; searching for eggs 136.

8. Heathcote, *St. Kilda*, 70.

9. Powell, *Life in Movies,* 237—38.

Appendix I:

Elaboration of Neurological Connections from Chapter Seven

A. "She cannot wake. We are talking in space, not in time."

As Peter and June are reclining under the rhododendrons, talking and kissing, Peter turns to pour a drink for her. He asks her if she wants a drink. Then Peter smells an unusual odor and sees Conductor 71, who tells him it is pointless to call for her. "She cannot wake. We are talking in space, not in time."

An Evocative Phrase
This concept made a deep impression on Michael Powell. He repeated it in his autobiography *A Life in Movies* on several occasions: The Conductor's visits take place in space, not in time.[1] He stated he had heard it in this way:

> On the *Queen Elizabeth* with 12,000 American troops on the ship, about ten of us in one cabin. On the way over I worked on the script from a medical point of view; I had all my notes in a special file on medical cases which I'd been looking up through my brother-in-law, who is a great surgeon. I don't think I ever stated what was wrong with the young flier (David Niven) after he's crashed in the bomber. A previous injury had caused adhesions on the brain... probably I didn't want to state it too much because so many people had had bangs and bumps during the war and you didn't want people to get too worried... anyway, these adhesions can produce pressures on various parts of the brain which can produce what are called "highly organized hallucinations." These can be comparable to an experience of actual life. I use this phrase because it was quoted to me by the surgeon who did the job in the particular case I was studying. And then he uttered another marvelous phrase which really altered the whole conception of

> the film. He said, "And this illusion can take place in space but not in time." And that's what we showed with the "frozen" ping-pong game and David Niven sitting up during the operation with everyone around him frozen in time—we had lots of fun then. There is this whole hallucination taking place in the thousandth of a fraction of a second.[2]

or he had read it:

> Everything was to be as real as possible in both worlds. I went back to my brother-in-law, Joe Reidy, the surgeon, who had had priceless experience during the war. He put me on to medical textbooks which gave me the idea of staging hallucinations in space, not in time.[3]

Michael Powell described his research process again in another part of his autobiography:

> I read that, "pressure on the brain can produce highly organized hallucinations, comparable to an experience of actual life, and which took place in space, but not in time."[4]

Where did such a pivotal concept come from? Does it refer to neurology or to Einstein? I went looking for a neurology paper or textbook that contained this phrase. What follows are the results of my search. I came close but did not find the exact words. As you review the works mentioned below, you will see that from 1850 on, psychologists and neurologists believed that an intact sense of both time and space are required for consciousness. We will recall that Peter Carter is having a serious problem with a disturbance of consciousness.

The History of a Neurological Idea

John Hughlings Jackson

The earliest reference to neurologic concepts of space and time came from John Hughlings Jackson. Jackson was influenced by psychologist Herbert Spencer's book *On Psychology*. In 1850, Spencer wrote that an awareness of time was essential to detect changes of the environment or space. In other words, the interior experience becomes recognizable to a person when he sees it as a combination of something which *exists* in duration of *time*. "A subjective state becomes recognizable as such, only when it has an appreciable duration: it must fill some space in the series of states otherwise it is not known as present."[5]

In 1876, Jackson went on to say that, "Time is required for consciousness."[6] Paraphrasing Herbert Spencer and suggesting that there is a discrete brain location for consciousness, Jackson said, "There is in the highest centres—the centres of centres [the location of consciousness and thinking]—a most intricate and yet orderly space and time co-ordination."[7] Emphasizing that idea, Jackson wrote, "A certain time, a certain duration is necessary for the smallest section of continuous energy to which consciousness is competent. Some minimum of time must be admitted as the condition of consciousness."[8]

Jackson, like the philosophers before him and all thinking people since, struggled to understand how our human brain makes us human and gives us qualities separate from other living creatures. Jackson put emphasis on the understanding of consciousness in his fundamental search for understanding "the organ of mind."[9] In his study of epilepsy, he discerned locations for several actions of the brain, but the understanding of consciousness eluded him.

Charles Sherrington

Sir Charles Sherrington was the Nobel Prize winner in 1932 for the mapping of single neurons communicating with muscles and sensory areas. He had similar questions considering consciousness and once again repeated the idea that consciousness required that a person experience both time and space. In *Integrative Activity of the Nervous System* he wrote, "Pure conjunction in time without necessarily cerebral conjunction in space lies at the root of the solution of the problem of the unity of mind."[10] The awareness of the self, he wrote, is not only "'here' but also as 'now.' The 'I' endures in time. Just as space is a continuum for it, so also is time…the 'I' in each is central."[11] Later in this chapter he quoted Andrew Marvell (just as Peter Carter did, and might agree with Sherrington's choice of lines!), who said, "Our loves so truly parallel though infinite can never meet."[12] Sherrington struggled with the limitations of his science in his era, which could describe the action of the enervation of muscle but could not explain consciousness:

> But indeed what right have we to conjoin mental experience with the physiological? No scientific right; only the right of Keats, with the superlative Shakespearian gift of his dubbed, "busy common sense."[13]…But when trying to collocate nerve action with mental activity we face something which not only transmits signals but reads them. Otherwise the signaling, whatever its complexity, remains just one red lamp showing itself to another."[14]

My point is that identifying concepts of space and time as factors underlying consciousness had neurological meaning from 1850 through 1950. Spencer conceives of it; Jackson hypothesizes it; Sherrington acknowledges it but cannot prove it.

Macdonald Critchley

This leaves one neurologist, a contemporary of Michael Powell who does describe epileptic hallucinations as having distortions of space and time. Macdonald Critchley (1900—1997), a neurologist practicing largely at the National Hospital, Queen Square, from 1927–1965, and President of the World Federation of Neurology (1965–1973), also wrote about concepts of time and space. Several of these cases were observed in the 1930s, but these words published soon *after* the release of *AMOLAD* were the closest I could come to a written reference of these words of dialogue. Could Michael Powell spoken with Dr. Critchley or one of his trainees? I do not know.

The following excerpts came from Critchley articles which describe visual hallucinations in seizures: "This phenomenon may perhaps be spoken of as a visual perseveration. The important point is that the perseveration *takes place in area and not in time* [emphasis mine]."[15] Additionally, "...the former phenomenon can be regarded as a sort of '*visual perseveration in time*,' and the latter representation a '*visual perseveration in space*.'"[16] By visual perseveration in time and space, Critchley referred to the experience, during a seizure or preceding it, of seeing one image or duplications of images no matter where the patient turned his eyes. As examples, he recorded his patients describing images of children playing, men playing cards, or stair railings superimposed on the real visual background.

Gordon Holmes

Even if Michael Powell did not encounter any of these references directly, the neurologic meaning of time and space as essential to consciousness was plain to neurologists of the day. The first three questions in the neurological exam evaluate the patient's sense of identity, time and space: "What is your name? What day is it? Can you tell me the name of this place?" The neurologic exam was formalized in the 1920s by Gordon Holmes, a prominent British neurologist, researcher and educator.

Critchley wrote the following about his mentor: "He could coax physical signs out of a patient like a Paganini on a violin. Perhaps it is not yet generally realized that every neurologist alive today—where ever he works—is unconsciously utilizing the routine clinical examination propagated, perfected, and perpetuated by Gordon Holmes."[17]

Peter Carter

So, for Peter Carter, our pilot and patient, if the events are taking place in space but not in time, then he does not fulfill the requirements for consciousness. By definition he is not conscious. That is the ironic situation of Conductor 71, a French aristocrat who lost his head in 1793.[18] Conductor 71 is an imaginary person, who might or might not possess his own head, having a very important conversation with a person who has his own head problem, altered consciousness. This is irony that Emeric Pressburger would surely enjoy!

Peter has a consciousness problem and Dr. Reeves, with Michael Powell's help, will determine the cause and the course of treatment.

1. Powell, Michael, *A Life in Movies*. (New York: Knopf, 1987), 496.

2. Badder, David, "Powell and Pressburger: The War Years," *Sight and Sound* 48, no.1 (1978/1979 Winter): 8.

3. Powell, 498.

4. Ibid., 458.

5. Spencer, Herbert, *Principles of Psychology,* 3rd ed. (New York: Appleton Press, 1908–1910), vol. 1, 107.

6. Jackson, John Hughlings "Investigation of Epilepsies" (1876) in *Selected Writings of John Hughlings Jackson,* Volume One, *On epilepsy and epileptiform convulsions,* edited by James Taylor (London: Stales Press, 1958), 205. (reprint of article from *Medical Press and Circular* October 14, 1874–December 13, 1876)

7. Ibid., 154.

8. Ibid., 291. (Initially published in *West Riding Asylum Medical Reports* vol. vi (1876), 143.

9. Ibid., 291.

10. Sherrington, Charles S., *The Integrative Activity of the Nervous System* (New York: Charles Scribner's Sons, 1906), 384.

11. Sherrington, Charles S., *Man on his Nature*: *Gifford Lectures 1937-8* (Cambridge: The University Press, 1940), 335.

12. Ibid., 323.

13. Sherrington, Charles S., *The brain and its mechanism: The Rede Lecture 12/5/1933,* (Cambridge: The University Press, 1933), 23.

14. Ibid., 25.

15. Critchley, Macdonald, "Metamorphosia of central origin, " *Transactions Ophthalmological Society of UK* 69 (1949): 111–21, quote on 119.

16. Critchley, Macdonald, "Types of visual perseveration: 'Paliopsia' and 'illusory visual spread,' " *Brain* 74 (1951): 267–99, quote on 267.

17. Critchley, Macdonald, "Gordon Holmes: The man and the neurologist," *The Divine Banquet of the Brain* (Raven Press New York: Raven Press, 1979), 228.

18. Powell, *A Life in Movies*, 489.

B. Poets and Neurologists:
"I haven't much modern stuff in my library, but you're there…I hope we shall have some talks together…"

A poet who is an R.A.F. pilot faces the choice of death by either fire or falling from the sky on the last day of the war. He will be cared for by a country neurologist—a widower who has been published in *Brain*—who likes poetry. A poet dies on the last day of the war. Could this describe a real situation?

Poets

There are some parallels to real life. The Georgians were young poets coming of age during World War I. They had the name Georgians to anchor them to the era of George V. A number of these poets appeared in the *Oxford Book of English Verse* that Michael Powell took with him across the Atlantic as he completed his script. These men included Siegfried Sassoon, Rupert Brooke, Wilfrid Owen, Walter de la Mare, and Edmund Blunden, as well as D. H. Lawrence, Robert Graves, and Robert Nichols. These poets wrote about their direct experiences as soldiers, and some of the poets railed against the terrible loss of young life.

Siegfried Sassoon's story was a part of this sacrifice of life to save the country. After having served in WWI for two years, being wounded, and losing close friends, Sassoon felt despondent and disillusioned. He composed an antiwar piece which he read in front of Parliament on July 30, 1917. He then threw the ribbon from his medal, the Military Cross, in the river. He went AWOL and expected imprisonment. Instead, because of his popularity, he was given the diagnosis of shell-shock and sent to Craiglocken Hospital near Edinburgh for treatment. There he met Wilfrid Owen, a soldier, a poet, and a fellow patient. Both men recovered and were sent back to the front. Wilfred Owen died in battle one week before the end of the war. On November 11, 1918 as the church bells were pealing the end to war, his mother received the telegram reporting his death.

The Early Morning of May 2, 1945

The narrator of *AMOLAD* specifically states the date, which is three days before the surrender of Germany. The time elapsed from Peter's fall at 4:10 AM to the surgery at 11PM is three days later—Peter lives as the war in Europe is ending. Tracing the events more closely, Peter jumps from the burning plane on May 2. 1945, at 4:10 AM British Double Summer Time, after he finishes dictating a telegram to his mother (the address of which is actually Emeric Pressburger's apartment). He washes up on the beach and sees June cycling by at 7:30 AM. By evening of the same day, they are in the garden and Peter sees Conductor 71. The next morning, May 3 at 11 AM, June comes over to see Dr. Reeves at his house. Dr. Reeves meets Peter at Lee Wood House at 4 PM. Peter and June go to Dr. Reeves' home where they are playing ping-pong at dusk while Peter has another meeting with Conductor 71. The next morning, May 4, Dr. Reeves rides on his motorcycle in the rain to meet with Dr. McEwen. He says that the trial takes place tonight and surgery must be performed tonight. In the evening, Dr. Reeves is killed in a motorcycle accident while Peter is taken by ambulance to the U.S. Base Hospital. The surgery is performed at 11 PM. The next day, May 5, Peter awakens in his hospital room. Thus this poet avoids the fate of Wilfred Owen of dying in the last days of the war. In June and Peter's embrace, the connection between America and England is assured for the future.

Henry Head M.D.,: A Physician for Poets and a Poet Himself

During World War I, there were several hospitals dedicated to the neurological and psychological treatment of soldiers and sailors. The chain of treatment began with mobile hospitals near the front and then continued with soldiers evacuated to an extensive network of military hospitals in Scotland and England for further treatment. In 1915, Henry Cushing headed up U.S. Base Hospital Number 5 in France, which was formed with volunteers from Harvard Medical School. Base Hospital Number 5 joined with the British Army No. 11 General Hospital Unit in May 31, 1917, in Camiers, France. In a diary entry for May 1917, he wrote that he sent his spinal injury patients along to Henry Head in London for further treatment once he had stabilized them.[1]

Henry Head was the civilian consultant to the Empire Hospital for officers in Vincent Square, London. Head invented the phrase "spinal shock." The neurologist and psychologist W. R. Rivers cared for Sassoon and Owen in Craiglocken, Scotland. Rivers was very kind and therapeutic, and Sassoon felt a life long connection to him. Before the war, Rivers and Head worked together on a set of groundbreaking experiments tracing how sensory nerves grew back after being severed. Rivers and Head worked together again at the end of the war when Rivers was appointed psychologist to the Royal Flying Corps, attached to the Central Hospital in Hampstead.

Dr. Head's life was vivid and full and has some parallels to the character of Dr. Reeves. He was an editor of *Brain* from 1909 to 1925. He moved from London and lived in a small country village. He was a great friend to younger adults, and not only in medicine. He counted as patients and friends some of the younger Georgians, including Sassoon, Robert Graves, and Robert Nichols. He was the doctor and friend of W. E. Henley (1849–1903), author of "Invictus":

> "....It matters not how strait the gate,
> How charged with punishments the scroll,
> I am the master of my fate:
> I am the captain of my soul."[2]

Head was a vigorous, gregarious, generous man; a very popular and inspiring teacher of medicine; a physiologist; and a published poet.[7,8] He was widely known as an accomplished imitator of neurologic conditions which he did in order to teach his students. In his hospital, the cry would go out among the medical trainees: "Come quickly! Henry Head is doing gaits!" He had wide-ranging interests in art, literature, the stage, and music. His wife Ruth compiled an anthology on the works of Thomas Hardy for which Dr. Head wrote the introduction:

> Tragedy is the struggle of man in the grip of forces he cannot master. To Hardy, Fate is not the wrath of a righteous Deity nor the ill-omened consequence of some outraged social custom; it is a sequence of natural events which are neither malevolent nor well-intentioned, but simply indifferent. [3]

When Dr. Head developed symptoms of Parkinson's disease, Sassoon suggested that he move to Dorset to become a neighbor of Hardy. He worked hard to complete his two-volume work on aphasia by 1920, as he knew the worsening impairments that he could expect from his illness. As his symptoms of Parkinson's intensified, he was sustained by letters from Robert Nichols and other poets; Nichol wrote letters almost weekly. In a letter to Dr. Head in 1925, he described his memories of being in the hospital in 1917 and cared for by Dr. Head:

> ...The most important event in my life to date was the occasion on which Dr. Henry Head F.R.S., a plump, bland, slightly Mephistophelean figure, pushed open the door in the hospital cell and sat down and asked me if I liked Conrad—the first sensible and honest question that had been put to me since I came out of France. You know Henry, I took to you from the very moment you sat down. It was your way of putting your bag down and settling into your seat. You settled yourself down with such an air of relish and of not being rushed—of guarding against any possibility of being rushed—for all the world as if you desired in me something in me and felt I might be worth, not a cure, but a chat.[4]

He was an attractive man with a red-brown goatee, who married at age 40. Cushing told a lovely story about Head who happened to be making a visit to a girl's school. Invited by the Superintendent to look through a peephole in the classroom door, (put there so classrooms could be observed without disturbing the students), Head looked in and was immediately struck with attraction for the young teacher, Ruth. They were a marriage of true minds and hearts, and they married soon after. Head, with a twinkle in his eye, claimed to be the cause of WWI in a story recounted by Cushing:

> Once when [Ruth and Henry] were cycling in France he with his strongly Teutonic cast of countenance and Van Dyke beard was heard talking German to his wife in an out-of the way countryside where there were military stores. The murder of the Archduke had recently taken place. The French were uneasy. A camera was found in their duffel bag. Explanations were useless. Complications ensued which reached international proportions. So the war was precipitated all because of a look through a peep hole.[5]

Even though the Parkinson's disease progressively affected his ability to speak and move, he was cared for lovingly by his wife. Many men of science and literature came to visit him, first in Dorset and later in Reading, Hartley Court.[6] Ruth died a year before Henry, who passed away from pneumonia on October 8, 1940. When he died, there was a long obituary in the *Times of London* and a lengthy remembrance written by Robert Nichols five days later.

Is it possible that this neurologist, who found the love of his life while looking through a visual device, could have provided some of the inspiration for the character of Dr. Reeves?

1. Fulton, John F., *Harvey Cushing: A Biography* (Springfield: Charles C. Thomas, 1946), 400.

2. Henley, William Ernest, "Invictus," in Quiller-Couch, Arthur, ed. *The Oxford Book of English Verse 1250–1918*, New edition, (London: Oxford University Press, 1940), 1027–28.

3. Head, Ruth, *Pages from the works of Thomas Hardy arranged by Ruth Head with an introduction by Henry Head, M.D., F.R.S.*, (London: Chatto and Windus, 1922), v–viii, quote on vii.

4. Charlton, Anne and William, *Putting Poetry First: A Life of Robert Nichols 1893–1944*, (Norwich: Michael Russell Publishing, 2003), 59.

5. Fulton, 533.

6. Brain, Russell, "Henry Head : The man and his ideas," *Brain*, 84 part V (1961): 561—66.

7. Gardner-Thorpe, C., "Henry Head (1861-1940)" in *Twentieth Century Neurology: The British Contribution,* ed. by F. Clifford Rose, (London: Imperial College Press, 2001), 9-30.

8. Gardner-Thorpe, C., "The poetry of Henry Head" in *Neurology of the Arts: Painting, Music, Literature*, ed. by F. Clifford Rose (London: Imperial College Press, 2004), 401-20.

C. Music in *A Matter of Life and Death*: A Musical Aura, a Precipitant of a Seizure, a Tribute to the First Brain Surgery, or All Three?

"Check," she answered.
There was no response from Peter...He seemed to be listening and then he sniffed sharply as though he smelt some indefinable odour.

As Peter sits in Lee Wood House playing chess with June, we first hear and see the *Overture to a Midsummer Night's Dream* playing on a phonograph player. As we see the record come to an end, we next see hands playing a theme on a piano. Peter looks slightly worried, distracted, or confused as he looks off to his right. June speaks to Peter but he does not seem to hear her. The piano theme continues until he responds to June's comment, "Your move, darling."

I think Peter is having an auditory aura at this moment. As you will recall, an aura is the first warning of more seizure activity, which in this instance does not progress any further. A number of my patients have told me that they have experienced auras that were so subtle that no one near by realized it. Just as in real life when auras might not be noticed by others, the audience of *AMOLAD* may not have been totally aware of it either. In the script and in the novel of the film, Peter is described as both listening to something and making a sniffing motion; in the film we seem him listening, but he does not make a sniffing gesture. But even if the audience does not fully understand the neurologic implication, they surely catch the change in tone of this short, disquieting piano theme. The audience does sense that something newly significant has been introduced.

As the film continues from this point, the audience comes to realize that this musical theme is a stereotyped musical phrase: This is the definition of a musical aura. Although he will not hear this phrase when he next meets Conductor 71 in Dr. Reeves' study, he will hear it on the subsequent visit as it heralds journeys on the stairway. It comes to represent a worsening of Peter's brain problem.

This brief segment of the story—hearing first the familiar classical piece, then the introduction of a new musical theme played by an unseen person on a piano, produces several layers of impressions for me. These interpretations can be supported by neurological and musical literature of the time. I ask the reader to consider the following observations while remembering that Michael Powell did have a conversation with an unnamed physician—who could have been a neurologist familiar with any or all of these contemporary concepts.

<u>The Overture to a Midsummer Night's Dream,</u> <u>Mendelssohn, and Victor Horsley</u>

Felix Mendelssohn's *Overture to a Midsummer Night's Dream* is playing on the record player in the Great Room in Lee Wood House as the American service men and women prepare to put on the play by Shakespeare. Some of the Americans struggle to capture the tone of portraying the story of "Pyramus and Thisbe" and to spell Shakespeare's name properly—although Michael Powell and Emeric Pressburger imply that the rough, broader nature of some Americans fits well with the tone of playing the character Bottom.

Hearing this music and thinking about epilepsy and brain surgery as I watched this film for the first time, I had recalled a statement made at an epilepsy surgery conference in 1985: that Mendelssohn was a family friend of the Victor Horsley family living in London, and this particular piece of music was first performed in the Horsley home.[1] I wrote about that in my article in *Seizure* in 1991 using the citation from the conference proceedings. The claim that the overture was first played in the Horsley home was also made in the 1966 book *The Citizen Surgeon: A Biography of Sir Victor Horsley*.[2]

To prepare for writing this book, I sought out more information from the musical literature. While I learned that it is not true that *Midsummer Night's Dream* was first performed at the Horsley home, I did learn the interesting actual connection between Felix Mendelssohn and Victor Horsley, the first British surgeon to successfully perform brain surgery for epilepsy. His professional descendent will operate on Peter for the same condition.

Victor Horsley belonged to the third generation of a well-known artistic family to have lived in the Kensington High Row home, purchased in 1823 by William Horsley from Muzio Clemente (1752–1832), himself a significant composer; friend of Mozart, Hayden, and Beethoven; and piano manufacturer. William Horsley (1774–1858), Victor Horsley's grandfather, was a well-known composer of Glees (musical arrangements for a cappella men's choruses). He married Elizabeth Callcott, and they had five children: Mary Elizabeth (1813–1881, who would marry Isambard Brunel, a prominent engineer and industrialist responsible for the Thames tunnel; Great Western Railway; and the Great Western Steamship Line, which laid the first transatlantic telegraph cables); Fanny (1815–1849); John Callcott—Sir Victor Horsley's father (1817–1903); Sophy (1819–1894); and Charles Edward (1821–1876).

The Horsley home was lively, friendly, and welcoming. They entertained many prominent visitors in the arts and sciences. Two of those visitors were Felix Mendelssohn (1809–1847) and his father Moses. They traveled to London in 1829 when Felix was 20. He had written both *Midsummer Night's Dream* and his *Octet* at age 16 (1825), and *Midsummer Night's Dream* had been performed in February

1827. In August 1829, after this visit in London, he continued on to Scotland, visiting the islands in the Hebrides, and saw Fingal's Cave, where he began musical sketches.

Mendelssohn loved visiting the Horsley home. His visits were described in a collection of letters written by Fanny and Sophy (collected and published in 1936 by Rosamund Brunel Gotch, Victor's younger sister).[3] After Felix departed in 1829, he wrote letters back to the Horsleys asking to hear about all the details of their days. Fanny and her younger sister Sophy were teenagers. On one visit in 1833, when Felix would have been 24, Fanny 18 and Sophy 14, they played music in the parlor and then ran outside in the garden playing Ghost: "they tore about in fine style," said Fanny."[4] By Fanny's description in her letter, the game sounded like tag. Felix looked forward to his visits and begged Mrs. Horsley not to let anything change before he visited again. "Oh pray, Mrs. Horsley," he wrote, "pray let me find no changes, let all be the same forever."[5] After Fanny and Sophy wrote an opera for their family, performed in their home on January 5, 1833, and to which Felix was invited, he wrote back and asked to be told all the details… "I had always had the idea of having acted the *Midsummer Night's Dream* in the open air, your garden would be splendid for that purpose but not exactly in Christmas-time." [6]

Sophy was a brilliant pianist, according to Gotch.[7] In her day, women were not encouraged to have formal education nor to develop their musical talents. But Felix recognized Sophy's talents. He developed a piano two-hands version of the *Overture of Melusine* for Fanny and Sophy Horsley, and he dedicated the *Caves of Fingal* (also known as *The Hebrides* and the *Isles of Fingal*) to Sophy. Later, younger brother Charles Edward Horsley would develop musical skills of his own and became a lifelong friend and pupil of Felix.

So while *Midsummer Night's Dream* was not first performed in the Horsley home, there was a connection between the composer and the surgeon. It is notable to mention Charles Edward Horsley's words:

> From this time [1832] Mendelssohn became the most intimate friend of my family. He used to come to us at all times while in London and especially to breakfast… We had a small garden attached to the house and it was Mendelssohn's great delight to spend hours in this, sketching the trees and talking not only about music but also about this friendships with Goethe and Zelter, and his future plans for his works. During these mornings we frequently heard the first germs of compositions that have now become immortal. The beautiful overtures to "Melusine" and "Isles of Fingal" were played at Kensington for some years, I may say before they were performed, and my sister [Mary] possesses a copy of the first MS totally different from those now published.[8]

I believe it is also fair to say that while *Midsummer Night's Dream* was not composed or first performed in the Horsley home, writers of the 1920s and '30s did assert that this was true.[9]

Finally, two other connections exist for Michael Powell and Mendelssohn's *Cave of Fingal*. One is that Mendelssohn wrote much of the sketches for the piece while staying overnight in Tobermory on the island of Mull, Scotland, which, as Powell/Pressburger scholars will recognize, is the location for the filming of *I Know Where I'm Going!*

The other observation comes from the Powell/Pressburger film *The Life and Death of Colonel Blimp*. In the scene where the German soldiers and Theo Kretschmar-Schuldorf are listening to an afternoon concert while in the English detention camp, we briefly glimpse a board announcing the works to be played. The second work is *The Cave of Fingal*.

Musicogenic Epilepsy

Macdonald Critchley, neurologist of Queen Square, published a 1936 monograph on a series of ten case histories in which a piece of music, often times classical, induced a seizure in a susceptible patient.[10] Critchley acknowledged that the fact that a seizure happened after the hearing of a particular piece did not by itself prove that the piece caused the seizure, but he set forward his data to make it available for further study.

In a 1989 collection of essays of the important developers of neurosurgery and neurology, Critchley told the story concerning the evaluation of his first patient with musicogenic epilepsy:

> I have a vivid memory of Derek Denny-Brown's residency at Queen Square. My patient was a ward maid at the hospital and I had been treating her epilepsy for some time. Once she mentioned as an afterthought that she only had an epileptic attack when she listened to music …it was "classical" music that was dangerous. She agreed to be put to the test…it transpired that Denny-Brown was the only one at Queen Square who owned a gramophone so I borrowed it and his records. The first one I played was a piece of jazz but the patient said, "It's not that sort that sets me off."…The others were of a similar type except one—Tchaikovsky's *Valse des Fleurs*…after a few bars the patient had a seizure…So two points were established. First, musciogenic epilepsy did indeed exist. Secondly, Denny-Brown was not a musical sophisticate.[11]

So it is suggestive that a classical piece by Mendelssohn seems to be followed directly by an aura experienced by Peter Carter. This further suggests the possibility that the physician providing information about epilepsy might have told this story to Powell.

An Unseen Hurdy-Gurdy and Frigyes Karinthy

In *A Journey 'Round My Skull*, Frigyes Karinthy described the six-week events of the worsening of his brain tumor and subsequent surgery with great detail.[12] His first symptom was hearing the sound of a freight train approaching and then passing. At first this train seemed to arrive each day punctually at 7 PM. Then as his condition worsened, the train sounds were accompanied by other symptoms. About four weeks after his first symptom, he began to notice noises that became more prolonged, louder, and more intrusive: "Somewhere behind me an unseen beggar with a hurdy-gurdy was grinding out a tune which I heard only as I walked. As soon as I stopped and swung around, it vanished. I was weary, unutterably weary of it all, weary of sickness and weary of death…just a nuisance, like some slinking treacherous dog forever tracking me down."[13] Karinthy is having a musical aura: The first symptom of his seizure is hearing a musical phrase resulting from abnormal activation of one location of the brain. Once again this sounds reminiscent of the scene of the unseen piano player in *AMOLAD*, except in this interpretation, the musical phrase is an aura.

So this brief moment in *AMOLAD*—when the music of the *Midsummer Night's Dream* becomes intertwined with a musical phrase that will come to stand for the ascent of imaginary stairs into Heaven—has a multilayered interpretation. Is it a musical aura, an example of musicogenic epilepsy, an acknowledgement of Victor Horsley, or all three? This is an example where a knowledgeable audience member might have the impression of authenticity intensifying the impact of the film, but alas, Powell and Pressburger did not explain if this scene has anything purposeful at all.

1. Taylor, David C., "One hundred years of epilepsy surgery: Sir Victor Horsley's contribution," in *Surgical Treatment of the Epilepsies*, edited by J. Engel Jr. (New York: Raven Press, 1987), 7–11, quote on 8.

2. Lyons, J.B., *The Citizen Surgeon: A Biography of Sir Victor Horsley* (London: Peter Dawnay Ltd, 1966), 10.

3. Gotch, Rosamund Brunel ed., *Mendelssohn and his Friends in Kensington: Letters from Fanny and Sophy Horsley written 1833-1836* (London: Oxford University Press, 1934).

4. Ibid., 4.

5. Ibid., 72.

6. Ibid., 10.

7. Ibid., 4.

8. Horsley, Charles, "Reminiscences of Mendelssohn by his English Pupil Charles Edward Horsley" in *Mendelssohn and his World*, edited by R. Larry Todd, (Princeton: Princeton University Press, 1991), 237–51, quote on 237.

9. Bond C. J., *Recollections of Student Life and Later Days* (London: H. K. Lewis & Co. Ltd., 1939); Paget S., *Sir Victor Horsley* (London: Constable & Co. Ltd, 1919).

10. Critchley, Macdonald, "Musicogenic epilepsy," *Brain* 60, (1936): 13–27.

11. Critchley, Macdonald, *The Ventricle of Memory*, (New York: Raven Press, 1990), 58–59.

12. Karinthy F. *A Journey 'Round My Skull*, (London: Faber and Faber, 1930).

13. Ibid., 127–28.

**D. "But it wouldn't explain how I could jump without a parachute and still be alive."
"No, it couldn't do that, but there might be a practical explanation, even of that."**

In *A Life in Movies*, Michael Powell mentioned that Emeric Pressburger had read a newspaper article of someone surviving a fall from a plane and used this as the premise of *AMOLAD*. The following describes an R.A.F. airman who fell from a plane and lived to tell about it.

Nicholas Alkemade, a crewman with the 115th R.A.F. squadron, jumped without a parachute on the night of March 24, 1944. His crew was flying in a Lancaster named *S for Sugar*. Alkemade was the tail gunner and in his small compartment, he had no room to wear his parachute. It was his habit to keep his parachute nearby but not wear it. On its way back from Berlin, the plane was shot down by a German Ju-88. Alkemade saw his crewmates jumping and he could feel the heat of the flames from the fire on his face. He escaped from his machine gun hatch and reached his own parachute, but it was on fire. He thought that death was certain, so he decided to jump rather than burn to death. "Better a clean and fast death than being roasted." After he jumped, he reported later, he felt calm and quiet, as if he were in a cloud or sinking into a comfortable mattress. "I remembered that I would not see my girlfriend, Pearl. Anyway I thought that if that was death, it wasn't so bad." He lost consciousness.

When he woke up, he thought for sure he was in the afterlife. He looked at his watch. It was 3:10 AM. When he felt the cold air and he saw the snow on the ground he decided he had not died after all. Although he was generally banged up, his most serious injury was to his knee. He couldn't move easily so he decided to light a cigarette, deciding that being captured as a POW probably would be the next event.

When the Germans found him a short time later, they thought he was a spy because he did not have a parachute. He could not speak German, and when they raised him up, he blacked out. They took him to a hospital in Berlin where he drifted in and out of consciousness. He told the truthful story but it was so fantastic, no one believed him. The doctors thought that either he was lying or that he had suffered a brain injury in the fall.

Alkemade told them that if they could locate the Lancaster wreckage, they would find his parachute in the tail of the plane. This was a tall order because first, he was suspected of being a spy and spies were usually shot; second, who would go look for wreckage of a plane that had probably been completely destroyed and third, why expect that a partially-burned parachute would survive even if the wreckage could be found? Amazingly, luck was with Alkemade once again. A German lieutenant, Hans Feidel, located the wreckage and found a portion of the parachute which matched a belt that Alkemade was wearing when he was found, so it was decided that he had been telling the truth all along. Alkemade returned to London in May 1945 and received much attention from the press. His fellow British prisoners wrote and signed a certificate attesting to the authenticity of the story.

Alkemade was certainly a man born under a lucky star. Three more times he survived very serious accidents at the chemical plant where he was employed after the war. On separate occasions, a beam fell on his head, he was burned by acid, and he fell into a chlorine pool. Each time he recovered and lived to tell the tale!

The source for this story was a translation from the Spanish book by Jesus Hernandez, *Hechos insolitos de la Segunda Guerra mundia*, (Barcelona: Inedita Editores, 2005). The English translation had been available from http://www.ww2incolor.com:80/phpBB2/viewtopic.php?p=34426&sid=9fe88c9229cf9183837f7eae902ba1cd

The story was posted on December 7, 2005, but it has since been removed.

E. "Do You Think I'm Cracked?"

Dr. Reeves asked Peter:
"Has she read your poems?...What were you doing in civil life?"
"I was at Oxford...specializing in European history."
"Called up?
"Volunteered. Trained in Canada. Went on ops in '41."
"Bomber"?
"Spell of Costal. Spell of Instructor. Back to Bombers. Lancasters."
"You must have done a good many operations."
"Sixty-seven."
"I'm surprised they let you go back, with your experience and seniority."
"New job. Master-bomber."
"Hmm. Tricky."
"Someone's got to do it."

Dr. Reeves argued with Dr. McEwen:
"The boy has a fine mind and it's over-taxed. That's the trouble. It's too fine a mind. A weak mind isn't strong enough to hurt itself...stupidity has saved many a man from going mad."

The study of the brain in the 1940s had an internal struggle among several lines of inquiry—neurology, psychology, psychiatry, and the new line of inquiry, psychoanalysis. Each sought to explain interior mental phenomena and external behavior of people from a common set of findings. Psychoanalysis was a controversial approach from some neurologists' point of view, made more perplexing by the fact that Freud had originally trained as a neurologist at the l'Hôpital de la Pitié in Paris. *AMOLAD* weaves traces of these approaches as the puzzle to understand what is going on in Peter Carter's mind unfolds.

What is it in Peter Carter's personality, experience, and intelligence that produces these visions?

Neurologist and psychiatrist C. P. Symonds, based at St. Hugh's (where Hugh Cairns and J. P. Reidy served),[1] was given the assignment by Air Marshall Sir Harold Whittingham to evaluate and advise on the operational limit of members of aircrews. Symonds wrote, "This represented a serious attempt to study the psychology of fear…We were empowered to interrogate any squadron leader or higher who were willing to discuss the two broad questions which began our investigations: What are the things that get men down? How do you know when a man has had enough?"[2]

The Kind of Injury and the Kind of Head

The portions of dialogue above connect with the aspects of Peter's three occupations: professor of European history at Oxford, poet, and Master Bomber for the R.A.F. During WWII, neurologists and the newly emerging subspecialty of neuropsychiatry were bringing all of their efforts to understand the human mind as yet another way to defeat the Nazis.

A number of papers in the psychiatric, neurologic, and ophthalmologic literature were written from 1890 to 1945 with the same goal—to try to determine a unifying explanation for the wide variety of visual hallucinatory phenomena. The 1940 review article "Visual hallucinations and their neuro-optical correlates" sought to evaluate the various phenomena including visions after staring at an object, after-visions while awakening from a dream, hallucinations during a narcoleptic episode, hallucinations during seizures, and hallucinations of psychosis.[3] The authors observed that the same brain lesion can produce different phenomena in different patients. They were baffled. How is it, they asked, "that the same lesion in one person produces relatively simple visual experiences and in another person provokes complicated visions?"

After a lengthy analysis, they concluded something pertinent for our discussion. "For persons having a high degree of visual imagery, the sensory presentations produced by the abnormal stimulation of the neuron-optic apparatus, such as occurs in association with irritations of the optic nerves, are projected as rich and elaborate images. In other words, the more intelligent and verbal and the more ability possessed to make mental images, the more complex the patient's experience, interpretation and communication of the mental phenomena."[3]

Hugh Cairns would endorse this opinion by saying at a 1939 conference on the diagnostic significance of hallucinatory phenomena, "It is the diplomat and not the servant from Whitechapel who sees the Japanese warrior."[4] C. P. Symonds said, "In other words *it is not only the kind of injury that matters but the kind of head.*"[5] So I believe that Peter Carter sees an eighteenth-century Frenchman because that was the subject of his teaching and writing before the war.

How Do You Know a Man's Had Enough?

In the early years of WWII, the R.A.F. took an enormous number of casualties. In a preface to his work on the psychological state of R.A.F. personnel, Symonds wrote:

> The heaviest load was carried by the home-based Bomber Command during the years 1942–1943, when the expectation of *survival* [emphasis mine] of the statutory operational tour of 30 sorties was probably less than 30%. After this came a period of instructional duty (not without its hazards and anxieties) and a second tour of 25 sorties." [2]

This seems to describe Peter Carter's service record pretty accurately. The words of a second neuropsychological researcher, D. D. Reid, help us understand a little more how we would feel in Peter's shoes:

> [In 1942] losses in any one raid by Bomber command rose at times in 1942 to 7%; and at this rate, the chance of surviving a tour of 30 operations could, when flying accidents were added in, fall to the insupportable level of 10%. No one was better aware of this grim actuarial outlook than the air crew themselves. They expressed the alternatives of either death or release from operational duty because of disabling neurosis in the pithy but macabre phrase "coffins or crackers."[6]

A psychological report was prepared in 1942 in which D. D. Reid wrote about the procedure used to interview flying personnel about psychological status:

> When a new air crew arrives the captain is given a *pro forma* with the names of all the sections to be visited. Among these is the medical officer. At the outset the subject must be made completely at ease and the impression conveyed that this is a slightly tiresome routine needed to complete the medical records demanded by a nebulous "higher authority." Such a reference usually enlists an attitude of sympathetic co-operation. Once a rapport is established, one proceeds briskly to the first routine questions. The emphasis must always be on the seemingly physical aspect of a man's past history, but disorders which might have a neurotic coloring are investigated.[7]

The tone and approach conveyed in this portion remind us of Dr. Reeves' tone as he interviews Peter Carter.

Findings from these investigations were released during the war as classified reports such as "The psychiatric assessment by wing commander J. Flind and squadron-leader B. Cates, of pilots under training at the personnel receiving centre Harrogate, and pilots at operational training units and heavy conversion units who had completed an operational tour in heavy bombers." Cambridge Psychological Laboratory, 1944.[7]

Just as neurologists and neurosurgeons published their findings in medical journals during the war, Symonds published his findings on psychological stress in pilots and air crews in the *British Medical Journal*.[8] Some of his findings are reminiscent of Peter's description of his work as a master bomber. First, Symonds describes a person whose limitations spare him from some feelings of fear:

> "Thus there is a kind of fearlessness which is associated with lack of intelligence or imagination. Fearlessness of this origin may be a source of strength in time of danger but carries with it a source of weakness. The same defect which prevents the acquisition of fear by conditioning or experience prevents the inhibition of fear by conditioning and experience…[but] the man whose lack of imagination prevents anticipatory fear is thereby saved much stress.[9]

Symonds went on to describe the psychological makeup of a confident, experienced pilot, recalling to us Dr. Reeves' comments about Peter Carter having too fine a mind:

> So long as he can make use of courage to conquer fears, he can preserve his confidence and tension and strain will be diminished…hav[ing] courage in reserve to balance exceptional stress…Distinguished men of great operational experience have told me that fear, especially before a trip, generally calls for conscious

control; but once the sortie has begun there is no fear in excess, and relatively little tension.[10]

Symonds experienced some unanticipated response after his papers on fear were published. For publishing these findings, Symonds was formally accused of being a traitor and of aiding the enemy:

> I was told a day or two later that a propaganda broadcast in English from Germany referred to [the articles] as evidence of low morale in the R.A.F. I therefore obeyed a summons to my D.G.M.S. with some trepidation. He told me he heard rumors of an attack to be made on me by some of the Air Staff but that as he had passed the letters for publication, his was the entire responsibility.[2]

In summary, *AMOLAD* presents Peter Carter as an intelligent squadron leader who communicated the satisfaction of confidence earned by surviving large numbers of operations through managing dangers and feelings of fear. This accurate presentation of a pilot is supported by neuro-psychological work of the 1930s and '40s. Possibly the neurologist who Michael Powell consulted could have been familiar with this work of the psychological makeup of experienced R.A.F. pilots. Or just possibly Charles Symonds, Hugh Cairns, or one of their trainees spoke with him directly about these findings.

1. Schurr, Peter, "The contribution to neurosurgery of the combined services hospital for head injuries at St. Hugh's College, Oxford, 1940–1945," *Journal of the Army Medical Corps* 134 (1988): 146–48.

2. Symonds, Sir Charles, *Studies in Neurology* (London: Oxford University Press, 1970), 20.

3. Weinberger, L. M., Grant, F. C., "Visual hallucinations and their neuro-optical correlates," *Archives of Ophthalmology* 23 (1940) 166–99, quote on 190.

4. Brown, R. Dodds, "Significance of auditory and visual hallucinations," *The Lancet* 2(August 19, 1939): 426–27, quote on 426.

5. Symonds C. P., "Mental disorder following head injury," *Proceedings of the Royal Society of Medicine* Vol. XXX part 2 (May–Oct. 1937), 1081–94, quote on 1092.

6. Reid , D. D., "The historical background to wartime research in psychology in the Royal Air Force," *Aircrew Stress in Wartime Operations*, (London: Academic Press, 1979), 3.

7. Reid, D. D., "The influence of psychological disorder on efficiency in operational flying FPRC, report 508, September 1942," in *Aircrew Stress in Wartime Operations*, (London: Academic Press, 1979), 46.

7. Flind, J., Cates B., "The psychiatric assessment by wing commander J. Flind and squadron-leader B. Cates, of pilots under training at the personnel receiving centre Harrogate, and pilots at operational training units and heavy conversion units who had completed an operational tour in heavy bombers." (Cambridge Psychological Laboratory, 1944).

8. Symonds, C. P., "The human response to flying stress," *British Medical Journal*, 2 (1943): 703–40, and reprinted in *Studies in Neurology*, 250–70.

9. Ibid., 259.

10. Ibid., 266.

F. The Intersection of Neurology and Literature

Conductor 71 asked Peter:
"I'd like to borrow this book."
"It's not mine. It's the doctor's."
"Oh doctors. They give me a lot of trouble in my job."

Neurology in Literature of the Time
Literature is an important aspect of neurology in the period from 1880 through 1945. Neurologists realized that neurologic conditions were being described in literary works, some of which referred to the neurological conditions of the writers themselves. Part of a neurologist's training is skill of observation, recall of patterns, and recognizing the variety of presentation of those phenomena. Because neurologists found the gradations of levels of consciousness so compelling, it was helpful to refer to these literary examples to communicate shades of meaning. Several articles refer directly to dreamy states or complex partial seizures with hallucinations. It is interesting for neuroscientists today to read the work of the neuroscientists of that period, seeking to glean some new understanding through these highly detailed descriptions. These descriptions are not colored by modern interpretation because that understanding would not be developed for another thirty years.

Quaerens and John Hughlings Jackson
The first connection of literature and epilepsy was made by a physician writing in 1874, who described his own epileptic seizures and contrasted them with experiences recorded by Dickens, Coleridge, and Tennyson. This physician-patient published his paper in *The Practitioner* under the pseudonym "Quaerens" (The Seeker) in May

1874. Quaerens argued that even though Coleridge and Tennyson suggested that these phenomena are universally experienced, they probably are indications of brain disturbance. Quaerens came under the treatment of John Hughlings Jackson, who combined Quaerens's case study with those of other patients in *Brain* 1888.[1] Jackson agreed with Quaerens that Coleridge and Tennyson were describing their own brain function disturbances, although he said that it would be unusual for a physician in 1888 to make the diagnosis of brain disease based on the report of a patient who was having "a curious sensation like transportation to another world lasting a second or so."[2] The article by Jackson goes on to describe a number of patients, several of whom experience an unpleasant odor as a beginning symptom of their seizure.

James Crichton-Browne

Crichton-Browne delivered the Cavendish Lecture in 1895 entitled "Dreamy Mental States."[3] He had left the West Riding Mental Asylum near Dumfries, Scotland, where he had been superintendent after his father's retirement from that position. Crichton-Browne moved to London and, with John Hughlings Jackson and David Ferrier, went on to found the new neurological journal *Brain*. The article on dreamy mental states sought to categorize several types of disturbance of consciousness.

Crichton-Browne's analysis of dreamy mental states began with the symptoms of *déjà vu*: "It consists of an impression suddenly taking possession of the mind that the passing moment of life has once been lived or must be once lived again…an echo of a life anterior to the present one…yet startles as if it were a revelation." He acknowledges that in superstitious ages, these experiences were interpreted as signs of the past or future fate. "It is ours to deal with from a purely medical point of view...not as intimations of immortality but as revivals of hereditarily transmitted or acquired states in new and special combinations."[4]

But what is remarkable in Crichton-Browne's article is the use of literary examples: " How often says Sir Walter Scott in *Guy Mannering* do we find ourselves impressed with an ill-defined consciousness?" "We all have some experience says Charles Dickens in *David Copperfield* of a feeling which comes over occasionally..." "Rossetti says in *Sudden Light* I have been here before..."[5]

Crichton-Browne also cites examples from Oliver Wendell Holmes, Edward Dowden, William Wordsworth, Russell Lowell, Thomas Hardy, and Coventry Patmore. Coleridge's example is especially telling. "Coleridge," he wrote, "who was very subject to dreamy states of all sorts and sizes seems to be disposed to take this view of their [dreamy states] hidden meaning...'oft o'er my brain does that strange fancy roll...'"[6] (Coleridge worried about epilepsy and mentioned "breezes of terror blowing up from the stomach to the brain" in his journal during a walking trip through Scotland in 1803 with Wordsworth.[7])

A second, more complex state, the *intellectual aura*, is then described in its elusiveness in Crichton-Browne's article. "The most general description of them is that they are indescribable—they consist in an exaltation of subject consciousness...and are almost invariably concerned with those ultimate scientific ideas—space, time, matter, motion, force and the like—which are beyond the domain of certain knowledge and according to Herbert Spencer, 'unthinkable'...there is a loss of a sense of proportion—in momentary black despair—in being at the Day of Judgment...it is impossible to put into words such strange and incomprehensible visitations..."[8] Tennyson is next described:

In these words it is not difficult to recognize an outline of *petit mal* and Tennyson himself names these seizures epilepsy..."weird seizures, Heaven knows what: On a sudden in the midst of men and day, And while I walked and talked as heretofore, I seemed to move among a world of ghosts, and feel myself the shadow of a dream."[9]

Crichton-Browne goes on to describe *epigastric auras* and *auras of fear and confusion*, which remind the modern reader of those symptoms experienced by George Gershwin fifty years later. He also mentioned "the distinguished men of letters whose confessions of dreamy mental states have been quoted—Scott, Dickens and Rossetti died of brain disease."[10] He reviews a family who has several members with epilepsy and dreamy states, speculating on the localization of the seizures: "There had been damage or disorder of the right hemisphere of the brain. Dr. Hughlings Jackson, whose guesses in neurology are more valuable, trustworthy and enlightening than most other men's lifelong observations and carefully reasoned conclusions, long ago suggested that [these states and symptoms] corresponded with involvement of the right or more subjective hemispheres of the brain..."[11]

The second part of the article first describes the mental states associated with anesthetic use and near-death experience. Then Crichton-Brown enumerates historical figures who have had epilepsy including Caesar, Marlborough, Napoleon, Wellington, Moliere, Sheridan, Balzac, Flaubert, John Addington Symonds, and Dostoyevsky.

The early articles by Quaerens, Jackson, and Crichton-Browne are all interesting because each describes epileptic phenomena in detail without the neuroscience that would develop in later years. These articles all describe details that are also present in *AMOLAD*—a dreamy, hallucinatory state; smelling an odor as an aura; disruption of space and time; and mentioning historical figures who have epilepsy. There is no direct evidence to indicate that Michael Powell read any of these particular articles. Crichton-Browne lived into his 90s and died in 1938, making him a contemporary of neurologists who could have spoken with Michael Powell.

Other examples of literature and neurology
A neurology conference in 1939 was focused on various causes of hallucination. Published proceedings summarize the comments made by C. P. Symonds, P. K. McGowan, Macdonald Critchely, Hugh Cairns, and others in attendance.[12] McGowan commented on the hallucinations of Byron, Luther, and Joan of Arc. Critchley referred to seizures whose visual symptoms produced a Lilliputian experience. Reviewing 100 cases of hallucinations in 800 cases of verified brain tumors, Cairns said that about ten had olfactory aura. These hallucinations were different than those of psychotic states. K. W. Todd discussed that "constructive intuitions took a hallucinatory form in cases like that of John Bunyan."[13]

As we will discuss later, stating that these historical figures had epilepsy has not held up over time to be completely accurate, as our knowledge of epilepsy and dreamy states has developed. What is important for our discussion was that this is the information available to neurologists and to Michael Powell in 1945.

Dr. Reeves' missing book of chess
Finally, I want to mention a unique connection between epilepsy and Charles Dickens which I connect with the "theft" of Alekhine's book of chess by Conductor 71 in *AMOLAD*. To review, Peter Carter has been reading *My 100 Best Games* in Dr. Reeves' study when he

falls asleep and has a seizure and a visit from Conductor 71. The Conductor states he would like to borrow the book. We next see the book as the Conductor returns it to Dr. Reeves when he greets the doctor, conducted by John Bunyan, arriving in Heaven. At the end of the film, Dr. Reeves throws the book down the Heavenly staircase and it appears in Peter's jacket pocket as we hear the Conductor say "Peter, don't forget your book!"

With great kindness and fondness, John Hughlings Jackson was eulogized by his friend and fellow neurologist E. Farquhar Buzzard and later by Macdonald Critchley:

> He was a great novel reader. Jackson had a quirk which has been mentioned by more than one of his biographers. He would refer to an imaginary Mr. Harris as being responsible for his day-to-day frustrations. He haunted Dr. Jackson in order to hide his things. Jackson would blame Mr. Harris for mislaying his papers or for disappointing changes in the weather. Mr. Harris was the make-believe husband of Sarah Gamp's mythical friend Mrs. Harris in *Martin Chuzzlewit*, written by Charles Dickens, said to be one of Jackson's favorite authors.[11, 12]

So John Hughlings Jackson, a neurologist, blamed an imaginary character when he mislaid his possessions. Wouldn't it be fun to think this little story is mirrored in the theft of the neurologist's book *My 100 Best Games* by the imaginary Conductor 71, who states, "I'd like to borrow your book."

1. Jackson, John Hughlings "On a particular variety of epilepsy 'intellectual aura;' one case with symptoms of organic brain disease."

Brain vol xi (1888): 179. Reprinted in *The selected writings of John Hughlings Jackson* vol. 1, ed. James Taylor (London: Staples Press, 1958), 385–405.

2. Ibid., 389.

3. Crichton-Browne, James, "Dreamy Mental States," *Lancet* vol. 2 (July 6, 1895): 1–5, and (July 13, 1895): 73–75.

4. Ibid., July 6, 1895, 1.

5. Ibid.

6. Ibid.

7. Vickers, Neil, *Wordsworth, Coleridge and the Doctors, 1795–1806* (Oxford: Oxford University Press, 2004), 138.

8. Crichton-Browne, 2.

9. Ibid.

10. Ibid., 4.

11. Ibid., 5.

12. Section of Neurology and Psychiatry, "Visual and Auditory Hallucinations," *British Medical Journal* vol 2 (Aug 12, 1939): 361-362.

13. Ibid., 362.

14. Buzzard, E. Farquhar, "Hughlings Jackson and his influence on neurology," *Lancet* (Oct 27 1934): 910.

15. Critchley, Macdonald, *John Hughlings Jackson* (New York: Oxford University Press, 1998), 163.

G. Dr. Reeves asked Peter: "Was it a pleasant smell? Can you place it?"
"Why yes … fried onions"

I have not been able to find a reference to explain why Michael Powell or Emeric Pressburger specifically chose the odor of fried onions to signify Peter Carter's aura. But I have found a number of medical sources available in 1945 that discuss the pleasant and unpleasant odors of olfactory auras. Here are details that are relevant: Almost all neurological textbooks state that an olfactory aura is usually an unpleasant smell, describing them as "vile," "rubbery," or "fumes."[1] However, there are a few references however to experiencing a pleasant smell: "The feeling…was always preceded by a strong olfactory hallucination, always pleasant;" "It is just as if I had been passing a perfume shop."[2] At one time, it was thought that pleasant smells might indicate that the lesion was in the right temporal lobe while unpleasant smells might reveal localization in the left. Recall that Peter Carter's lesion is in the right temporal lobe.

Dr. Frederic Schreiber announced in 1940 that he had conducted a small retrospective study using Dr. Cushing's case series:

> My first acquaintance with Dr. Cushing began in 1922 when, as a fourth year medical student, I asked him to give me an *arbeit*. He wrote on a slip of paper which I have kept: "Are uncinate seizures of lateralizing value?" In reviewing the 39 cases of verified tumors in the series of the Peter Bent Brigham Hospital at the time, I found that in all those in which pleasant or nauseatingly sweet odors were present, the tumor was in the right temporal lobe. In three-fourths of those in which foul or disagreeable odors were present the tumor was on the left side. The findings in such a small series of cases may not be significant, but the study

marked the beginning of my interest in this subject and led to my later association with Dr. Cushing as a surgical pupil.[3]

Case reports of persons with olfactory symptoms were available in the medical literature. Cushing described his own cases with pleasant auras and temporal lobe locations for seizures.[4] Case Six described an eleven-year-old boy who had visual symptoms of various hallucinations. At times he saw another boy, a man sitting by the fire tying his shoe, and later, some children sitting around a desk. He also had symptoms of smelling and tasting roasted peanuts and at other times smelling and tasting peaches.[5] Case Seven found her olfactory symptoms difficult to describe "but [they are] like something from another world; nothing that is in the environment—I can't describe it."[6] This person also had visual hallucinations of a woman friend and a man with a golden helmet on his head. Case Nine smelled fresh paint "so distinct she is surprised others do not detect it."[7]

1. Wilson, S. A. K., *Neurology*, ed. A. Ninian Bruce, vol. 2 (London: Edward Arnold and Co., 1940), 1620.

2. Wilson, 1631.

3. Schreiber, Frederic, *Archives of Neurology and Psychiatry* 43 (1940): 1046.

4. Cushing, Harvey, "The field deficits produced by temporal lobe lesions," *Brain* 44 (Jan 1921): 341–96, quote on 367.

5. Ibid., 370.

6. Ibid., 367.

7. Ibid., 378.

H. The Staircase and the Statues

As the story of *AMOLAD* progresses, Peter's condition worsens. He spends time in Dr. Reeves' study, surrounded by tall piles of books. Among these piles of books are little statues. During his seizures, Peter finds himself on a white stairway lined by tall statues of famous people. I see an additional interpretation within a neurological context: I think it is possible that Michael Powell intended that the stairway and the statues reflect a neurologic phenomenon in which Peter perceives himself as being smaller than the objects in his environment. I think the white pages of the books seen on edge in the study resemble stair steps. The famous people represented by the statues may have in common a diagnosis of epilepsy.

<u>Lilliputian seizures: micropsia and macropsia phenomena</u>
A particular subtype of neurologic visual phenomena is called "Lilliputian" or micropsia phenomena, in which the person sees himself as being larger than the objects in the environment. Other patients experience the converse, "Macropsia," perceiving themselves to be markedly smaller than surrounding objects. People can experience these phenomena in delirium, during migraines, and also during complex partial seizures. Lewis Carroll is thought to have some experience with these symptoms, as he depicts Alice as being bigger than her surroundings as well as smaller in various scenes of *Through the Looking Glass*. I myself have taken care of a patient in delirium who misapprehended the flower patterns of the bed sheets that covered her as she exclaimed repeatedly, "I'm shrinking!" because she believed that the sheets were her pants and thus excessively large with respect to her body size.

In 1923, Gilbert Horrax wrote an extensive article on visual phenomena as a clue to localizing the source of a brain problem.[1] He made several statements that resonate with details within *AMOLAD*. He describes one case history in which "[The patient] saw a man dressed in white sitting by the fire bending over to tie his shoe...The patient was sure he was not asleep, as he closed and opened his eyes several times and the figure was always there..." This is reminiscent of Peter Carter opening and closing each eye as he sees the heavenly messenger in Dr. Reeves' study. With regards to micropsia and macropsia, Horrax summarizes Cushing's published findings of visual hallucination:

> The usual story obtained from the patient is that during the few moments of "unreality" or "dreamy state" often while experiencing the olfactory or gustatory aura, there appear, usually to one side or another, the shadows of people, animals or inanimate objects. These figures are sometimes grotesque, sometimes fairly natural. Often they are diminutive or more rarely, enlarged. In some cases the hallucination is stationary, in others it may be seen to be coming toward or going away from the patient."[2]

This article then describes several case histories, including one in which a woman sees the figure of a woman friend and at other times "a man with a gold helmet on his head sitting in a chair beside the examiner." Another case described the recurring vision of a group of men playing cards, with the game invariably ending in a fight among the players.[3] With regards to objects appearing larger, Horrax stated, "A physician suffered from uncinate gyrus seizures...so far as vision was concerned, this manifested itself by making objects appear abnormally large to him, a condition noted by Josefson in 1913...[who] gave the name *macropsia* to this phenomenon."[4] Horrax then goes on to discuss the three possible explanations for the phenomenon: pressure on structures (as Dr. Reeves endorses), local irritation of local structures, or irritation of nerve pathways passing through but joining up with brain locations as a distance to the actual lesion and expressing the function of the distant location.[5]

Thomas Johnson wrote a medical review article in 1933[6] in which he describes a case recorded in 1836 by James Craig of a seventy-six-year-old man:

> A well-to-do Retired British Official, noted as a linguist, who saw repeatedly "an elderly female with a brilliant eye, an arch and playful expression, appeared ready to address him. She was dressed in an old-fashioned Scottish tartan plaid drawn like a hood over the head and fastened beneath the chin"... Figures seen were almost always of an agreeable character and varied in size and distance they stood from him.[7]

Horrax (1932) had a patient who also saw figures:

> [Such as] Dante, which resembled the well-known profile with a long nose and a wreath on the head. Twice he saw the figure of Theodore Roosevelt, once in a white vest and once in a frock coat. One of the few figures which had any motion was a white Punchinello with a white face who kept bowing from the waist. He also saw strange men walking, dogs, goats, and lions, a Japanese warrior in tortoiseshell armour, a fat man blowing his nose, and a host of unrecognized figures."[8]

Later in 1939, Macdonald Critchley referred to this article and indicated that, "Lilliputian hallucinations are most often associated with pituitary or juxtapituitary tumors,"[9] very near the location of Peter Carter's problem.

The identify and significance of the statues

In Michael Powell's handwriting, a list of names of the statues appears on page 49 of the script and the page facing page 50. Ian Christie compiled the list: "Alexander the great! Homer, Beethoven, Plato, Socrates, Abraham Lincoln, Confucius, Julius Caesar, King Solomon, Shakespeare, Mohamed, Michael Angelo, Moses, Benjamin Franklin, Chopin, <u>Murillo</u>, [Powell's underline], Swift, Rembrandt, Beethoven etc., etc." Richelieu is also mentioned, as well as Sophocles. Chopin is mistaken for Talleyrand. Capt. Scott, RN, is written in.[10]

Most of these people have in common a characteristic beyond their prominence in politics, arts, and philosophy. In 1945, almost all of them were believed to have epilepsy. Mentioning the names of famous people with epilepsy as evidence of either overcoming a disability to achieve greatness, or being the neurological cause of greatness or special sight, was found in the neurological literature as well as mentioned by doctors to be a comfort to patients.

I reviewed several sources that mentioned prominent historical figures. John Bunyan, although not depicted in a statue, is the conductor for Dr. Reeves. Neurologists in 1939 thought Bunyan had epilepsy, or at least "constructive intuitions."[11] One prominent book concerning epilepsy in history, *The Falling Sickness*, was published in 1945.[12] The author, Owsei Temkin, presented a compilation of famous people with epilepsy adapted from a list created in 1602 that included Hercules, Ajax, Bellerophon, Socrates, Plato, Empedocles, Julius Caesar, and Maracus of Syracuse and the Sybils.[12] The 1946 book *Science and Seizures*, written by the Harvard neurologist William Lennox, contains a long list of famous people with epilepsy including Caesar and Alexander the Great.[13]

Others thought to have epilepsy included Pythagoras, Aristotle, Hannibal, Dante, Leonardo da Vinci, Michelangelo, Cardinal Richelieu, Blaise Pascal, Sir Isaac Newton, Jonathan Swift, George Frederick Handel, William Pitt, Ludwig von Beethoven, Sir Walter Scott, Lord Byron, Percy Shelly, King Louis XIII of France, Jean-

Baptiste Poquelin-Moliere, Hector Berlioz, Edgar Allen Poe, Alfred Lord Tennyson, Charles Dickens, Robert Schumann, Fyodor Dostoevsky, Gustav Flaubert, Leo Tolstoy, Lewis Carroll, and Pytor Ilyich Tchaikovsky.[14]

In 2005, the medical information of these prominent people was reviewed in the article, "Did all those famous people really have epilepsy?"[14] Reviewing the medical information available concerning forty-three historical figures, new diagnoses were made to explain symptoms ranging from fainting to seeing visions to paroxysmal attacks of unconsciousness. Those diagnoses range from true epilepsy to migraine, anxiety, alcohol withdrawal, and other problems.

For our purposes, though, we should focus on what information was available to neurologists of 1945, the time the film was created. I believe that most of the statues represent prominent people thought to have had epilepsy. However, not all of the statues depict people in this category. I could find not references mentioning Confucius, Benjamin Franklin, Chopin, Lincoln, Murillo, Rembrandt, or Captain Scott, RN.

1. Horrax, G., "Visual hallucination as a cerebral localizing phenomena," *Archives of Neurology and Psychiatry* 10 (1923): 532–47, quote on 537.

2. Ibid., 539.

3. Ibid., 542.

4. Ibid., 543.

5. Ibid., 544.

6. Johnson, Thomas, "Visual hallucinations accompanying organic lesions of the brain with special reference to their value as localizing phenomena," *Transactions of American Ophthalmological Society*, 31 (1933): 334–94.

7. Ibid., 350.

8. Horrax, G., Putnam, T., "Distortions of the visual fields in causes of brain tumor," *Brain* 155 (1932): 499–523, quote on 519.

9. Critchley, M., comments in "Visual and auditory hallucinations," *British Medical Journal* 2 (1939): 361–62.

10. Christie, Ian, *A Matter of Life and Death* (London: British Film Institute Publishing, 2000), 48.

11. Todd, K. W., comments in "Visual and auditory hallucinations," *British Medical Journal* 2 (1939): 361–62.

12. Temkin, O. *The Falling Sickness: A history of epilepsy from the Greeks to the beginnings of modern neurology* (Baltimore: Johns Hopkins, 1945), 152.

13. Lennox, W. *Science and Seizures* (New York: Harper Bros., 1946), 59.

14. Hughes, John R., "Did all those famous people really have epilepsy?" *Epilepsy and Behavior*, 6 no.2 (March 2005): 115–39.

I. "Frank's had an accident."

As Emeric Pressburger noted, the outcome of *AMOLAD* hinges on the doctor dying in order to save his patient. Earlier in the film, we see that Dr. Frank Reeves, wearing his leather cap and goggles, loves to ride his motorcycle at high speed on the narrow country lanes. He loves to race and knows each turn and dip of the road by heart, as pointed out in the book of the film, when Frank rushes to the American Hospital in the thunderstorm:

> Between the lightning flashes it was pitch dark, and his headlight, reflected back from the drenched surface of the road, was of very limited service. But it picked out the dripping hedge as he tore along, and he drove by that and by his great familiarity with the route which he could have almost have covered blindfold[ed]. It was an exhilarating drive, the violence of the storm emphasizing his sense of power and of dependence upon his own skill and strength…The sheer uncomplicated thrill appealed to that one small side of the Doctor that had never quite grown up…"[1]

But then Frank meets his end, in the same way that T. E. Lawrence met his, by swerving his motorcycle to avoid running into someone. (See discussion in Chapter Two.)

Powell had another connection with motorcycles and physicians. Described in Chapter Six, Powell's friend, the actor and surgeon Niall MacGinnis, was famous for riding his motorcycle at Ashridge, the country college temporarily housing over 1,200 patients evacuated from Charing Cross from 1939 to 1946.

I see another neurosurgical connection with Frank and his motorcycle. If we pretend that Frank was a real neurologist of 1945, then he would have been very familiar with the research of Hugh

Cairns in the prevention of motorcycle injury with the mandatory wearing of properly designed motorcycle helmets.[2,3,4] When Cairns was called to Lawrence's bedside he felt frustrated that he could not save him. Over the next years, Cairns took note of the effectiveness of different crash helmet designs. By nature, Cairns was a very determined surgeon, and he maintained his focus on trying to prevent the death and disability from head injury. He pointed out in 1941 that among motorcyclists, head injuries were the most common cause of death, but those wearing helmets were far less likely to have fatal injuries. When helmets were made compulsory in 1941 for Army motorcyclists and their passengers, the rate of motorcycle fatalities from all causes fell markedly. In his 1946 article, Cairns showed that the statistics for all fatal motorcycle injuries were far less during the days leading up to the Normandy invasion in 1944 when compared to 1939 and the outbreak of the war.[5] When published in the *British Medical Journal*, Cairns' findings on crash helmets and motorcycle injuries appeared as the lead article in each issue.

Should we consider Frank a physician who does not follow his own advice, like a lung specialist who smokes or a trauma surgeon who does not wear his seat belt? Would Michael Powell have paid attention to the detail of wearing a motorcycle helmet? The only evidence we have is that, in *The Life and Death of Colonel Blimp*, the motorcycle riders are all wearing their helmets with the hard outer shell. The *AMOLAD* script states that Frank pulls on his helmet as he goes out in the thunderstorm, although we see him with his leather cap both on the motorcycle and when he arrives in Heaven.

There is one other interesting coincidence about degrees of separation between Hugh Cairns and Michael Powell, in addition to the fact that the plastic surgeon, Mr. Joe Reidy, Frankie Powell's brother, had patients in common with Mr. Cairns. Hugh Cairns, born in Australia in 1896, came to Oxford as a Rhodes Scholar in 1919. This scholarship led him to meet Rudyard Kipling, then a trustee of the scholarship fund. Athletic abilities were part of the qualification for the scholarship and Cairns was a strong rower. This brought him a new friendship with a rowing teammate, Raymond Massey.[6]

While we are talking about Hugh Cairns, one element in the film that is an unanswered question for me is why Peter Carter would be taken to an American hospital for his surgery? It does work in the story as an example of the symmetry and reciprocity of American and British cooperation. But Hugh Cairns had worked very hard to develop Harvey Cushing's findings of expert neurosurgical treatment to reduce disability and save lives of military personnel from the beginning of WWII. Cairns developed an extensive network of neurosurgical hospitals and support services for injured British military. He pushed his concept of mobile neurosurgical units. Staffed with a neurosurgeon and a surgical team as well as outfitted with sufficient supplies to support 200 surgeries without restocking, the units provided expert treatment close to the front lines.[7] These units were called MNSUs—Mobile Neurosurgical Units.[8] Cairns also had developed a network of neurosurgical hospitals in England, financed in part by the British financier Lord Nuffield. Cairns was remarkably determined in collecting very detailed notes on each surgical case, allowing him and his colleagues to continue to ask research questions and publish throughout the war. It is remarkable to consider the intensity of effort in saving lives, organizing surgical systems, and conducting research and publishing findings, all while Oxford had its share of bombings.

1. Warman, Eric, Adaptation of Michael Powell and Emeric Pressburger's *A Matter of Life and Death: The book of the film*, (London: World Film Publications, 1946), 74.

2. Maartens, N. F., Wills, A. D., Adams, C. B., "Lawrence of Arabia, Sir Hugh Cairns and the origin of motorcycle helmets," *Neurosurgery*, 50, no.1 (Jan 2002): 176-80.

3. Cairns, H., "Head injuries in motor-cyclists: the importance of the crash helmet," *British Medical Journal* (Oct. 4, 1941): 465–71.

4. Cairns, H., Holbourn, H. "Head injuries in motor-cycles with special reference to crash helmets," *British Medical Journal* (May 15, 1943): 590–98.

5. Ibid., Maartens, 178.

6. Fraenkel, G. J., *Hugh Cairns First Nuffield Professor of Surgery*, (Oxford: Oxford University Press, 1991): 34.

7. Aziz, T. Z., Adams, C. B. T., "Neurosurgery at the Radcliffe Infirmary Oxford," *Neurosurgery* 37 no. 3 (1995): 505–20.

8. Fraenkel, Ibid., after page 207.

J. The Camera Obscura

I have not been able to determine if any Scottish or English neurologists or neurosurgeons had interests in the camera obscura, but I have found one connection linking Michael Powell and a camera obscura. From personal correspondence with Joanne Turner, Museums Assistant—Collections, Dumfries Museum and Camera Obscura, in Dumfries, Scotland, I learned that John Laurie, who appeared in Michael Powell's films *Edge of the World* and *Life and Death of Colonel Blimp*, was born in a house two streets from the Camera Obscura observatory in Dumfries. The Dumfries camera obscura is built in an old wooden windmill. "The camera obscura was installed at the top of the old windmill tower in the 1830s. This was undertaken by the newly formed Dumfries and Maxwelltown Astronomical Society for the purpose of saving the windmill, still a prominent landmark, from demolition in 1832."[1] The image projects onto a wooden tabletop, just as in Dr. Reeves' camera obscura. The image is controlled by the use of levers hanging from the ceiling, much like the ones in Dr. Reeves' house.

One of the people who served on the committee for the maintenance of the camera obscura in the 1870s was James Crichton-Browne, neurologist, superintendent of the nearby West Riding Asylum, author of an early work on dreamy state, and an early supporter of humane and enlightened treatment of people with mental illness. He was an employer of John Hughlings Jackson early in Jackson's career.

Michael Powell was not listed as a visitor in the visitor books of the 1930s, as determined by Ms. Turner's kind search. However, in *A Life in Movies*, he writes about brief visits he made to Dumfries. In 1943 when his mother had taken a cottage nearby in the shadow of the Dun, near a waterfall called the Linn:

This break from London to the Lowlands was so precious to me that I would often do it (by train) when I only had 24 hours to turn around in. I would catch the sleeping car express from London at nine o'clock at night and arrive at the Linn [he would walk much of the way from Thornhill to Penpoint to Tynron and beyond] for breakfast the next morning, spend the whole day in the open air and then get a car into Dumfries to catch the express back to London the next night. Sometimes I would go earlier into Dumfries and drop in for tea with John Laurie's two sisters, who kept a clothier's and haberdashery shop on the Square. They were delighted with his performance as Murdock in *Colonel Blimp* but of course being his sisters, they couldn't understand why he hadn't been offered the leading role. I would usually return home with a haggis or a black pudding tucked away somewhere in my rucksack." [2]

I wonder if the reader will be struck by the similarity of the pictures from the Dumfries camera obscura with the scene of Dr. Reeves and his camera obscura.

1. Joanne Turner, Museums Assistant—Collections, Dumfries Museum and Camera Obscura. Personal correspondence, October 7, 2007:

Dear Diane Friedman

Thank you for your enquiry (22 September) regarding the camera obscura here at Dumfries Museum. The camera obscura was installed at the top of the old windmill tower in the 1830s. This was undertaken by the newly formed Dumfries and Maxwelltown Astronomical Society, for the purpose of saving the windmill, still a prominent landmark, from demolition.

Later, a gallery was added to the rear of the tower, to accommodate the artefacts that had begun to accumulate. The Dumfriesshire and Galloway Natural History and Antiquarian Society (DGNHAS) was also involved in the buildings activities by then. Both these organisations collections were housed here and mainly assumed into the care of what is now Dumfries Museum, in the 1930s.

It does not seem unreasonable to suppose that prominent members of the community were associated with one or both of these societies. Add in the local connection with Robert Burns and the Dumfries Burns Club and the cultural landscape of that time was very active. The Mechanics Institute was another such organisation.

The camera obscura has been in operation throughout all this time and local people would know if it. Others in Scotland are of course the one in Edinburgh, and the one at Kirriemuir. The latter was donated to the people of Kirriemuir in 1929 by Sir J. M. Barrie who went to school in Dumfries.

Yes—the camera obscura does project onto a disc table top.

John Laurie was born about two streets from the camera obscura, by the river. He performed at the local theatre with his sister. He must have known of it, but I do not know if he was in a position to influence / inspire Powell's later use of a camera obscura. www.dumgal.gov.uk/museums

2. Powell, Michael, *A Life in Movies* (New York: Alfred A. Knopf, 1986), 445.

K. "The trial takes place tonight, and that's why we must operate tonight." Echoes of Dr. James Collier (1870–1935)

Dr. McEwen said, "Hullo Frank. Anything new?"
"Deterioration all around," Frank said. "We ought to operate tonight!"
"We're swamped. There's no crisis in such a thing. Any day will do."
"No it won't! I'll tell you why it won't and why there is a crisis."

As we have watched a doctor examine someone we love, we have all experienced the delicate moment of wondering what is being seen and what does it all mean. That moment comes in *AMOLAD* when Peter is examined by Dr. Reeves in Dr. Reeves' study after Peter has seen Conductor 71. Dr. Reeves looks into Peter's right eye and then removes the shoe and sock from Peter's left foot and checks a reflex. What Dr. Reeves sees heightens his concern. The momentum of the story intensifies, the film images focus more closely on Peter's face, and the surroundings fade in importance and distinctness. What exactly did Dr. Reeves conclude that leads him to ride his motorcycle in the rain the next morning to the American Base Hospital and tell the surgeon, Dr. McEwen, "There's deterioration all around…we must operate tonight!"

Dr. Reeves concludes through the appearance of Peter's pupil, the abnormality of Peter's Babinski reflex, and Peter's more anxious demeanor, that a critical point is approaching: there are signs of increasing intracranial pressure. That increasing pressure can compress the soft brain tissues against the hard skull, permanently damaging brain areas, sometimes those that control heart beat and respiration. These signs indicate a sudden turn for the worse, and were not apparent mere hours earlier. For me there is a residue here of the influence of James Collier, a British neurologist at the turn of the century.[1] He was not only a researcher but also a significant teacher of neurologists and general internists and the author of a widely read neurology work.

A neurologist in the audience in 1946 might quickly reflect on Collier's paper in *Brain* from 1904, "The false localizing signs of intracranial tumor."[2] He had collected 161 cases from the National Hospital Queen Square during the years 1894–1904 seeking an answer to the question: What made the patient suddenly change?

While surgeons such as William Macewen, Victor Horsley, and others were working out the techniques for successful brain surgery and for correctly localizing the source of problem in the brain, the neurologists and surgeons also needed to understand the problem of timing. Because surgery had the promise of being so much more effective, the new question arose of determining when the patient was running out of time. What process was at work so that a patient might seem unchanged for months or more, and then die suddenly? What can we observe in a patient that will reliably alert us to a sudden deterioration of brain function? What does it mean when abnormal signs come on slowly or disappear?

It is important to recall once again that scientists and physicians at this time had very little technology to draw upon. They used what they had to the fullest; the most fundamental were their skills of careful observation, rigorous and faithful narratives of the events of the patient's illness, and combining that information with surgical and pathological findings. Collier's conclusion was that the sooner one suspected the presence of a brain lesion, the more reliable the deficits were in pointing the way to the source of the problem and the sooner action could be taken.

This finding was not an obvious one in 1904. Already there was a tension between neurologists and surgeons. Which physician, and which specialty—medicine or surgery—would be responsible for the patient's care? Who would determine the diagnosis, and who would determine the timing of the surgery? Would surgery make the patient better or worse?[3] In *AMOLAD*, you see that debate depicted between Dr. Reeves and Dr. McEwen at the Base Hospital, using the real-life findings of Dr. Collier to inform the decision.

At the time of his unexpected death from pneumonia in 1935, Collier had attracted students from other countries for training at Queen Square Hospital because of his inspirational and effective teaching style. In 1930, Collier and his close friend William Adie,[4] a neuro-ophthalmologist also at Queen Square, had written a three-hundred-page "chapter" on diseases of the nervous system within the 1800-page *Textbook of the Practice of Medicine* by Frederic Price.[5] This chapter was so influential to students and physicians that some neurologists, including Macdonald Critchley, bought the book, tore out the neurology chapter and had it bound for personal use.[6] I think that when a neurologist in the audience in 1946 saw that little moment in Dr. Reeves' study, he could have easily thought of Dr. Collier.

Here is a portion of Dr. Collier's chapter referring to complex partial seizures with hallucinations:

> A patient of mine suddenly found himself approaching a level railway-crossing in a picturesque village in high sunlight. Out of a little guard-house on the farther side came a woman dressed in the conical beaver hat and scarlet cloak of the Welsh national dress, who greeted him with a smile. He hastened forward to meet her, but found the gates rapidly closing upon him. As they closed, but before they touched him he

lost consciousness. In this case the hallucination was always the same in every detail...[7]

1. Pearce, J. M. S. "Historical note: James Collier and uncal herniation," *Journal of Neurology Neurosurgery and Psychiatry* 77 (2006): 883–84.

2. Collier, James, "The false localizing signs of intracranial tumor," Brain 27 (1904): 490–508.

3. Pool, J. Lawrence, *Brain Surgeon Anecdotes 1932–1972*, (Connecticut: Rainbow Press, 1992), 22.

4. Adie, W. J., "Tonic pupils and absent tendon reflexes," *Brain* 55 (1932): 98–115.

5. Collier, James and Adie, W. J., "Diseases of the nervous system," in *Textbook of the Practice of Medicine*, edited by Frederic Price (London: Humphrey Milford/Oxford University Press, 1930), 1371–1690.

6. Critchley, Macdonald, "James Collier," *The Black Hole and Other Essays* (London: Pittman Medical Publishers, 1964).

7. Collier and Adie, 1534.

L. The Authors of Two Brain Atlases—William Macewen, John Lizars and Landon Rives and the Names of the Three *AMOLAD* Doctors— Dr. McEwen, Dr. Leiser and Dr. Reeves:

Three loose threads of information may be significant or may be a total coincidence. First, I see a similarity between the names of three of the four physicians named in *AMOLAD* and three surgeons of the 1800s who were responsible for publishing two brain atlases. Second, it appears that an outsized book of the size of a typical brain atlas is visible as a set decoration in Dr. Reeves' study. Third, many historians of neuroscience are uncomfortable with the title of "Father of Modern Neurosurgery" being given to Victor Horsley because William Macewen performed successful brain surgeries in Glasgow before Horsley. Could the names of these characters in *AMOLAD* be a purposeful choice with neurosurgical significance? This could be a coincidence, but I am going to include this information in case another researcher can make something more out of these ideas. I believe that it might not be a coincidence because of Michael Powell's life-long attraction for maps.

John Lizars's (1783-1860) Brain Atlas

An anatomical atlas contains illustrations intended to be as faithful as possible so that a surgeon or researcher can have a reliable guide. An atlas might measure 12 x 24 inches to permit small details to be illustrated. At the time of the first editions of the Lizars atlas in the early 1800s, the need was especially acute because autopsies for medical education were not permitted in England and Scotland.[1] W. H. Lizars was a prominent publisher in Edinburgh. Among many other items, they also published a map of the railway lines in western Scotland.[2] John Lizars was a professor of surgery.

The atlas was republished in Cincinnati in 1854 with an additional editor, Landon Rives, M.D. The color, size, and style of the drawings in the atlas are very similar, although not identical, to paintings used as set decorations in *AMOLAD* and are discussed in the final chapter of this book.

Sir William Macewen (1848-1924), Atlas of Head Sections

Sir William Macewen was revered in Scotland for his surgical talents, adoption and promotion of Joseph Lister's recommendations for asepsis and antiseptic surgical techniques, medical education, and hospital administration.[3-9] Harvey Cushing modeled his structure of scientific reports and data keeping after Macewen.[7] He was trained as a general surgeon, but he performed a number of successful brain operations to treat brain abscesses and meningiomas in 1879, eight years before Victor Horsley's report of ten cases of successful brain surgery. He took some notice of the title of pioneer brain surgeon being given to Victor Horsley, citing Godlee and others in a historical review of Scottish scientific accomplishments for the *ninetieth* meeting of The British Medical Association in Glasgow in 1922.

After service in World War I as Surgeon Rear Admiral, he continued to work both in Glasgow and as superintendent of Erskine Hospital for Limbless Sailors on the River Clyde near the Firth of Forth. Two anecdotes from that period will describe the respect in which he was held by fellow surgeons and patients: [6]

> Macewen was determined...to enlist the interest and help of the Clyde shipbuilders and engineers...who lent not only their technical assistance but also their best tradesmen and craftsmen...to devise a series of artificial limbs to meet practically every need...by

dexterous political maneuvering fortified by his persuasive personality.

The problem of the provision of suitable timber [for prostheses] was a pressing one but Macewen had his own characteristic ways of making good any deficiency. Sir Donald MacAlister has related that, "One day I met Macewen at an outlying part of the university grounds. He was standing before two old trees of no great significance. 'These are willows,' he said. 'We are short of willow timber for artificial limbs at Erskine. Can I have these?' 'I have no objection,' I said, 'and I am sure if you ask, the University court will give them to you if you ask for them.' 'If you are sure of that then I'll ask afterwards." That same afternoon the willows disappeared and no request ever came to the University!"

[A house painter was observed applying his trade with a little awkwardness. When asked he said,] "Why I have no left arm. I left the limb behind me at the Somme. How do I carry on my trade? Sir William Macewen fixed me up. I feel as good as new. In fact my arm is new!"

1. Lizars, John, *A System of Anatomical Plates of the Human body* (Edinburgh: W. H. Lizars and Daniel Lizars, 1822); *Anatomy of the Brain*, edited by Landon Rives (Cincinnati: Derby Publishers, 1856).

2. Lizars W. H., *Lizars' Guide to the Edinburgh and Glasgow, Glasgow, Paisley, Kilmarnock, Ayr, and Greenock Railways*, (Edinburgh: W. H. Lizars, 1842).

3. Macewen, William, *Atlas of Head sections: Fifty-three Engraved Copperplates of Frozen Sections of the Head, and Fifty-three Key Plates with Descriptive Texts* (Glasgow: Maclehose, 1893).

4. Mackey, A. M., "Great teachers of surgery in the past: A sketch of Sir William Macewen," *British Journal of Surgery* 54 (1967):1–7.

5. Macewen, Sir William, "President's address on brain surgery," *The British Medical Journal* (July 29, 1922): 155–65.

6. Bowman, A. K. *The Life and Teaching of Sir William Macewen: A chapter in the history of surgery*, (London: William Hodge and Co., 1942), 390–95.

7. Canale, Dee J. "William Macewen and the treatment of brain abscesses: Revisited after one hundred years," *Journal of Neurosurgery* 84 (1996), 133–42. Quote on 135.

8. Macmillan, Malcolm "Localization and William Macewen's early brain surgery" "Part I: The Controversy," *Journal of the History of the Neurosciences* 13 (2004): 297–325; "Part II: The cases," *Journal of the History of the Neurosciences* 14 (2005): 24–56.

9. Keller, T. M. "Sir William Macewen's visit to California as the first Lane Medical Lecturer, 1896" *Western Journal of Medicine* 165 (1996): 279–82.

M. A Joke in the History of Neurology

In the Heavenly court, Dr. Reeves for the defense argues against Abraham Farlan, the Revolutionary War soldier from Boston, over whose democratic country is preferable. At one point, each counsel turns on his personal radio to illustrate a point from contemporary popular culture.

At this moment (on page 78 of the script), Farlan was to say, "The whole world knows that it takes a surgical operation to get a joke into an Englishman's head." This passage is crossed out. These lines did not appear in the film or in the novelization of the film. Yet this comment has a neurologic significance.

The first brain operation in which neurological symptoms were used to determine the location of the brain problem and guide the surgeon to the correct spot to operate was performed May 25, 1886, in London at the National Hospital Queen Square by Victor Horsley, surgeon, John Hughlings Jackson, neurologist, and David Ferrier, neurophysiologist. When the surgery was completed and all were very pleased with the success of the procedure, Jackson turned to Ferrier:

> The physicians watched the operation with keen interest: and when it was over, Hughlings Jackson let himself enjoy the relaxation of a strained mind. He beckoned to Ferrier: "Awful, perfectly awful," he said. Ferrier was shocked: the operation had seemed to him faultless. Again Hughlings Jackson murmured that an awful mistake had been made. "Here's the first operation of this kind that we have ever had at this hospital: the patient is a Scotsman. We had the chance of getting a joke into his head, and we failed to take advantage of it."[1]

I believe that if a neurologist had heard these lines spoken in the movie, an instant connection to Jackson would have been made. But for an unknown reason, these lines were not spoken in the film. I don't know whether it was because the joke was offensive or simply removed for economy of film running time.

1. Paget, Stephen, *Sir Victor Horsley: A study of his life and work* (London: Constable and Co, 1919), 120. Also described by Taylor, David C. "One Hundred Years of Epilepsy Surgery: Sir Victor Horsley's contribution," in Jerome Engle, Ed., *Surgical Treatment of the Epilepsies* (New York: Raven Press, 1987), 7.

N. Why Chess?

I have found a variety of connections between the game of chess and *AMOLAD*. Some are tangential, but I will include them here in case another researcher would like to pick up the thread.

Vision, Philidor, and Alekhine

Francois-Andre Philidor lived from 1726 to 1795 and was considered the best chess player of his time. He operated a chess club in Paris that attracted a number of prominent people including Diderot, Voltaire, Gibbon, and Talleyrand.[1] This club made chess very fashionable. The French Revolution came as a blow to Philidor, because he was dependent on honorariums from the club. He then moved to London, where he opened another chess club and made the game even more popular there. Alexander Alekhine (1892–1946) was a prominent twentieth-century player who wrote *My 100 Best Games*, but I did not find any details within the book that clearly connect with *AMOLAD*.[2] The only connection I can see with the film and details concerning vision is that both Philidor and Alekhine were famous as blindfolded chess players. Philidor was the first chess player to play blindfolded, while Alekhine once played thirty-nine people simultaneously while blindfolded.[3]

Neuroscience and Philidor

Santiago Ramon y Cajal was a prominent neuroanatomist who lived from 1852 to 1934. He wrote an autobiography, *Recollections of my Life*. In it, he wrote, "I should like to tell here how I freed myself [in 1887, at the age of 33] from a tenacious and inveterate vice, the game of chess, which seriously menaced my evenings. Knowing my fondness for the noble game of Ruy Lopez y Philidor, various members of the *Casino Militar* invited me to join"[4] He described in detail how he became entranced with chess, thinking about moves and strategy every waking moment, progressing until he could play four people at once. His scientific work suffered as his compulsion intensified. How would he free himself from the grip of this game? For one final week, he decided to play every competitor, eventually defeating them all. "Fearful of a relapse I abandoned my place in the casino and did not move a pawn again for twenty-five years…now able to devote [my modest intellect] to the noble worship of science."[4]

Philidor and Phillimore
The reader will recall that when Peter Carter is speaking with Conductor 71 in Dr. Reeves' library, Peter hears that a prosecutor has been assigned to his case. Peter mistakenly believes it is "Phillimore." John Swinnerton Phillimore (1873–1926) was a professor of classics at Glasgow University and a poet who studied at Oxford. He translated Latin poetry, one of Michael Powell's favorite subjects. One poem of Phillimore's, "In a Meadow," is included in the *Oxford Book of English Verse,* a book that Michael Powell carried with him on the Queen Elizabeth, copying out portions of verse for Peter Carter's dialogue, as he made the final changes to the script of *AMOLAD*.[5]

Chess and Chaucer
Geoffrey Chaucer wrote *The Canterbury Tales* and a number of other works. One of those was *The Book of the Duchess,* written in 1368. In one part of this poem, Chaucer wrote about his brother in law, John of Gaunt, and his wife Blanche in an allegory about a knight and his lost love. The *Book of the Duchess* describes how a poet cannot sleep, so he starts reading a tale from Greek mythology about the love of Ceyx and Alcyone and their tragic deaths. Ceyx was a warrior who drowned at sea when the gods heaved a thunderbolt at his vessel. Alcyone was the love of his life who died soon after she saw his dead

body wash up on the beach. (She asked her father Aeolus, god of the winds to help, so he stoppd the winds for seven days. The cessation of winds for a period is now referred to as *Halcyon days*.)[6,7]

The poet reading this story falls asleep over his book and begins to dream about a knight who loved his wife, the White Lady. When she dies, he plays chess with Lady Fortune to try to appeal his wife's fate, although he doesn't succeed.

This story within a story has echoes with *AMOLAD*. Peter Carter, the warrior, should die when his vessel is struck by fire; he falls into the ocean without a parachute and should be drowned; and his body washes up on the beach. His new love June is deeply upset. Luckily, Peter and June are reunited because he didn't die after all. In the black and white portion of the film, Lady Fortune appears, sending Conductor 71 to claim Peter Carter. Later, Peter, who is also a poet (and who the doctor says never sleeps unless the doctor drugs him), is reading in the study. He dozes. Then he has an uncinate seizure, during which he has some dialogue about chess with Conductor 71 and makes plans to appeal his fate.

1. Murray, H.J.R., *A History of Chess* (Oxford: Oxford University Press, 1913), 861.

2. Alekhine, Alexander, *My Best Games of Chess 1908-1937* (New York: Dover Press, 1985).

3. Wikipedia. "Alexander Alekhine," http://en.wikipedia.org/wiki/Alexander_Alekhine "Blindfold Chess," http://en.wikipedia.org/wiki/Blindfold_chess (Accessed March 19, 2008.)

4. Ramon y Cajal, Santiago, *Recollections of My Life* (Cambridge, MA: MIT Press, 1989), 326–28.

5. Quiller-Couch, Arthur, ed. *The Oxford Book of English Verse* (Oxford: Oxford University Press, 1940), 1102.

6. Taylor, M. N., "Chaucer's Knowledge of Chess," The *Chaucer Review* 38, no.4 (2004): 299–313.

7. Chaucer, Geoffrey, "The Book of the Duchess." From *The Modern Reader's Chaucer*, ed. John S. P. Tatlock and Percy MacKaye (New York: Free Press, 1912).

O. "Abraham Farlan! The American War of Independence! Killed by a British bullet!"

Conductor 71 declared these words to Peter Carter as an introduction to the person who would lead the prosecution for Heaven. Having come this far, I am still puzzled about one detail. Michael Powell states that Emeric Pressburger was doing research in the British Museum Reading Room at the same as Michael Powell. They would compare ideas as Pressburger focused on details of the American Revolution.[1] "He [the first person to be killed] was a school teacher, Michael. He was the first American to be killed by a British bullet in the Revolutionary War." In the script, it is emphatically stated that Abraham Farlan was the first person to be killed by a British bullet. Unfortunately, I have not been able to come to the same finding.

I have spent time looking through the Revolutionary War collections at the Public Libraries of Lexington and Concord, Massachusetts, but I could not find any reference to the name "Abraham Farlan" as having participated in or being wounded or killed in either the Boston Massacre (March 7, 1770) or the Battles of Lexington and Concord (April 19, 1775). I found no reference to "Farlan" as I read the extensive listings of families from Massachusetts involved in the American Revolution, listings from which the Daughters of the American Revolution draw their information. Reviewing the book *The battle of April 19, 1775 in Lexington, Concord, Lincoln, Arlington, Cambridge, Somerville and Charlestown Massachusetts*, written in 1912, there is no mention of Farlan's name or any one with a name that resembles it. In this book, the name of each participating American from each muster roll is listed individually. The killed and wounded are listed separately.[3] The forward to the book, dated March 19, 1912, states, "I am glad to add that the bitterness and hatred, so much in evidence on that long-ago battle day, no longer exist between the children of the great British nation [and America]."

I also looked at *The Boston Massacre* by Hiller B. Zobel. The names of the people shot and killed on March 7, 1770, were Crispus Attics, Samuel Maverick, James Caldwell, and Samuel Gray.[4] In reading this history, it is a sad realization of these times and events to imagine these British troops caught in an impossible situation. The situations are reminiscent of modern conflicts.

1. Powell, Michael, *A Life in Movies*, 459

2. Coburn, Frank Warren, *The battle of April 19, 1775 in Lexington, Concord, Lincoln, Arlington, Cambridge, Somerville and Charlestown Massachusetts* (Lexington Mass: self-published, 1912). The Lexington, Massachusetts library has copy 10/160.

3. Ibid., 157–58.

4. Zobel, Hillier B., *The Boston Massacre* (New York: W. W. Norton, 1970).

APPENDIX II:

Some Additional Neurologic Ideas

What follows is a small section containing neurologic writing I came across in preparation for this book. They do not directly support my main discussion about the film. But I believe they add richness concerning the thinking that went on at the time between 1850 and 1950. When we read works from that time, it is important to recall that they represent a crystallization of ideas and impressions that had arisen from the fabric of preceding years or decades. These passages express a wish to see into the future, a novel solution to a current problem, or a fresh snapshot of that day. When I came across these ideas, I did not want to lose track of them.

• •

Excerpts from *Brain Surgeon Anecdotes 1932-1972*, written by J. Lawrence Pool (Torrington, Connecticut: Rainbow Press, 1994)

Pg. 25:
[Dr. Pool, talking about the prodigious work and influence of Dr. Cushing with L. Eisenhardt in their book *Meningiomas: Their classification regional behavior and surgical results* C.C. Thomas (Springfield, IL: C.C. Thomas, 1938) 785 pages.]:

"During the grimmest part of the war, my friend Dr. Louis Pouyanne of Bordeaux explained, 'The Nazis imposed a curfew on my city, decreeing that everyone stay off the streets from six in the evening until nine the next morning. Why not use those hours of house arrest for some useful purpose? So I translated *Meningiomas* into French. As I did so I realized that Cushing had been waging a war—a war against meningiomas, and that in spite of grim defeats at first he had finally achieved victory. I said to myself: This is an example of American spirit and determination. It tells me that American help will win the war for the Allies. For two long years this thought kept me going.'"

Pg. 3–4

[In 1947, Pool, based in New York City was asked to go out to Long Island to perform brain surgery on a 65-year-old man, a very wealthy man's butler, who had been hit by a car. At surgery, Dr. Pool found a characteristically horseshoe-shaped scar, evidence of earlier brain surgery.]

"Two days after my operation (in 1947), the patient had fully recovered his senses and was up and about. I now asked him when, why, and by whom his head had been operated on.

"'Oh naow that you arsk,' said he with a Cockney accent, 'hit was done when I was but a lad of heighten or so and at work in dear old London. The hoperation must 'ave been done in the year nineteen 'undred or about that toime. Why? Because I used to 'ave fits--lot's of 'em. Just about cured 'em too. 'Ardly 'ad any since.'

"'Do you remember who operated on you?'

"'Indeed I do. 'Ow could I forget? 'Is nyme was 'Orsley—Mister Victor 'Orsley 'e was, until 'e got to be Sir Victor.'"

A happy twist to the story of my butler patient was the thrill it gave me to have operated on a person who had once been cared for by the father of modern neurosurgery. It gave me the humble feeling that I had momentarily been in vicarious contact with Sir Victor and had perhaps been touched by the outstretched finger tip of that great pioneer in the way a certain Finger Tip on the Ceiling of the Sistine Chapel touches a mere mortal. It is more likely, however, that Sir Victor's finger would have given me a good poke for entertaining such a brash thought."

• •

Wilder Penfield, in *Epilepsy and Cerebral Localization*, 1941, found this idea by Jacob Henle meaningful.
From the *Life of Jacob Henle* by Victor Robinson (New York: Medical Life Company, 1921), 113.
Jacob Henle had this to say in his 1846 *Handbook of Rational Pathology*:

"The day of the last hypothesis would also be the day of the last observation. A hypothesis which leaves dispossessed by new facts dies an honorable death; and if it has already called up for examination those truths by which it was annihilated, it deserves a moment of gratitude."

• •

I can imagine that Michael Powell would find very evocative the following comments by Sherrington, recalled by Macdonald Critchley in his Harverian Oration and reprinted in *The Banquet of the Brain and Other Essays* (New York: Raven Press, 1979, pg. 267):

"Wonder of wonders, though familiar even to boredom. So much with us that we forget it all our time. The eye sends into the cell-and-fibre forest of the brain throughout the waking day continual streams of tiny, individually evanescent, electrical potentials. This throbbing streaming crowd of electrified shifting points in the in the sponge-work of the brain bears no obvious semblance in space-pattern and even in temporal relation resembles but a little remotely, the tiny two-dimensional upside-down picture of the outside world which the eye ball paints on the beginnings of its nerve-fibres to the brain. But that little picture sets up an electrical storm. And that electrical storm so set up is one which affects a whole population of brain-cells. Electrical charges have in themselves not the faintest elements of the visual—having for instance, nothing of 'distance,' 'right-side-upness,' nor 'vertical,' nor 'horizontal,' nor 'colour,' nor 'brightness,' nor 'shadow,' nor 'roundness,' nor 'squareness,' nor 'contour,' nor 'transparency', nor 'opacity,' nor 'near,' nor 'far,' nor visual anything—yet conjure up all these. A shower of little electrical leaks conjures up for me, when I look at the landscape; the castle on the height; or, when I look at him, my friend's face, and how distant he is from me, they tell me. Taking their word for it, I go forward and my other senses confirm that he is there."

• •

Leeson, John Rudd, *Lister As I Knew Him* (New York: William Wood, 1927), 182–87.

[Lister developed his practice of antisepsis in Edinburgh, drawing on the research of Pasteur and others. For his pioneering work, Lister was held in the highest regard not only in Scotland, but also in Germany and France. Lister proved that microbes associated with trauma and surgery could be permanently abolished and with that, the products of infection. One of his lines of evidence were three sealed large beakers of urine, sterilized by heat 10 years previously, which still had no evidence of infection. But the practice of antisepsis had not made its way to London. Aspects of surgery—including hand washing, sterile instruments, clean hospital dress for nurses and surgeons, and sterile operating theatres—had not been adopted. These aspects were thought by many London surgeons of the day to be silly. Infection and death were thought to be inevitable in many cases.]

"[In London] in February 1877 Sir William Fergusson died. For over thirty years he had been professor of surgery at King's College London. The authorities of King's College in the choice of a successor turned to Lister [in Edinburgh]...The removal of his antiseptic treasures to London was a serious and perplexing problem, particularly those three flasks of boiled urine of which I have spoken...He told me the only method he could devise was to carry them upon his knees; so for four hundred miles he and Mrs. Lister journeyed in a specially reserved first-class carriage bearing these strange treasures upon their laps, their attention riveted to every jog and jostle to counteract each serious shake or menacing splash. Those who have made the long journey under ordinary circumstances know how wearying it is but to have it augmented by unremitting attention upon three vibrating flasks of epoch-making fluid for ten consecutive hours is a feat of endurance few could have achieved. However, they survived and biogenesis survives them all...His reception at King's College was cold in the extreme. At his introductory lectures the students were bored and after the uncouth manners of the times, actually shuffled their feet to express their impatience...It must have been a sad contrast, the apathy and indifference. He was no longer revered [in Edinburgh] as the founder of a new system that was to revolutionize surgery, but was regarded as a crank who was crazed upon exploiting a method that acknowledged heads of the profession [in London] rejected..."

• •

The Diagnosis of Nervous Diseases by Sir James Purves-Stewart, ninth ed. (Baltimore: Williams and Wilkins Co, 1945)

Pg. vii
"Even this book has had its modest war adventures. In 1939 and 1943 I traveled to the United States of America to study American neurological methods. I collected a number of fresh references and new illustrations. Alas! They were destined never to appear. During

the voyage back to England all my manuscripts were sunk in Mid-Atlantic by enemy action. I myself happening to travel in another ship, had a fortunate escape…

Returning to my native land, I found my old Lighthouse home on the Sussex cliffs reduced by shell-fire to a heap of rubble. I then became a war refugee for over two years in Kilmarnock, a Scottish country town…"

Appendix III:

For Further Reading

Epilepsy:

The British Epilepsy Association http://www.epilepsy.org.uk/
Epilepsy Foundation of America http://www.epilepsyfoundation.org/

Leppik, Ilo, *Epilepsy: A guide to balancing your life* (New York: Demos Medical Publications, 2006).

Wyllie, Elaine, Gupta, Ajay, Lachwani, Deepak K., *The Treatment of Epilepsy: Principles and practice* (Philadelphia: Lippincott, Williams & Wilkins, 2006).

Wyllie, Elaine, *Epilepsy: Information for you and those who care about you* (Cleveland: Cleveland Clinic Press, 2008).

Michael Powell and Emeric Pressburger:

Dumfries Museum and Camera Obscura http://www.dumgal.gov.uk/museums

The Powell and Pressburger pages http://www.powell-pressburger.org/

Ashridge http://www.berkhamsted.info/localhistoryashridgethehospital.htm

Christie, Ian, editor, *Powell, Pressburger and Others*, (London: British Film Institute, 1978).

Christie, Ian, *A Matter of Life and Death* (London: BFI, 2000).

Gough-Yates, Kevin, *Michael Powell in Collaboration with Emeric Pressburger* (London: John Player and Sons, 1971).

Lazar, David, editor, *Michael Powell Interviews*. (Jackson: University of Mississippi Press, 2003).

Macdonald, Kevin, *Emeric Pressburger: The life and death of a screen writer*, (London: Faber and Faber, 1994).

Powell, Michael, *The Edge of the World: The making of a film (200,000 Feet on Foula)*, published 1938. (London: Faber and Faber, 1990).

Powell, Michael, *A Life in Movies*. (New York: Knopf, 1987).

Books of Interest in Medical History:

Bliss, Michael, *Harvey Cushing: A Life in Surgery* (Oxford: Oxford University Press 2005.)

Bowman, A. J., *The Life and Teaching of Sir William Macewen* (London: William Hodge and Co., 1942).

Critchley, Macdonald, *The Citadel of the Senses*, (New York: Raven Press, 1986).

Fraenkel, G.J., *Hugh Cairns* (Oxford: Oxford University Press 1991).

Leeson, John Rudd, *Lister As I Knew Him* (New York: William Wood, 1927).

Penfield, W., Erickson, T. C., *Epilepsy and Cerebral Localization* (Springfield: C. C.Thomas, 1941).

Penfield, Wilder, *No Man Alone* (Boston: Little Brown and Co. 1977).

Pool, J. Lawrence, *Brain Surgeon Anecdotes 1932–1972* (Torrington CT: Rainbow Press, 1994).

Rose, F. Clifford, *Twentieth Century Neurology: The British Contribution* (London: Imperial College Press, 2001).

Sherrington, Charles S., *The Integrative Activity of the Nervous System* (New York: Charles Scribner's Sons, 1906).

Sherrington, Charles S., *Man on his Nature: Gifford Lectures 1937–8* (Cambridge: The University Press, 1940).

Truax, Rhoda, *Joseph Lister: Father of Modern Surgery* (Cornwall NY: Cornwall Press, 1944).

Appendix IV:

"Chiasmal Arachnoiditis" by A.J.B. Goldsmith

Transillumination threw an opaque shadow in the upper part of the globe. The peripheral visual field was full, but there was a scotoma corresponding to the affected area of the retina. There was a shallow detachment of the lower part of the retina.

General medical examination.—No evidence of metastases found. X-ray of skull and chest normal. Ear, nose and throat examination negative. *Diagnosis.*—Choroidal sarcoma in right eye.

Discussion.—The PRESIDENT said that he thought S/Ldr. Cashell's case was one of malignant melanoma and should be excised.

S/Ldr. CASHELL said that a similar case was shown by Air Commodore Livingston; this was taken to be innocent, but later the growth increased and the eye had to be excised. It was found to contain a neoplasm.

Mr. G. W. BLACK said that he would like explored the relationship between the swelling and the history of injury. He had lately seen a case in a man aged 22 who had attended a neighbouring hospital following a blow on his eye from a large missile. He was treated for a time and then one day it was discovered that the vision was very dim. When he first saw the patient he had a large sarcoma.

Chiasmal Arachnoiditis

By A. J. B. GOLDSMITH, F.R.C.S.

THE inclusion of arachnoiditis among diseases giving rise to the chiasmal syndrome is comparatively recent, and is due to the rapid advances made by neuro-surgery during and since the last war. Quincke in 1893 described the condition of generalized serous meningitis, or idiopathic internal hydrocephalus, the symptoms of which resemble those of tumour or meningitis but differ from these diseases in that repeated lumbar punctures afford good prospects of alleviation or even cure. Since then there has developed the conception of external hydrocephalus due to diffuse or localized chronic leptomeningitis. The later or localized serous meningitis may occur on the surface of the brain or in and around the basal cisternæ.

Horrax in 1924 from Cushing's clinic described 33 cases of arachnoiditis of the posterior fossa simulating cerebellar tumour, but it was not until 1929 that Cushing and Eisenhardt included arachnoiditis in the differential diagnosis of chiasmal lesions. In the same year, at the Amsterdam Congress, Gordon Holmes reported two cases of chronic localized basal cystic arachnoiditis comparable to chronic localized spinal meningitis and due to trauma or inflammation. These two cases had been operated on by Sargent on account of progressive failure of vision, and both had shown marked functional improvement. Further cases were described by Cushing in 1930 and by Craig and Lillie in 1931. The subject was fully reviewed in a study by Bollach, David and Puesch published by the French Ophthalmic Society in 1937, from which most of my knowledge has been derived. In that paper 63 cases were collected from the literature and a further 66 were added which had been operated on by Clovis Vincent and his assistants at the Hôpital de la Pitié.

The disease appears to be either rare or to have attracted little attention in this country. Hinds-Howell in his Presidential Address to the Section of Neurology in 1936 said that these cases must be sought for and that search was worth while, for, on the whole, operation results were strikingly good. Williamson-Noble in the Doyne Memorial Lecture in 1939 discussed the condition among chiasmal lesions.

In the past year while working in Mr. McKissock's neuro-surgical unit I have seen three cases, all of which have been operated on. The series is small compared with the numbers collected by the French workers, but I have thought it worth recording them. One which followed an air raid injury is of some topical interest, and the results of surgical treatment have been at least encouraging. It may be argued that the diagnosis and treatment of these cases lies more in the sphere of the neurologist, the rhinologist or the neuro-surgeon, but even if we cannot afford, like Bacon, to take all knowledge to be our province, the subject is of some importance to us in that the first complaint, that of failing vision, will bring the patient to the ophthalmologist. Further, the findings of perimetry and campimetry and the fundus appearances, though, as we shall see, by no means pathognomonic, may suggest the diagnosis.

I shall describe the three cases which we have dealt with first, and then discuss briefly the main features of the disease and the views which are held as to its ætiology.

The first patient was a woman, M. H., admitted to hospital in April 1942. She was aged 32, married, no children, occupation—house-work, formerly a worker in an aircraft factory. There was nothing in her family history nor in her personal history except for a motor-cycle accident fourteen years ago following which she was unconscious for twelve hours, but suffered no sequelæ. In 1939 she began to have attacks of violent frontal and temporal headaches, worse with coughing and sneezing, and associated with vomiting and giddiness. These attacks lasted for two to three days and recurred at intervals of about ten days. Her menses ceased at about the same time and had not returned. On admission she was still having attacks of headache, but they were less severe. In September 1941 when starting work in an aircraft factory she found that her right vision was seriously defective, and had since noticed a progressive deterioration in her left eye also. Other symptoms elicited by questioning were that for several months she had noticed increased appetite and thirst, polyuria and lack of energy.

On examination she was a rather obese woman showing a normal hair distribution. The ocular findings were: A slight divergent right squint with no limitation of movement; pupils equal and reacting normally; the optic discs showed well-marked temporal pallor, especially in the right eye, the disc margins being clear cut and the vessels of normal size. The visual acuity was R. H.M.s; L. 6/36. The right visual field showed a large complete central scotoma to a 20/330 white object. The left field was full to 5 and 1 mm. object on the perimeter, but on the screen there was a temporal hemianopia to a 1/2,000 white object; temporal contraction to a 2/2,000 object as well as a concentric contraction of the nasal field to both these objects. For the rest, there was no abnormality of any part of the C.N.S. nor of her condition generally. X-rays showed a normal sella turcica. Clinical and radiological examination of the nasal sinuses was negative. The C.S.F. showed a normal pressure, chemistry and cell content, and the W.R. of blood and C.S.F. was negative.

The ocular findings suggested a pituitary lesion, particularly taken in conjunction with the symptoms of polyuria, polydipsia, polyphagia and obesity. However, ventriculograms taken after replacement of ventricular fluid by air revealed no evidence of a space-occupying lesion in the neighbourhood of the floor of the third ventricle.

We therefore considered the possibility of arachnoiditis as a cause of the symptoms, and in view of the progressive loss of vision it was felt that an exploratory operation was justified. Mr. McKissock operated on May 5, 1942. A right frontal osteoplastic flap hinged on the temporalis muscle was turned down, the ventricular fluid was evacuated through a brain needle and the dura was stripped off the roof of the right orbit. After division of the dura along the edge of the lesser wing of the sphenoid the chiasmal region was exposed. It was found that the nerves and chiasm were much pinker than normal and that masses of fine avascular meningeal adhesions were present binding the optic nerves to the overlying brain, to the internal carotid, to the diaphragma sellæ and to the anterior part of the chiasm. In addition a thick band of avascular adhesions stretched between the chiasm and the brain. All adhesions were very carefully divided by blunt dissection. There was no hæmorrhage, and no evidence of tumour was seen in the operation field.

Convalescence was uneventful. On May 6, two days after operation, the right vision had improved from hand movements to 5/60 and the left from 6/36 to 5/12. Seven days after operation the patient was up, and I plotted the visual fields. The right eye was then full to 20 and 5 mm. objects on the perimeter, but showed concentric contraction to small objects and a small central scotoma to a 2/2,000 object on the screen. The left eye showed only a slight temporal contraction to small objects on the screen.

Three weeks after operation the vision was: R. 6/60; L. 6/12, and with a small astigmatic correction: R. 6/36; L. 6/9. The visual fields showed no further alteration.

This patient was seen again at the end of September, five months after operation. There had been no deterioration in vision, her headaches were relieved and symptoms of polyuria, polydipsia and polyphagia had cleared up, and her menses had restarted. She had a right-sided anosmia, an almost inevitable result of the operative disturbance.

I did colour fields in all these cases, and while there was contraction of the fields to red and green, the results were no more informative than with the varied sizes of white objects used.

The second case was a man aged 38, a Czechoslovak corporal in the R.A.F. There was nothing relevant in either his family or personal history and he had been perfectly well until June 16, 1941, when he was struck on the right temple by a fragment of shrapnel during a bombing attack on his aerodrome. He sustained a superficial wound and was unconscious for twelve hours. On recovering consciousness he found that with his right eye he could see his hand only when it was held close to his face although the left was unaffected. We could not obtain any information as to his ocular condition at that time. He was kept in bed for seven weeks, after which he suffered from headaches and had a tendency to fall to the left. Since that time he has noticed no change in the right eye, but there has been a progressive deterioration of the left.

When examined on admission to hospital in April 1942 the ocular movements were full and the pupil reactions normal. The right fundus showed generalized pallor of the disc, which was whitish in colour and had clear-cut margins. The vessels were normal in size. The left fundus was normal. The right vision was H.M.s (hand movements); the left 6/60. In the visual fields, the right could be examined only by confrontation with hand movements and appeared grossly contracted. The left, to perimetry, showed a marked pure concentric contraction without scotomata.

In the general examination of the C.N.S. he had right anosmia, partial anæsthesia

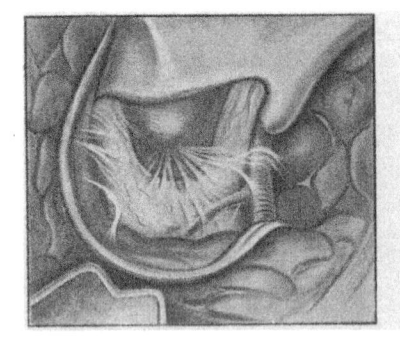

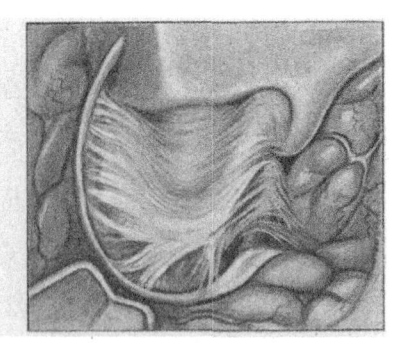

FIGS. 1 and 2.—Arachnoid adhesions involving the dorsum sellæ, optic and olfactory nerves, chiasm and brain.

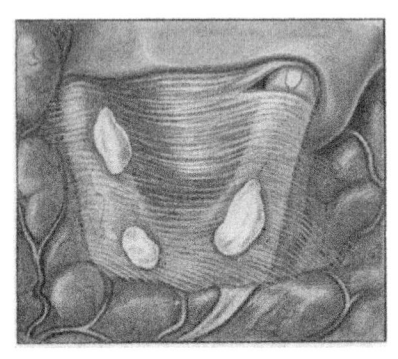

FIG. 3.—Arachnoid adhesions with small calcareous plaques.

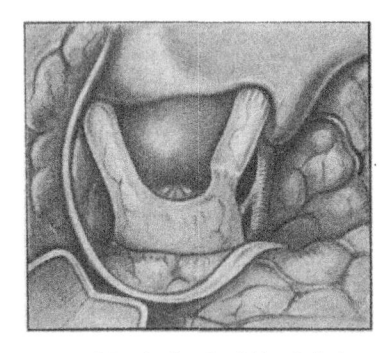

FIG. 4.—Chiasmal region after division of adhesions showing increased vascularity and also compression of the right optic nerve.

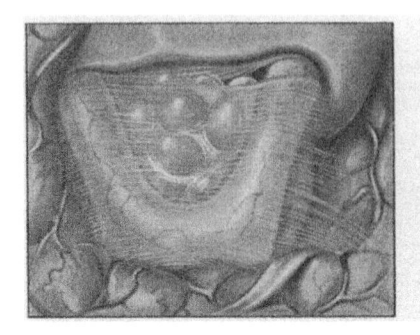

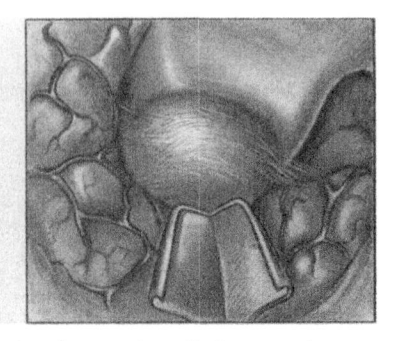

FIGS. 5 and 6.—Types with cyst formation. 5 showing multiple small cysts; 6 a large unilocular cyst concealing the nerves and chiasm.

With acknowledgment to " Les Arachnoidites Opto-chiasmatiques ", by Bollach, David and Puesch, Paris, 1937.

1. *J. B. GOLDSMITH : Chiasmal Arachnoiditis*

FEB.—OPHTH. 2

of the first and second divisions of the right fifth nerve, and a partial involvement of the right eighth nerve with some unsteadiness of gait. The X-ray findings were inconclusive and suggested a fracture of the posterior wall of the right frontal sinus running into the anterior ethmoidal cells.

The history and findings here suggested a progressive involvement of the left optic nerve, probably resulting from scar tissue, and operation was thought to be justifiable. Mr. McKissock operated in May, the exposure being the same as in the previous case. He found adhesions between the brain of the frontal lobe and the dorsum sellæ. The right optic nerve was covered by small convoluted vessels and had adhesions binding it to the brain, carotid, chiasm and left optic nerve. There was a loculated collection of fluid between the right nerve and the carotid artery. The left optic nerve and chiasm were similarly surrounded by adhesions, all of which were carefully divided by blunt dissection.

His convalescence also was uneventful, but improvement in his sight, which has been very marked, was less dramatic than in the first case. One week after operation the right vision was H.M.s; left 6/36. After one month the right vision was 6/60; left 6/12. After ten weeks the right vision was still 6/60, and the left 6/9. Last month, five months after operation, the right vision was the same, but the left had improved still further to 6/5 partly. The right visual field is grossly contracted, but the left has shown a gradual opening out paralleling the improvement in his vision, and is now practically normal.

The third patient was a man of 38, a G.P.O. telephonist, who discovered twelve months before admission that his right eye was weak. He had then consulted an optician and had been comforted by reassurances and a pair of glasses. He gave a history of having been knocked down in the black-out some four months prior to this, when he had been very dazed but not unconscious. He had also had severe headaches for the past year, and had noticed that his left eye had been failing for several months. There was nothing relevant in his family or personal history, nor in his habits.

On ocular examination the only positive findings were some 1·5 D of swelling of both discs without optic atrophy, and reduction of vision in the right eye to H.M.s, and in the left to 6/60. The visual fields in both eyes were full peripherally to 5/330 objects, but in the right eye there was a large central scotoma to 20/330, and in the left eye a small central scotoma to 5/2,000.

Examination of the C.N.S. and of his general condition was negative. X-rays and ventriculography showed a normal sella turcica and no evidence of a space-occupying lesion in the pituitary region. Clinical and X-ray examination of the accessory sinuses was negative as were the W.R. in blood and C.S.F. C.S.F. pressure and chemistry were normal. There was no history to suggest intoxication by tobacco or other poisons.

Here again in view of the length of history and of the negative findings of ventriculography the most probable cause of this man's visual defect was thought to be a chiasmal arachnoiditis, and Mr. McKissock operated in June 1942. The nerves and chiasm were markedly pink and masses of fine adhesions were present involving both optic nerves, the chiasm and the overlying brain. These were carefully divided as in the previous cases, and the wound was closed. Convalescence was again entirely uneventful. The papillœdema subsided rapidly, but unfortunately the patient since operation has shown a progressive deterioration in vision, and in the past few weeks has developed a marked temporal pallor of both discs. The vision in each eye is now only H.M.s, there is concentric contraction of the fields, and absolute central scotomata extending some 15° round the fixation point are present in each eye.

The types of lesion found in chiasmal arachnoiditis are fairly well exemplified in these cases. Arachnoid adhesions bind the optic nerves and chiasm to the brain, to each other, to the great vessels and to the dorsum sellæ. Congestion of vessels is usually present, though the adhesions are often avascular. In the most advanced cases small calcareous plaques have been described. In addition, as in the second case, cysts may be present resulting from loculation of fluid between the adhesions. The nerves themselves may be atrophic or œdematous, or kinked by bands, or show simple congestion. Pathological examination has shown thickening of the pia and arachnoid, vascularity, infiltration by lymphocytes and demyelination and atrophy of peripheral and central nerve fibres. The mechanism by which vision is affected is not entirely clear. It may be that the arachnoiditis and visual disturbances are separate manifestations of an infection, that the arachnoiditis is secondary to a lesion of the nerve fibres, or that visual loss is due to the meningeal changes. The improvement effected by operation suggests that the last is the most likely factor, and if this be so the arachnoiditis may act either mechanically by the direct pressure of adhesions or cysts or indirectly by compression or by causing spasm of blood-vessels.

Causes of the inflammatory changes.—Arachnoiditis is a common concomitant of tumours and occurs in close proximity to them. The type we are discussing arises *de novo* and in these cases tumour has been excluded by operation or ventriculography. Owing to their propinquity the accessory nasal sinuses have been indicted as the source of a low grade chronic infection either by direct spread or via lymphatics. As Cushing has pointed out sinusitis may cause meningeal reactions in the chiasmal space just as middle-ear infections can cause reactions in the middle or posterior fossæ, and a meningeal inflammation once started may survive the infection which gives rise to it. Secondly syphilis, excluding tabes, figures as the presumed cause in some 15% of the cases in the French series. The chiasmal lesions here form part of the generalized leptomeningitis for which at any rate preliminary medical treatment is indicated. Schiff-Wertheimer has pointed out that meningeal adhesions around the optic nerves are common in tabetic atrophy, and has reported some cases that have been improved by division of these adhesions. Thirdly, other infections, such as localized tuberculosis or residual meningeal lesions may affect the chiasm, or the disintegration products of pathological processes in the C.N.S may set up an aseptic inflammation. Finally, trauma appeared to be an operative factor in the second case I have reported, and in the two cases described by Gordon Holmes in 1929. In the French series it figures in 10% of cases. The nature, intensity and point of application of the injury appear unimportant, and in view of the large number of cases of head injury that are seen and the small proportion that develop this trouble it would seem that injury *per se*, acts as a predisposing rather than an exciting cause.

The incidence as given by the French authors is surprisingly high. Of 254 exploratory operations performed on the chiasmal region between 1930 and 1936, 71 cases or 27% were of primary arachnoiditis, and this series does not include presumed cases treated medically. The disease is one of adult life, 60% of cases occurring between the ages of 20 and 40, and males are more commonly affected than females, the ratio being almost 2:1.

The ocular symptoms are usually early and important, but there is no diagnostic pattern. An early complaint is of loss of visual acuity, which may be sudden or gradual and may progress either evenly or with sudden relapses to complete blindness. It is usually unilateral at the start with the second eye failing weeks or months afterwards. The findings of perimetry, as might be expected from the extent of the visual pathway affected, are very variable. In the French series of 129 cases central scotoma was the commonest finding, in 31% of cases, concentric contraction in 23%, temporal loss in 17%, while the other cases showed nasal or horizontal loss or homonymous hemianopia. Temporal hemichromatopsia, common in tumour cases, is said not to occur in arachnoiditis. The fundus appearances also are variable. The French series show primary optic atrophy to be the commonest finding, followed by post-papillitic atrophy, papillœdema and then temporal pallor. In about 10% of cases the fundi are normal. Other ocular signs are rare except in syphilitic cases. Extra-ocular symptoms include severe headache, which as in our first case may precede the eye signs. There may also be symptoms referable to involvement of the infundibulum such as increased appetite, thirst and polyuria, obesity or adiposo-genital dystrophy. General neurological examination is usually entirely negative, as are X-ray of the sella, and ventriculography.

Diagnosis, therefore, is a matter of elimination and involves co-operation between the neuro-surgeon, the rhinologist and the oculist. It is in general based on: (1) Signs of chiasmal or neural involvement. (2) The presence of ætiological factors. (3) The capricious progress with successive exacerbations. (4) The negative findings of X-ray and C.S.F. examinations. Space does not permit of a detailed discussion of the differential diagnosis. Of non-tumour conditions the retrobulbar neuritis of disseminated sclerosis is excluded fairly easily by the pupil reactions, the early functional recovery, disproportion between the functional recovery and the degree of optic atrophy and other factors. Devic's and Schilder's diseases present a typical course after their initial onset. Toxic neuritis is bilateral in its onset and steadily progressive; the fundus remains normal for some time and the ætiological factor is usually discoverable. Except in the early stages of tabes other signs of this disease are present, and the W.R. is helpful. Leber's disease is hereditary and familial and does not progress to complete blindness. Other conditions in this group to be excluded are syphilitic basal meningitis, vascular atrophy and the optic neuritis due to sinusitis. This last debatable condition presents considerable difficulty, but in cases in which clinical sinusitis is present its treatment should obviously precede any exploration of the chiasmal region. Tumourous conditions such as meningeomata of the olfactory groove, lesser wing of the sphenoid or of the dorsum sellæ, frontal gliomata, pituitary adenomata and craniopharyngiomata, are excluded by X-rays and ventriculography.

TREATMENT

Chiasmal arachnoiditis is not a homogenous group; its ætiology is doubtful, and diagnosis is often not made until the late stages and even then is usually confirmed only by operation.

For medical treatment mercury and iodides have been suggested on general grounds, whether or not the cases are syphilitic. The treatment of infection in the nasal sinuses is of importance, but the efficacy of medical or rhinological treatment will depend on the anatomical conditions around the nerves and chiasm. If these are still in the stage only of œdema or vascular spasm, resolution is possible, but with definite cicatrization it is difficult to see what benefit will accrue.

Direct surgical intervention has passed through two stages, the first an incidental one in the exploration of a supposed tumour, the second, elaborated by Vincent, undertaken as a definite therapeutic measure with the object of freeing all adhesions present. This must, of course, be done as carefully as possible to avoid forming a starting point for fresh adhesions.

Mortality from the operation in skilled hands is small. In Vincent and Puesch's series there were seven deaths in 95 cases of operation on this region, of which three occurred before their operative technique had been fully elaborated. Of the survivors 28% showed permanent improvement of vision. It is pointed out that many cases show an immediate improvement followed after three to four weeks by progressive deterioration, but that relapses later than one month after operation are rare. It would seem advisable to continue the treatment of any particular ætiological factor found, such as sinusitis or neurovascular syphilis, after the direct attack on the chiasmal region.

The improvement is seen, as in our first two cases, in the visual acuity and the fields of vision. The fundi except in cases with papillœdema show no change, as one would expect. The extraocular symptoms of headache and diabetes insipidus are usually much ameliorated. A permanent anosmia usually confined to the right side, results from the operation, but if successful most patients will agree that recovery of function in the second cranial nerve will compensate for its loss in the first.

While the French authors are most enthusiastic about the prospects surgery holds out for this condition, our knowledge of its pathogenesis and diagnosis does not yet rest on sure foundations, and much remains to be elucidated especially in regard to its relationship to nasal sinusitis. The presence of arachnoid adhesions has been described in Leber's disease and, as I have mentioned, in tabes dorsalis. To what extent their action can be blamed for the visual loss in these diseases yet remains to be worked out.

In conclusion I must express my thanks to my colleague, Mr. Wylie McKissock, in whose department these cases were investigated and treated and who has allowed me to make use of his case records and operation notes.

REFERENCES

BOLLACH, DAVID, and PUESCH (1937) Les Arachnoidites Opto-chiasmatiques, Paris.
CRAIG and LILLIE (1931) *Arch. Ophthal.*, N.Y., **5,** 558.
CUSHING (1930) *Arch. Ophthal.*, N.Y., **3,** 505.
—— and EISENHARDT (1929) *Arch. Ophthal.*, N.Y., **1,** 1 and 168.
HINDS-HOWELL (1936) *Proc. R. Soc. Med.*, **30,** 33.
HOLMES (1929) *13th Int. Ophthal. Congr.*, **3,** 65.
HORRAX (1924) *Arch. Surg.*, **9,** 95, Chicago.
SCHIFF-WERTHEIMER (1932) *Bull. Soc. Ophtal. Paris*, **44** (in Supp.), 1.
WILLIAMSON-NOBLE (1939) *Trans. Ophthal. Soc. U.K.*, **59,** 627.

Goldsmith, A.J.B "Chiasmal Arachnoiditis," Proceedings of the Royal Society of Medicine (1943, xxxvi): 163-68. Article reproduced with permission of the Royal Society of Medicine Press, London.

Appendix V:

Emeric Pressburger's application for the British Museum Reading Room

Emeric Pressburger's application to use the British Museum Reading Room May 1938. Reproduced with the kind permission of the British Museum.

30, Ascot Court,
Grove End Road,
N.W.8.

8th March, 1938.

The Director,
British Museum,
W.C.1.

Dear Sir,

Would you kindly let me have a ticket of admission to the Reading Room of the Museum. As a film scenario writer I frequently need during the course of my work to refer to various works of reference on divers subjects. I enclose a letter of recommendation from Mr. Stapenhorst of London Film Productions Limited.

Yours faithfully,

Emmerich Pressburger.

LONDON FILM PRODUCTIONS LIMITED
DENHAM   UXBRIDGE   MIDDLESEX

Telegrams: Londufilm Telex Denham   Cablegrams: Londufilm Denham
Telephone: Denham 2345

Directors:
Alexander Korda (Hungarian), Chairman and Managing Director,
Sir Connop Guthrie, Bart., K.B.E.,
H. A. Holmes,   John Richard Sucro,
E. H. George,   C. Holmes Brand.

8th March, 1938.

The Director,
British Museum,
W.C.1.

Dear Sir,

The writer of the enclosed letter, Emmerich Pressburger, is personally known to me: I confirm his statement and can recommend him as a suitable person to have the use of the Museum Reading Room.

Yours faithfully,

Film Producer.

NEW YORK: 720 Seventh Avenue.   PARIS: 61 Avenue Victor Emmanuel III.   BERLIN: 10 Friedrichstrasse.   ROME: 48 Via Firenze.

Index

A

A Canterbury Tale   10, 50, 51, 93, 94, 95, 118
A Journey 'Round My Skull   24, 102-9, 180
Alekhine, Alexander   80, 81, 198-99, 228
Alkemade, Nicholas   121, 183-5
A Matter of Life and Death, novelization of the film   77, 80, 81, 91, 109, 174, 211, 226
Arachnoid adhesions   60, 65, 86, 87, 88, 159
Arachnoiditis   85, 86-9, 143, 249-55
Ashford, County Wicklow, Ireland   xv, 99-100
Ashridge Business School   xv, 95, 96-100, 211, 245
Atlas   132, 146-7, 222-5,
Aura   40, 41, 42, 50, 105, 120, 174-181

B

Berger, Hans   129
Black Narcissus   84, 85
Book of the Duchess   229-30
Brain   xiii, 120, 167, 169, 195, 219
British Epilepsy Association   37, 245
Byrne, Joseph Grandson   130-1

C

Cairns, Hugh   20, 21, 25, 43, 90, 105, 122, 133, 187, 188, 191, 198, 212-13
Cajal, Santiago Ramon y   228-9
Camera obscura   xv, xxiv, 53, 54, 75-7, 123, 144, 145, 215-7, 245
Cane   xxiv, 39, 42-3, 144
Charing Cross Hospital   xv, 95-100, 211
Chaucer, Geoffrey   4, 110, 229-30
Chess   80-1, 123, 174, 198, 228-30
Chiasma, optic   71, 72, 73, 78, 81, 85, 86-9, 143, 148, 249-55, 257

Chiasmal arachnoiditis 85, 86-9, 143, 249-55
Christie, Ian xii, 64, 118, 129, 140, 151, 152, 207-8
Clarke, Arthur 117
Collier, James 60, 102, 218-21, 123, 133
Complex partial seizures 23, 30, 35, 38-43, 47, 58, 65, 100, 142, 194, 205, 220
Crichton-Browne, James 139-40, 133 195-8, 215,
Critchley, Macdonald 103, 121, 132-5, 163-4, 179, 198-9, 207, 220, 239
Crook, Steve xvi, 58
Crowther, Bosley 141-2
Cushing, Harvey 20, 21, 23, 24, 31, 84, 105-6, 133, 169, 171, 202, 206, 213, 223, 237

D

Diagnosis of Nervous Diseases 84-5, 72, 79, 241-2
Dickens, Charles 194, 196, 197, 198, 199, 209
Documentary 11, 106
Dumfries Museum and Camera Obscura xv, 76-7, 123, 215-7, 245
Dumfriesshire & Galloway Natural History and Antiquarian Society xv, 215-7, 245
Dreamy State, see aura
Dreifuss, Fritz 142

E

Edge of the World 9, 10, 12, 48, 95, 18, 153, 154, 215
Edwards, Vivian xv, 97-9
EEG xxii, 33, 100, 129

Epilepsy xi, xii, 32, 36, 100, 102, 122, 140, 161, 175, 194, 196-8, 205-9, 245
Epilepsy Foundation of America 37, 245
Epilepsy surgery xxii, 120, 123, 142, 175

F

49th Parallel 9, 10, 95
Farlan, Abraham 123, 226, 232-3
Ferrier, David 123, 134, 195, 226
Flaherty, Robert 11, 154
Fried onions, (also see aura) 40, 50, 51, 56, 58, 122, 202-3
Freud, Sigmund 89, 186

G

Gershwin, George 20, 22-4, 40, 60, 197
Goldsmith, A.J.B. 86-9, 135, 143, 249-55

H

Hallucinations, (also see aura) 24, 30, 40, 41, 50-9, 65, 69, 81, 87, 89, 90, 91, 103, 104, 106, 129, 132, 141, 159, 160, 163, 187, 194, 198, 202-3, 206-7, 220
Head, Henry 120, 133, 169-72
Henley, W.E. 169
Hippocampus 42, 43
Holmes, Gordon 133, 134, 163, 164
Homonymous Hemianopsia 38, 39, 55, 79, 144
Hôpital de la Pitié 87, 88, 89, 186
Horrax, Gilbert 205-7
Horsley, Victor 20, 36, 84, 120, 123, 133, 134, 175, 176, 178, 180, 219, 222, 223, 226

Family-Sophy and
Fannie   176-8
Hurdy-gurdy   105, 180

I

I Know Where I'm Going!   11,
48, 51, 52, 65, 141, 178
International League Against
Epilepsy   142
Intracranial pressure   23, 50,
51, 57, 60, 78, 85, 89, 105,
123, 159, 160, 206, 218, 219
Isles of Fingal   177-9

J

Jackson, John Hughlings xiii, 32,
33, 36, 41, 84, 123, 133, 134,
161-2, 194, 195, 197, 215, 226-7

K

Kaplan, Bernard   89, 91-2
Karinthy, Frigyes   20,
24, 102-9, 180

L

Laurie, John   76-7, 123, 216-7
Lawrence, T.E. (Lawrence of
Arabia)   20-2, 122, 211, 212
Lister, Joseph   20, 133, 223, 240-1
Lizars, John   123, 124, 125,
132, 146, 147, 222-3

M

Macdonald, William
George   89, 93-100, 135
Macewen, William   20, 123, 132,
133, 219, 222, 223, 224, 246
MacGinnis, Niall Patrick   xv,
89, 93-100, 135, 154, 211
Maps   8-11, 13, 123, 127,
139, 145, 152, 153, 222

Marvell, Andrew   110,131, 162,
Mendelssohn, Felix   175-178
*Midsummer Night's Dream
Overture*   120, 174-180
Motorcycle   19, 21, 80, 97, 122,
145, 168, 211, 212, 218
Mr. Harris   198-9
Musicogenic Epilepsy   179-80
My 100 Best Games   198, 199, 228

N

Nanook of the North   11, 154
Neurologic exam   30,
52-66, 133, 164
Nichols, Robert   167, 169, 170, 172

O

Olivecrona, Herbert   20, 24, 105
Optic chiasm, (also see chiasmal
arachnoiditis)   57, 71, 72,
73, 78, 81, 85, 144, 148
Owen, Wilfrid   111, 167, 168, 169
*Oxford Book of English
Verse*   109-11, 167, 229

P

Parachute fall   18, 53, 56,
96, 121, 183-5, 230
Patton, George   20, 25
Penicillin   xxii, 99
Philidor, François-
Andre   80, 81, 228-9
Phillimore, John
Swinnerton   110, 229
Physiology of the Eye   130-1
Pool, J. Lawrence   237-8
Powell, Mabel   2-6
Prevention of Malaria   131
Purves-Stewart, Sir James   72,
79, 84, 85, 86, 241-2

Q
Quaerens   194-7
Queen Elizabeth   30, 52, 109, 159, 229

R
Reidy, Joseph P.   xii, 51, 83, 89, 90, 93, 94, 95, 160, 187, 212
Rhododendrons   97-99, 159
Rivers, W.R.   169
Rives, Landon   123, 124, 146-7, 222-3
Ross, Ronald   131
Royal Society of Medicine   xx, xxi, 86, 92

S
Saccade   73, 78, 145
Sassoon, Siegfried   111, 167, 169, 170
Schoonmaker, Thelma Powell   xii, xvi
Scott, Walter   110, 196, 208
Seizures   xxii, 23, 24, 35-6, 33-37, 40-3, 58-60, 65, 78, 90, 100, 101, 102, 105, 129, 133, 143, 144, 163, 174-80
Sherrington, Charles   133, 162, 239
Society for Psychical Research   129
Spencer, Herbert   32, 161, 162, 196
Spruce, Irene   xv, 96
Symonds, C.P.   62, 121, 187, 188, 190, 191, 198

T
Tennyson, Alfred   110, 194, 195, 196, 197, 209
The Red Shoes   140, 151

The Life and Death of Colonel Blimp   11, 64, 178, 212, 215, 216
The Thief of Bagdad   69
Thompson, Mick   xvi, 96
Turner, Joanne   xv, 215-7

U
Uncus   42-43, 57
Uncinate seizure, (see also complex partial seizure)   xiii, 23, 43, 58, 144, 202, 206, 230

V
Visual field   54-6, 58, 71, 73, 75-9, 81, 84, 85, 86, 145

W
Warman, Eric   91
Wyllie, Elaine   245

About the Author

Diane Broadbent Friedman is a nurse practitioner with a focus on neurological disorders. She is currently in a course of study leading to a PhD in Neuroscience.

Printed in Great Britain
by Amazon